CAMBRIDGE LIBRARY COLLECTION

Books of enduring scholarly value

Travel and Exploration

The history of travel writing dates back to the Bible, Caesar, the Vikings and the Crusaders, and its many themes include war, trade, science and recreation. Explorers from Columbus to Cook charted lands not previously visited by Western travellers, and were followed by merchants, missionaries, and colonists, who wrote accounts of their experiences. The development of steam power in the nineteenth century provided opportunities for increasing numbers of 'ordinary' people to travel further, more economically, and more safely, and resulted in great enthusiasm for travel writing among the reading public. Works included in this series range from first-hand descriptions of previously unrecorded places, to literary accounts of the strange habits of foreigners, to examples of the burgeoning numbers of guidebooks produced to satisfy the needs of a new kind of traveller - the tourist.

The Historie of Travaile into Virginia Britannia

The publications of the Hakluyt Society (founded in 1846) made available edited (and sometimes translated) early accounts of exploration. The first series, which ran from 1847 to 1899, consists of 100 books containing published or previously unpublished works by authors from Christopher Columbus to Sir Francis Drake, and covering voyages to the New World, to China and Japan, to Russia and to Africa and India. Volume 6 (1849) is the first published edition of a collection of manuscript records gathered by William Strachey (?1572–1621), the first Secretary of the English colony of Virginia. It includes Strachey's own account of a shipwreck off Bermuda, which is believed by some scholars to have inspired passages in Shakespeare's *The Tempest*, and a list of words in Powhatan which is the only source of information about that language apart from the account of Captain John Smith. This is the second Hakluyt volume to have been edited by R.H. Major of the British Museum.

T0371119

Cambridge University Press has long been a pioneer in the reissuing of out-of-print titles from its own backlist, producing digital reprints of books that are still sought after by scholars and students but could not be reprinted economically using traditional technology. The Cambridge Library Collection extends this activity to a wider range of books which are still of importance to researchers and professionals, either for the source material they contain, or as landmarks in the history of their academic discipline.

Drawing from the world-renowned collections in the Cambridge University Library, and guided by the advice of experts in each subject area, Cambridge University Press is using state-of-the-art scanning machines in its own Printing House to capture the content of each book selected for inclusion. The files are processed to give a consistently clear, crisp image, and the books finished to the high quality standard for which the Press is recognised around the world. The latest print-on-demand technology ensures that the books will remain available indefinitely, and that orders for single or multiple copies can quickly be supplied.

The Cambridge Library Collection will bring back to life books of enduring scholarly value (including out-of-copyright works originally issued by other publishers) across a wide range of disciplines in the humanities and social sciences and in science and technology.

The Historie
of Travaile into
Virginia Britannia

Expressing the Cosmographie and Comodities
of the Country, together with
the Manners and Customes of the People

WILLIAM STRACHEY
EDITED BY RICHARD HENRY MAJOR

CAMBRIDGE
UNIVERSITY PRESS

CAMBRIDGE UNIVERSITY PRESS

Cambridge, New York, Melbourne, Madrid, Cape Town, Singapore,
São Paolo, Delhi, Dubai, Tokyo

Published in the United States of America by Cambridge University Press, New York

www.cambridge.org
Information on this title: www.cambridge.org/9781108008037

© in this compilation Cambridge University Press 2010

This edition first published 1849
This digitally printed version 2010

ISBN 978-1-108-00803-7 Paperback

WORKS ISSUED BY

The Hakluyt Society.

———— ✳ ————

THE HISTORIE OF TRAVAILE

INTO VIRGINIA.

M.DCCC.XLIX

THE

HISTORIE OF TRAVAILE

INTO

VIRGINIA BRITANNIA;

EXPRESSING THE

COSMOGRAPHIE AND COMODITIES OF THE COUNTRY,
TOGITHER WITH THE MANNERS AND
CUSTOMES OF THE PEOPLE.

GATHERED AND OBSERVED AS WELL BY THOSE WHO WENT
FIRST THITHER AS COLLECTED BY

WILLIAM STRACHEY, GENT.,

THE FIRST SECRETARY OF THE COLONY.

———

NOW FIRST EDITED FROM THE ORIGINAL MANUSCRIPT, IN THE
BRITISH MUSEUM, BY

R. H. MAJOR, ESQ.,

OF THE BRITISH MUSEUM.

LONDON:

PRINTED FOR THE HAKLUYT SOCIETY.

M.DCCC.XLIX.

THE HAKLUYT SOCIETY.

Council.

EDITOR'S PREFACE.

THE prophetic quotation which the author of this work has placed upon his title-page, seems to indicate an anticipation on his part, that his manuscript would one day be printed; and its interesting date and curious details, have given the Editor reason to congratulate himself upon the fact, that the Hakluyt Society is the " generation" prognosticated.

Two copies of the manuscript, both in the author's handwriting (for there are a sufficient number of instances of it in the British Museum to prove its identity), are all that have come under the Editor's notice; one in the Sloane Collection, No. 1622, in the British Museum, from which the present publication has been transcribed; and the other among the Ashmolean Manuscripts, No. 1754. The only difference between these two, is an alteration in the title of the second book, and the addition to the titles, both of the first and second books, of the motto of *Alget qui non ardet*. The Museum copy is dedicated to Sir Francis Bacon, " Lord High Chancellor"; and that in the Ashmolean Library to Sir Allen Apsley, " Purveyor to His Majesties Navie Royall."

That the author was a man of an intelligent and observing mind will be evident from a perusal of the following pages. That he was a man of considerable learning will be likewise evident; although it must be acknowledged that he was not without a tincture of the pedantry common to the age, which has led him occasionally to illustrate his descriptions by the employment of classical expressions, and those of such an unusual character, that the Editor has been compelled, in his duty to the reader, to make annotations apparently but little suited to the general tenour of the narrative. This defect, however, it is hoped, will be found to be amply compensated by the intrinsic merit of the work itself, especially when the date at which it was written is taken into consideration.

R. H. M.

INTRODUCTION.

THE EDITOR was extremely desirous of commencing
this introduction with a short biographical notice of
William Strachey, the author of the following pages ;
but notwithstanding that he has used his best exertions, he has been unsuccessful in discovering anything more respecting him, than such few points as
connect him immediately with the subject of the work
itself.[1] The place and date of his birth, as well as those
of his death, are unknown.   That he was a person of
importance in Virginia we shall hereafter show.   But
in the absence of sufficient materials to make even the

[1] The Editor having communicated with Sir Henry Strachey,
Bart., of Sutton Court, Somersetshire, as to the possibility of his
connexion with the Strachey of this MS., was kindly permitted,
through the obliging medium of Edward Strachey, Esq. of Clifton,
and William Strachey, Esq. of London, to inspect the family
pedigree. From this it appeared that there was a William Strachey
of Saffron Walden, who was married in 1588, and was alive in
1620, a range of years including the period of our MS. : but
no mention was made of his having been to Virginia.   It is
remarkable, however, that his grandson of the same name is especially referred to as having emigrated to that place.   It would
appear not improbable that the former of them may be identical
with the Virginian adventurer, and that the latter may have gone
to America under the influence of his grandfather's distinguished
connexion with the colony.   Mention is made twice or thrice in
various of the Harleian MSS. of a William Strachey of Saffron
Walden about the same period.

b

slightest biographical sketch, the Editor has thought
it better simply to introduce his name at those points
of the following introductory outline of the progress
of the colony, where it naturally falls in with the
thread of the narrative.

It is presumed that the two following questions will
most naturally suggest themselves, upon the perusal
of our title-page.   First, what is the period of this
Historie of Travaile? and secondly, what degree of
interest does the date of the narrative involve, with
reference to the history of the country of which it
treats?

The period referred to in our title-page, ranges over
1610, 1611, and 1612; and if we call to mind that
the first definite settlement of Virginia, or in other
words, the first permanent colonization of America by
the British, took place only in 1607, it must be evident
that this period is one of the highest interest to all
who read with pleasure what Hakluyt calls "the
industrious labors and painefull travels of our countrymen."

The title of the English to the soil of which we
eventually gained possession, as well as the description
of the principal previous visitations of our countrymen to the western coasts of America—both points
forming suitable introductory matter to a work like
the present—have been dealt with by the author himself, all quaintly and briefly though it be, in the succeeding pages.   His "premonition to the reader" leaves
all allusion to the first question unnecessary; and
the second book (which might more correctly have
been the first instead of the second), embodies the
narrative of those earlier voyages, which though un-

successful in effecting settlements, paved the way to the ultimate colonization of the country.

Many attempts at this great object had been made by the English, under the command of Sir Hugh Willoughby and Martin Frobisher, and finally under patents granted by Elizabeth in the early part of her reign to Sir Humphrey Gilbert and Sir Walter Raleigh, but without any permanently favourable result.

These several voyages, however, though falling short of the purpose for which they were originated, were not unproductive of interesting narratives (brief, it is true, but unitedly too lengthy even for a digested repetition here), which may yet, perhaps, be appropriately enumerated for the reader's advantage for reference.

G. Best. Discourse of the late voyages and of discoveries for the finding of a passage to Cathaya by the nord-weast, under the conduct of Martin Frobisher, general, with a particular card thereunto adjoined of Meta Incognita, 4to. *London, Bynneman,* 1578.

Reprinted in Hakluyt.

A prayse and report of Maister Martyne Forboisher voyage to Meta Incognita, now spoken of by Thomas Churchyard, gentl. Imprinted for Andrew Maunsell in Paules Churchyard, at the sign of the Parrot, 8vo. *s. l. (circ.* 1580.)

R. Hakluyt. Divers voyages touching the discoverie of America and the Islands adjacent unto the same, made first of all by our Englishmen, and afterwards by the Frenchmen and Bretons, 4to. *London,* 1582.[1]

A discourse upon the intended voyage to the hithermoste parts of America, written by Captaine Carleill for the better inducement to satisfie such merchauntes, as in disburseing

[1] This rare book, the first publication of Hakluyt, is now in progress of preparation for the Hakluyt Society, under the editorial care of J. Winter Jones, Esq. of the British Museum.

their money, do demaunde forwith a present returne of gaine; albeit their saied particular disbursement are in such slender sommes as are not worth the speaking of, 4to. 1583.
Reprinted in Hakluyt.

A briefe and true report of the new found land of Virginia, &c., discovered by the English Colony there seated by Sir Richard Greinville, Knight, in the yeere 1585... by Thomas Hariot, 4to. *London*, 1588.

Hakluyt. The principal navigations, voyages and discoveries made by the English nation, folio. 1589.
Reprinted with additions in 1599.

De Bry. America, sive navigationes in Indiam Occidentalem. *Francofurti*, 1590.

A brief and true report of the new found land of Virginia, [being the first part of the preceding collection which was not continued in English] T. de Bry, 4to. *Frankfort*, 1590.

A briefe and true relation of the discovery of the north part of Virginia . . . . by Captains Gilbert, Gosnold, &c., J. Brereton, 4to. goth. *London*, 1602.

A prosperous voyage in the discovery of the north part of Virginia, by Capt. G. Waymouth, written by G. Rosier, a gentleman employed in the voyage, 4to. goth. *London*, 1605.

Nova Britannia offering most excellent fruits by planting in Virginia, 4to. 1609.

Virginia richly valued by the description of the maine land of Florida, her next neighbour, &c., written by a Portuguese gentleman of the city of Elvas, and translated by R. Hakluyt, 4to. 1609.

At the time of the death of Queen Elizabeth, one hundred and eleven years subsequent to the great discovery of the Western World by Columbus, the Spaniards, on whose behalf his discovery had been made, were the sole permanent settlers in this wide and wealthy continent. In 1606, the French began to make settlements in Canada and Acadie, now Nova Scotia, but it was not till 1607 that the enterprise, which was finally destined to lay the foundation of British occupancy of American soil, was undertaken. Twenty-three years had expired since the patent had been granted to Sir Walter Raleigh to discover and take possession, with little less than royal privileges, of remote heathen and barbarous lands, hitherto not actually possessed by any Christian prince; and yet not an acre of American soil had hitherto become the property of the English.

The attainder of this enterprising and highly gifted man would seem to have been, by some inexplicable decree of Providence, a signal for the commencement of that success which had been denied to nearly thirty several voyages, the furnishing of which had cost him a fortune and the persevering exertions of the best portion of an energetic and influential life. It was shortly after this period, viz., A° 1605-6, that Richard Hakluyt, the "*presidium et dulce decus*" of our society, to whom, as Robertson justly remarks, "England is more indebted for its American possessions than to any man of that age", used influential arguments with various gentlemen of condition, to induce them to present a petition to King James, to grant them patents for the settlement of two plantations on the Coast of North America. This petition issued in the concession of a charter, bearing date the 10th of April, 1606, by which the tract of country lying between the thirty-fourth and forty-fifth degrees of latitude was to be divided into nearly equal portions, between two companies; that occupying the southern portion to be called the first colony (subsequently named the London Company), and that occupying the northern, to be called the second colony (subsequently named the Plymouth Company). The patent also vested in each colony a right of property over fifty miles of the land, extending along the coast each side of the point of first occupation, and a hundred miles inland. The chief adventurers in the London or South Virginian Company, with which as the first settlement we now have principally to do, were Sir Thomas Gates, Sir George Somers, Richard Hakluyt, and Edward Maria Wingfield. The command of the expedition was committed to Captain Newport.

By a strange caprice of the king—who, with a pedantry in keeping with his general character and little consonant with the wisdom necessary for the direction of important enterprises, had undertaken the personal dictation of the instructions for the colony, and the appointment of the members of the council,—these instructions were sent carefully sealed up and enclosed in a box not to be opened till after the arrival in Virginia. The result of this absurdity was, that the main body of the adventurers knew not to whom they had to look as president, so that in the absence of specified authority, the preponderance of personal talents or energy in any individual among their officers, would naturally attract the attention and respect of those who felt the need of an able and determined leader. Such an one presented himself in Captain John Smith, who had already distinguished himself by feats of surpassing skill and daring in the wars of Transylvania and Hungary.

It was in April 1607, that the expedition approached the shores of America, and after encountering a violent tempest and being driven out of their reckoning, came in sight of the magnificent bay of Chesapeake. Upon opening the box containing the instructions drawn up by King James, the name of Captain Smith was found mentioned in the list of council. The members mentioned, were to choose their president for one year, who, in conjunction with the council, was to govern the colony. By whatever motive actuated, it appears that the council endeavoured, under the most trifling pretences, to exclude Smith from a seat amongst them, and it was only by the judicious and earnest exhortations of Mr. Hunt, the chaplain, that the royal authority was in this respect deferred to, and he was admitted into the council. His prudence and courage subsequently produced effects which obtained for him, as is well known to every reader of American history, a patriarchal rank among British colonists in America. It is not our business here to enter into a repetition of the oft-repeated story of his chivalrous conduct among the Indians, of his steady determination and politic endurance, when having to contend with the disaffection of his own people, nor of the romantic tale of his own life and Englishmen's lives, for his sake, being saved once and again by the personal devotion of the generous but ill-requited Pocahontas. Suffice it to say, that by this expedition, and prominently under the management of Captain Smith, the first permanent settlement of the English in América was effected in the construction of a town on the river Powhatan, now called James' River, and which they named James Town, in honour of the king.

Misfortune, however, seemed to haunt the infant colony. The storehouse at James Town caught fire accidentally, and was consumed.[1] Although the

---

[1] See Stith's *Virginia*, 59 ; and Smith's *Virginia*, 52. By this fire, Mr. Hunt, the chaplain, lost his library and all that he possessed.

colonists were abstemious,[1] yet an over-amount of toil in the extremity of the heat, together with unwholesome food and comfortless lodging, produced considerable mortality amongst them; which again was increased in the winter of the following year 1608, by the remarkable severity of a frost, which has been the subject of notice by several writers of the period. In the summer of this latter year, Captain Smith, whose wisdom and vigour had by this time gained him the presidency of the colony, made an exploratory excursion amongst the great rivers which fall into the Chesapeake, and drew up a map (a fac-simile of which accompanies this volume, frequent reference being made to it by our author), together with a short description of the country and of the natives, which he transmitted to the council in England. This was subsequently published under the title of " A map of Virginia, with a description of the countrey, &c., written by Captaine Smith, whereunto is annexed the proceedings of those Colonies since their first departure from England, &c., &c., taken faithfully as they were written, out of the writings of Doctor Russell, Tho. Studley, &c., &c., and the relations of divers other diligent observers then present there, and now many of them in England. By W. Strachey." Oxford, 1612, 4to. A considerable portion of this small work has been adopted by Strachey, and interwoven into his own narrative in the following MS.

In the interval Captain Newport, who had returned to England, arrived with a second supply for the colony at Virginia, and brought over with him seventy persons, many of whom were men of rank and distinction. It

---

[1] See Smith, fo. 44, and Purchas, v. 1706-1707.

is to be deplored, however, that gold, and not the permanent establishment of the colony, appears to have been the predominating incentive; inasmuch as, according to Chalmers, the company's instructions which were sent with this expedition, imperatively required that the interior should be explored for gold; and threatened that, in the event of failure, the colonists "should be allowed to remain as banished men in Virginia." Although these hopes of the company were not realized, the confirmation which the narratives of the more recent adventurers gave to the accounts of those who had preceded them, excited an enthusiasm that led to the best results at this very critical period. Individuals of the highest rank, tempted by the descriptions of the extent and fertility of the country. and induced, through the medium of commendatory pamphlets, to believe that an enterprise on a more extensive scale would completely nullify the obstacles which had hitherto stood in the way, obtained from the king a new charter, in which he was prevailed upon to relinquish some of those claims of sovereignty, which in the former patent had been so uncompromisingly reserved. By this charter, the lands which had formerly been conveyed only in trust were now granted in absolute property. The principal restrictive clauses comprised the administration of the oath of supremacy to all emigrants, the exclusive establishment of the Church of England, with an especial veto against Roman Catholics.[1]

It is in this second patent, which exists at the present day in the state paper office, that the first mention occurs,

[1] See *Nova Britannia*, by R. J.   London, 1609.

which we have been able to light upon, of the name of our author as William Strachey, gentleman. Copies of it are preserved in Stith's *Virginia*, appendix No. 2; in Smith's *Virginia*, fol., where the names are alphabetically arranged; and in Hazard's *Historical Collection*, vol. i. fol. 58-72.[1] Thomas, 11th Lord Delawarr, was therein appointed governor for life; Sir Thomas Gates was appointed lieutenant governor; Sir George Somers, admiral; and Christopher Newport, vice admiral. Seven ships, attended by two small ketches, were equipped with five hundred emigrants for the colony. Lord Delawarr did not, himself, leave England immediately, but delegated the command, in the meantime, to Sir Thomas Gates, Sir George Somers, and Captain Newport, and it is interesting to notice, in connexion with the subsequent events of the voyage, a curious circumstance related by Smith in his *Virginia*, p. 89.

As each of these officers held a commission which entitled him to recall the commission previously granted for the government of the colony, they agreed, in order to avoid disputes respecting precedence, to sail in one ship. The nine vessels weighed anchor on the 15th of May, 1609; but that in which these officers sailed, was separated, by a tempest of uncommon violence,

[1] It is worthy of mention that George Sandys, the celebrated author of "A Relation of a Journey begun A.D. 1610," whose name is entered in the list of adventurers in this patent, made his translation of Ovid in Virginia, as he himself mentions in his dedication of the edition of 1632 to King Charles, where he says, "It needeth more than a simple denization, being a double stranger sprung from the stock of the ancient Romans, but *bred in the new world, whereof it cannot but participate, especially having wars and tumults to bring it to light, instead of the muses.*

from the rest of the squadron, and was wrecked upon
the Bermudas; but the company, consisting of one
hundred and fifty persons, was saved by an act of
Providence, often spoken of as most remarkable.
Strachey also was in this vessel, and wrote a description of the storm, which is to be found in *Purchas*,
vol. iv. fol. 1734.[1] The remainder of the fleet, meanwhile,
with the exception of one of the ketches which was
lost, had reached James Town on the 11th of August;
and in the absence of the commissioned officers, Smith,
who had been the practical leader of the principal
undertakings of the colony, assumed with justice the
virtual presidency. The new comers, however, consisted, as he graphically says at p. 90 of his *Virginia*,
"of many unruly gallants, packed hither by their
friends to escape ill destinies." These shewed little
inclination to obey a man who held no appointed authority over them, and of whose qualities and actions
they had had no experience as entitling him to assume
a rank unwarranted by written authority. Anarchy
soon spread through the colony, but the evils which
ensued before long reduced them to the necessity of
requesting that protection which the order, consequent
upon his influence, would procure them. Good effects
immediately resulted from this improved state of
affairs; the people built houses, prepared tar and pitch,
with various other desiderata for success in their settlement; dug a well, constructed a block-house, and

---

[1] This description was supposed by Malone to have been the
foundation of Shakespeare's *Tempest*, and there is, in the British
Museum, a small octavo volume, privately printed by him, written
for the express purpose of substantiating his opinion. The idea
has been however completely controverted by the Rev. Joseph
Hunter, in a pamphlet also privately printed. London, 1839, 8vo.

laid out in cultivation some thirty or forty acres of
ground.[1] Smith also made exertions to fix two advan-
tageous settlements at Nandsamund and at the falls
of James River. Companies, of one hundred and
twenty each, were detached for these separate locali-
ties, but both of them imprudently offended the Indians and lost a great number of their men. It was
on his return from the latter place, that Captain Smith
received a severe accident from the explosion of a bag
of gunpowder, which dreadfully mangled his person,
and drove him suffering with extreme torture to England; disgusted with the unfair opposition and the
difficulties which he had met with in a colony that had
been so greatly indebted to him, and to which he never
afterwards returned. By his departure the authority,
which kept the Indians in awe, was removed, and the
English, now undisciplined, became an easy prey to
their revenge or jealousy. Captain[2] Sickelmore, who
bore the pseudonym of Ratcliffe, imprudently ventur-
ing himself with thirty men, for the purposes of trade,
within the power of the king Powhatan, was killed
together with his people. These various losses, com-
bined with the heedless waste of provisions which
this reckless band had exhibited, reduced the four
hundred and ninety persons which were left in the
colony at Captain Smith's departure, within the space
of six months, to only sixty. This fearful period was
called "the starving time."[3]

Meanwhile Sir Thomas Gates and Sir George
Somers, who had been wrecked on the Bermudas,

[1] See Stith, fo. 97.   [2] See Stith, 116; Keith, fo. 120.
[3] See Smith's *Virginia*, fo. 105-106; Chalmers, vol. i. fo. 30;
and Stith, fo. 110.

employed the winter in forming a settlement there and
constructing[1] two small vessels, in which they set
sail on the 10th of May 1610, and arrived at James
Town on the 23rd of the same month. To their
intense disappointment, in lieu of a numerous and
flourishing colony, they found the small remnants
of the large expedition with which they had started
from England, in the last stage of wretchedness and
famine. No hope was left for the rescue of the miserable settlers but an immediate return to England. It
was at this critical juncture that, on the 6th of June,
every preparation being made, the whole colony was
on board and actually descending James River on their
return voyage, when they met a long boat announcing
the arrival of Lord Delawarr, with three ships, one
hundred and fifty men, and a plentiful supply of provisions, to take the command. This apparently special
interposition of Providence, thus bringing not only
life but good hope for the future to men in an almost
desperate condition, aided by the circumstance, that
the government was now invested in one, over whose
deliberations there could be no control, and with whom
there could consequently be no rivalry, caused them
all to return with cheerfulness to James Town, and
resume with steady obedience the resettlement of the
colony. The account of Lord Delawarr's arrival is
given by Strachey, in *Purchas*, vol. iv. fol. 1754, as well
as in a letter addressed by his lordship to the patentees
in England; which the editor has discovered amongst
the Harleian manuscripts in the British Museum, and
has added to this introduction by way of appendix.
This letter would appear for several reasons to have

[1] See Keith, fo. 120; Stith, fo. 115.

been indited by Strachey himself; the first reason is that both it and Strachey's description mention, in the enumeration of the appointments made upon Lord Delawarr's arrival, that of William Strachey as secretary and recorder, an office which would in all probability entail on him the dictation of the letter in question: in the second place, the diction of the letter and the description in *Purchas*, contain passages repeated almost verbatim; and thirdly, the date and address of the letter are supplied in Strachey's hand-writing, which would seem to imply that it was written for him by a scribe, and finally completed by him in his official position as secretary. It is signed by his lordship, Sir Thomas Gates, Sir George Percie, F. Henman, and William Strachey. This letter, dated, " James Town, June 7th, 1610", embodies not only the description of his lordship's outward voyage and his arrival, but the events which ensued in the intervening period.

Under his enlightened and beneficent auspices, the colony soon assumed a wholesome and active appearance. Every man had his own duty to do, and officers were appointed to see that duty done; and it was not long before the disturbances and confusion which had been the natural consequence of disaffection and revolt, were succeeded by the happy fruits of peaceful industry and order. While discipline, and the worthy example together with the rank of the governor, were producing this favourable effect upon the colony at Virginia, Lord Delawarr had the prudence to dispatch Sir George Somers and Captain Argol to the Bermudas for supplies of provisions; favourable accounts having been brought thence by the officers whom he had sent in advance in 1609. The expedition was unfortunate.

Argol being separated from his companion, made his
way for New England and finally returned to Virginia;
and Sir George Somers, though he reached the Bermudas, was so exhausted, being now above sixty
years of age, with the toil of the journey, that he sunk
under his fatigues and died soon after his arrival.
Short intervals of relief to the colony seemed thus
only to be succeeded by depressing misfortunes. The
excellent Lord Delawarr, whose virtues, rank, and
talents, had promised the best results for Virginia, was
seized (as is shown by his own *Relation*, published,
London, 1611, 4to.) with a severe ague, followed by a
flux, which threatened entirely to destroy his health.
He was, therefore, compelled to relinquish the anxieties
of his office and return home. He set sail on the 28th
of March 1611, leaving Sir George Percy in the command of the colony. The departure of Lord Delawarr
immediately opened the door to anarchy, and its natural
consequence, adversity; but Sir Thomas Dale arriving
soon after, in the month of May, with a fresh supply of
emigrants, and provisions for a whole year, matters
again assumed a more prosperous appearance. It is to
be presumed, that Strachey did not accompany his lordship to England, although the editor has not been able
to ascertain the precise date of the secretary's return.
That he was in London in 1612 is certain, from his own
statement in the " Address to His Majestie's Councill
for the colony of Virginia Britannia", prefixed to his
" Laws for Virginia"; published, Oxford, 1612, 4to.,
the dedication of which is signed thus: " From my
lodging in the Blacke Friers, at your best pleasures,
either to returne unto the colony or to pray for the
successe of it here. W. S."

In this year, 1612, a new charter was granted by the king, in behalf of the adventurers. Not only were all the privileges that had been conceded to them confirmed, but a grant was made to them of all the islands lying within three hundred leagues of the coast.[1] The Bermudas, which came within this range, were sold to a number of the company's own members, who gave to the group the name of the Somers Islands, in honour of their lately deceased deputy governor, Sir George Somers.[2] Sir Thomas Gates arrived in the colony in August 1611, and held the post of governor till 1614. It was during this period that the first hostilities took place between the English and French colonies in America; but the former gained a complete ascendancy, under the bold and vigorous management of Captain Argol.

Sir Thomas Gates was succeeded in the government by Sir Thomas Dale, under whose administration the right to landed property in Virginia was first established. In the year 1615, fifty acres of land were allotted to each emigrant and his heirs, with a grant of a like quantity to every new comer. Early in the year 1616, Sir Thomas Dale returned to England, and the government was consigned to Sir George Yeardly. It was in this year that the English first cultivated tobacco in Virginia. Sir George was succeeded, in 1617, by Captain Argol, the tyranny of whose admi-

[1] For copies of this charter see Hazard's *Hist. Coll.* vol. i. fo. 72-81, and Appendix No. 3 to Stith's *Virginia*.

[2] The name of these islands has been strangely misconceived by map makers, through a long series of years. Not only have the English almost universally designated them the Summer Islands, but this nomenclature has been ludicrously translated by the French into the " Isles d'Été."

nistration caused great dissatisfaction. The necessities of the colony now demanded the attention of a more active and influential government, and Lord Delawarr, the captain general, was again sent out in the year 1618, with two hundred people, in a vessel of two hundred and fifty tons burthen. He died, however, on the voyage, in or near the bay which bears his name. The great Indian king, Powhatan, whose description is so fully and interestingly given in the following pages, also died this year.

The second book contains the only detailed account which has hitherto been printed of the voyage of Captains George Popham and Raleigh Gilbert, and the formation of the colony at Saghadehock, which, like so many of the attempts at colonizing Virginia, proved ultimately abortive.

Upon the death of Sir John Popham, Chief Justice of England, his son and successor, Sir Francis Popham, who was sent out, and who now likewise became governor of New England, dispatched thither vessels on his account to fish and carry on the fur trade. This adventure proving profitable, gave considerable impulse to colonization, and in the year 1614, Captain John Smith, who had so greatly distinguished himself in the history of Virginia, was sent out at the expense of four English merchants to form a settlement. He sailed on the 3rd of March, and reached Manhegin Island on the 30th of April. He directed his attention principally to the fur trade, as a means of producing what had in the previous attempts been too little attended to, a profitable return for the expenses of the enterprise, and realized by his traffic in this commodity nearly fifteen hundred pounds. He also

d

laid down, from the observations which he had made, a map of the coast from Penobscot to Cape Cod, which he presented to Prince Charles, to whom in consequence the country owes the designation of New England, which it has ever since retained. When Captain Smith returned to England, he left one of his ships behind, with instructions to the master, whose name was Thomas Hunt, to sail for Malaga when he had laden his vessel with the fish that he might catch on the coast. This "wicked varlet", as Hubbard rightly calls him, kidnapped twenty-four of the natives, whom he carried to Malaga, and sold as slaves. The result of this infamous outrage was that Captain Hobson, who arrived shortly after in perfect ignorance of the crime that had been committed, was attacked by the Indians, who visited his vessel under the pretext of trading, and he and several of his men were severely wounded. The resentment kindled by Hunt's atrocious conduct presented a serious impediment to the establishment of the contemplated colony, although Smith, in his *New England's Trials*, published London, 1622, 4to., while he reprobates the crime, endeavours to make light of the disasters which must naturally have been its consequence.

In 1615, Smith was again sent out in command of two vessels, one of two hundred, and the other of fifty tons, equipped by Sir Ferdinand Gorges, and Dr. Sutcliffe, Dean of Exeter, but encountering a storm soon after he had put to sea, which broke the masts of his largest ship, he was compelled to return to Plymouth. Thomas Durmer, the commander of the smaller vessel, continued his voyage, and though the main intention of the enterprise was frustrated as to effecting a settlement, he was successful in the fishery,[1] and moreover sailed along the coast from New England to Virginia, thereby for the first time proving its continuity. He was subsequently wounded severely by a band of savages, and died soon afterwards in Virginia.

The indefatigable Captain John Smith meanwhile showed no relaxation in his exertions to infuse the spirit of colonization amongst his countrymen. He circulated seven thousand copies of books and maps among those whom he thought most likely to sympathize with his plans; but he complains in his *New England's Trials*, 2nd edition, 1622, that he might as well have attempted to " cut rocks with oyster shells." The ill-success of his former voyages was adduced as an argument against him, and the present thriving condition of Virginia was contrasted, to his prejudice, with its unprosperous condition while under his presidency, no allowance being made for the fact that his own excellent management had paved the way for this subsequent prosperity.

Finally it was not till 1620, after so many abortive efforts had been made both by government and powerful bodies to form an establishment in North Virginia, that at length it received, under unexpected circumstances, an influx of settlers which soon rendered it by far the most prosperous of all the colonies in North America. This was the emigration of a large band of Puritans, who suffering under the intolerance of the English government, on account of non-conformity, first passed into Holland, and afterwards found an asylum in America.

[1] He freighted a ship of three hundred tons with fish for Spain. See Purchas, vol. v. p. 1833.

The Editor has thus far led the reader cursorily through the history of the attempts which our countrymen made at effecting settlements in the two divisions of Virginia, and has done so because the English colonization of America seemed to be the pivot upon which the interest of the MS. turned. If he has mistaken his duty in so doing, he hopes that his explanation will involve his excuse. An additional reason for his having given the foregoing consecutive narrative in this introduction, has been that Strachey's MS., although unavoidably borrowing so much of its interest from the date at which it was written, and although giving many most interesting details about the natives, especially the great king Powhatan, that have never been hitherto printed, does not continue the description of the progress of the two colonies up to the period at which we have reason to conclude that he finished his narrative. It is at the same time right to observe, that Strachey appears to have entertained the project of carrying on the work to a much greater extent, inasmuch as he designates the first of the books now published " the First Book of the First Decade"; and the second book, " the Second Book of the First Decade."

It is difficult to say precisely in what year the narrative was written. That it was subsequent to 1612, we are informed by Strachey himself, in the " Address to His Majesties Councell for the Colonie of Virginia Britannia", prefixed to his *Laws for Virginia*, printed at Oxford, 1612, where he says,— " When I went forth upon this voyage (right worthy gentlemen), true it is, I held it a service of dutie (during the time of my unprofitable service, and purpose of stay in the colonie, for which way else might I adde unto the least hight of so heroicke and pious a building) to propose unto myself to be (though an unable) remembrancer of all accidents, occurrences, and undertakings thereunto adventitiall; in most of which, since the time our right famous sole governour then, now Lieutenant General Sir Thomas Gates, Knight, after the unsealing of his commission, hasted to our fleete in the west, there staying for him, I have, both in the Bermudas, and since, in Virginia, beene a sufferer and an eie-witnesse, and the full storie of both in due time shall consecrate unto your viewes, as unto whome by right it appertaineth. . . . .

" Howbeit, since many impediments as yet must detaine such my observations in the shadow of darknesses, untill I shall be able to deliver them perfect unto your judgements, I do, in the meantime, present a transcript of the *Toparchia*, or state of those duties by which their colonie stands regulated and commaunded," &c. &c.

If the MS. copy from which the present publication has been printed had been the only one remaining, we should have been compelled to have quoted 1618 as the earliest possible date of the work, since the rank of lord high chancellor, which is appended to the name of Sir Francis Bacon in the dedication of this copy, was not conferred on him until later. But as there is a duplicate[1] copy among the Ashmolean manuscripts at Oxford, dedicated to Sir Allen Apsley, to whose name is appended the title of

[1] The only difference appears to be in the title of the second book, and the addition to each of the title-pages of the sentence, " Alget qui non ardet."

" Purveyor to His Majestie's Navie Royall"; and as Sir
Allen Apsley was, according to Mrs. Hutchinson, in
her celebrated life of Colonel Hutchinson, made Lieutenant of the Tower fourteen years before his death in
1630, *i.e.*, 1616, it is presumed that that copy was
written prior to that period; inasmuch as it is not
reasonable to suppose, that the latter and more important of the two titles would have been omitted in an
author's dedication. At the same time, it is but right
to observe, that some authors have quoted the year
1619 as the date of Sir Allen Apsley's appointment
to the lieutenantcy of the Tower.

The glossary at the end of the voyage has included
the Indian and English names promiscuously in one
alphabetical series; but the Editor has thought it
better not to interfere with the original arrangement.

It only remains for the Editor to express his best
thanks to Mr. Bennett, of the British Museum, and
Secretary of the Linnean Society, for his obliging
assistance in the botanical portions of the work. He
also feels it to be only a just expression of gratitude
to his wife, to acknowledge here her kind aid in supplying the illustrations,—a " labour of love" which it is
hoped that the reader will criticise with a lenient eye,
as they are her first efforts at etching, and would for
that reason not have been made in connexion with a
work like the present, but from a natural desire to
share in the Editor's labours, and an earnest wish to
add, in however feeble a manner, to the interest of the
narrative.

LETTER FROM THE LORD DELAWARR,

GOVERNOR OF VIRGINIA,

TO THE PATENTEES IN ENGLAND.

[MS. Harl. 7009, fol. 58.]

" Right Honourable and the rest of our very loving friends,—We are not ignorant how divers perplext and jealous eies mae looke out, and keepe more then freindly espiall over this our passive and misconceived bewsines, and now (more especially, haply, then at any other time), in these our early dayes, and after the aspersions of so many slanderous and wandering discourses, which have bin scattered by malignant and ill-disposed people against it ; for which we have conceived it essentiall with the birth of the worke itself, to give up unto your noble knowledges the truith of the state of the same, and of some consequences most materiall following it, since it tooke protection and fostering from us.

" You shall please then to know, how the first of Aprill 1610, in the good shipp the De-la-warr, admirall, accompanied with the Blissing of Plinmouth, viz-admirall, and the Hercules of Ry, reere-admirall, we weyed from the Cowes, getting out of the Needles, and with a favourable passadge holding consort ; the 12th day we fell with the Treseras, and recovered that evening (within three leagues) the westermost part of St. George's Island, where we lay that night becalmed ; but the next morning with the sunn-rise did the wind likewise rise, west and west-by-south, a rough and lowde gale, at what time the master of the Reere-admirall told me of a roade fitt for that winde at Gratiosa, whereupon I willed him to go before and I would follow, and so we stood for that roade ; but it was my fortune to lead it in, where we came to an ancor at fortie fathom, when it blew so much winde presently, that our ancor came home, and we were forced to sea againe : the same time the Blissing was compeld to cutt her cable at haulfe, for in the weying of it the pale of her capstan brake, and dangerously hurte 12 of our men : the Hercules was likewise forced from the roade, and brake her ancor; yet the next day we mett altogether againe. The 15th, we lost sight of the Hercules, betweene the Treceras and Gratiosa, and we saw her no more untill the 6th of June, at what time we made land to the southward of our harbour, the Chesiopiock Bay, where, running in towards the shoare, steering away nor-west, before noone we made Cape Henry, bearing nor-west and by west ; and that night came to an ancor under the Cape, where we went ashoare, as well to refresh ourselves as to fish, and to sett up a cross upon the pointe (if haply the Hercules might arrive there) to signify our coming in. Whilst we were a fishing, divers Indians came downe from the woods unto us, and with faire intreatye on both sides, I gave unto them of such fish as we tooke, which was good store, and was not unwelcome unto them, for indeed at this time of the yeare they live poore, their corne being but newly putt into the ground, and their old store spent; oysters and crabbs, and such fish as they take in their weares, is their best releefe. As we were returning aboard againe, our master discried a sayle close by the pointe at Cape Henry, whereupon I commaunded him to beare up the helme, and we gave it chase, when within an hower or a little more, to our no little [joy], made her to be the Hercules, our reereadmirall, whome we had now lost

. . . weekes and odd dayes ; and this night (all praise be to God for it) came to an ancor under Pointe Comfort; from whence the captaine of the forte, Co[lonel] James Davies, repaired unto us, and soone had unfolded a strange . . . tion of a double quallitie, mixed both with joy and sorrow. He let us to understand first (because thereof I first inquired) of the arrivall of Sir Thomas Gates and Sir George Sumers, in 2 pinnisses, with all their company safe from the Bermudas, the 21 of May (about some fortnight before our now coming in), whome, he tould us, were now up our river at James Town. I was heartily glad to heare the happines of this newes; but it was seasoned with a following discourse, compound of so many miseries and calamities (and those in such horrid chaunges and divers formes), as no story, I believe, ever presented the wrath and curse of the eternall offended Maiestie in a greater measure. I understood moreover, by reason I saw the Virginia to ly then in Roade, before the pointe ridg, and prepared to sett sayle out of the river, how that Sir Thomas Gates and Sir George Sumers were within a tide or two coming downe againe, purposing to abandon the countrie, whilest they had meanes yet lefte to transport them and the whole company to Newfoundland.

" For most true it is, the straunge and unexpected condition and . . . in which Sir Thomas Gates found the colony, gave him to underst[and] never was there more neede of all the powers of judgement, and . . . . knowing, and long exercised vertue, then now to be awak . . . . calling upon him to save such whome he found so fo . . . . as in redeeming himself and his againe from falling into the . . . . . . ties. For

e

besides that he found the forte unfurnished (and that
. . . . . and many casualties) of so lardge an accompte
and number . . . . . as he expected, and knew came
alonge the last yeare, trained in . . . . . fleete with
himself; so likewise found he as empty and unfurnished a . . . . entering the towne. It appeared raither
as the ruins of some auntient [for]tification, then that
any people living might now inhabit it: the pallisadoes
he found tourne downe, the portes open, the gates
from the hinges, the church ruined and unfrequented,
empty howses (whose owners untimely death had taken
newly from them) rent up and burnt, the living not
hable, as they pretended, to step into the woodes to
gather other fire-wood; and, it is true, the Indian as
fast killing without as the famine and pestilence within.
Only the blockhouse (somewhat regarded) was the
safetie of the remainder that lived; which yet could not
have preserved them now many dayes longer from the
watching, subtile, and offended Indian, who (it is most
certaine) knew all this their weaknes, and forbare too
timely to assault the forte, or hazard themselves in a
fruitles warr on such whome they were assured in
short time would of themselves perish, and being pro-
voked, their desperate condition might draw forth to
a valiaunt defence; yet were they so ready and prepared, that such whome they found of our men stragled
single beyond the bounds, at any time, of the block-
house, they would fiercely chardge (for all their peices),
as they did 2 of our people not many dayes before Sir
Thomas Gates was come in, and 2 likewise they killed
after his arrivall 4 or 5 dayes.

" But that which added most to his sorowe, and not
a litle startled him, was the impossibilitie which he

conceived (and conceived truly) how to amend any
one whitt of this.   His forces were not of habilitie to
revenge upon the Indian, nor his owne supply (now
brought from the Bermudas) sufficient to releive his
people; for he had brought no greater store of provision (as not jealous that any such disaster could have
befalne the colony) then might well serve 150 for a
sea voyage; and at this time of the yeare, neither by
force (had his power bin sufficient) nor trade, might
have amended these wants, by any help from the
Indian: nor was there any meanes in the forte to take
fish, for there was neither a sufficient seave to be
found, nor any other convenient netts; and, to saye
true, if there had, yet was there not aneye sturgion
come into the river.

" All these considered, he then entered into consultation with Sir George Sumers and Capt. Newporte,
calling unto the same the gentlemen and counsaile of
the former government, intreating both the one and
the other to advise with him, what was to be don: the
provision which they both had aboard, both Sir George
Sumers and Capt. Newporte, was examined and delivered, how it being rackt to the uttermost, extended
not to above 16 dayes, after 2 cakes a day.   The gentlemen of the towne (who knew better of the countrie)
could not give them any hope, or wayes how to recover
oughts from the Indian. It soone then appeered most
fitt, by a generall approbation, that to preserve and
save all from starving, there could be no readier course
thought on, then to abandon the countrie, and accom-
modating themselves the best that they might in the
present pinnasses then in the roade (as, namely, in
the Discovery, and the Virginia, the 2 brought from,

and builded at, the Bermudas, the one called the Deli-
veraunce, of about 70 tonn, and the other, the Patience,
of about 30 tonn), with all speed convenient, to make
for the New-found-land, where, it being then fishing
time, they might meete with many English shipps,
into which, happily, they might disperce most of the
company.

" This consultation taking effect the 7th of June, Sir
Thomas Gates having appointed to every pinnass his
complement and nomber, and delivered likewise thereunto a proportionable rate of provision, caused every
man to repaire aboard; and bycause he would preserve the towne (albeit now to be quitted) unburned,
which some intemperate and malitious people threatened, his one company he caused likewise to be cast
ashoare, and was himself the last of them, when, about
noone, giving a farewell with a peale of small shott,
he sett sayle, and that night, with the tide, fell down
to an island in the river, which our people here call
Hogg Island; and the next morning the tide brought
them to another island, which they have called Mulberry Island, at what time they discovered my long
boat.   For I, having understood of the resolution by
the aforesaid pinnas, which was some 4 or 5 days come
away before, to prepare those at Pointe Comforte, with
all expedition I caused the same to be man'd, and in
it, with the newes of our arrivall, dispatched my letters
by Captaine Edward Brewister to Sir Thomas Gates,
which, meeting to[gether] before the aforesaid Mulberry Island, the 8th of June aforesaid, upon the re-
ceite of our letters, Sir Thomas Gates bore up the helm
againe, and that night (the wind favourable) re-landed
all his men at the forte; before which, the 10th of

June being Sonday, I brought my shipp, and in the
afternoon went ashoare, where after a sermon made by
Mr. Buck, Sir Thomas Gates his preacher, I caused
my commission to be read, upon which Sir Thomas
Thomas Gates delivered up unto me his owne commission, both patents, and the counsell seale: and then I
delivered some few wordes unto the company, laying
some blames on them for many vanities and their idle-
nes, earnestly wisshing that I might no more find it
so, leaste I should be compeld to drawe the sworde
of justice, to cut of such delinquents, which I had
much rather drawe in theire defence, to protect from
enimies; heartening them with the knowledge of what
store of provisions I had brought for them; and after,
not finding as yet in the towne a convenient house, I
repaired aboard againe, where the 12th of June, I did
constitute and give places of office and chardge to
divers captaines and gentlemen, and elected unto me
a counsaile, unto whome I administred an oath of faith,
assistance, and secresy; their names were these:—

Sir Thomas Gates, Knight, Lieutenant Gen[eral.]
Sir George Sumers, Knight, Admirall.
Capt. George Percey, Esq.
Sir Ferdinando Wenman, Knight, M . . . .
Capt. Christopher Newport, ...
William Strachey, Esq., Secretary [and Recorder?]¹
As likewise I nominated Capt. John Martin Master of
the B . . . . workes for steele and iron; and Capt.

¹ The paper of the original is destroyed where the dots, &c., are
inserted. The wordes " and recorder" are supplied from Strachey's
description of the same appointments in Purchas. The almost verbatim similarity of the two, leads to the inference that this letter
was indited by Strachey himself.

George Webb, Serjeant . . . . . of the forte; and Mr. Daniell Tucker and Mr. Robert Wild, clarkes of the store.

" Our first care was to advise with our counsaile for the obtaining of such provisions of victualls, for store and quallitie, as the countrey afforded for our people. It did not appeare unto us that any kind of flesh, deere, or what els, of that kind could be recovered from the Indians, or to be sought in the countrey by us; and our people, together with the Indians (not to friend), had the last winter destroyd and kild up all our hoggs, insomuch as of five or six hundred (as it is supposed), there was not above one sow, that we can heare of, left alive; not a henn nor chick in the forte (and our horses and mares they had eaten with the first); and the provision which we had brought concerning any kind of flesh was little or nothing: whereupon it pleased Sir George Sumers to propose a voyage, which, for the better releife and good of the colony, he would performe into the Bermudas (which, lying in the height of 32 degrees and 20 minutes, 5 degrees from our bay, may be some seve[n] skore leagues from us, or thereabouts; reckoning to every degree that lyes nor-west and westerly, 28 English leagues); and from thence he would fetch 6 monthes' provision of flesh and fish, and some live hoggs, of which those islands (by their owne reporte, however, most daungerous to fall with) are marveilous full and well stored; whereupon, well approving and applauding a motion relishing of so faire hopes and much goodnes, we gave him a commission the 15th of June, who, in his owne Bermuda pinnas, the Patience, accompanied with Capt. Samuell Argall, in the Discovery

(whome we sware of our counsaile before his departure),
the 19th of June fell with the tide from before our
towne, whome we have ever since accompanied with
our hearty prayers for his happy and safe returne.

" And likewise bicause at our first coming we found
in our owne river no store of fish after many tryalls,
we dispatched with instructions the 17. of June,
Robert Tindall, master of the Delawarr, to fish unto
all along and betweene Cape Henry and Cape Charles
within the bay, who the last of the same returned
unto us againe, but mett with so small a quantitie and
store of fish, as he scarce tooke so much as served the
company that he caried forth with him. Nor were
we in the meane while idle at the forte, but every day
and night we hayled our nett sometimes a dozen times
one after an other, but it pleased not God so to bless
our labours, that we should at any time take one
quarter so much as would give unto our people one
pound at a meale a peice (by which we might have
better husbanded and spared our peaz and oatmeale),
notwithstanding the greate store we now saw dayly in
our river.

" Thus much in briefe concerning our voyadge
hether, our meeting with Sir Thomas Gates heere, and
our joynt cares and indevours since our arrivall : nor
shall we be fayling on our parte to do the uttermost
that we may for the happy structure and raysing
againe of this too much stooped and dejected imployment. It rests that I should now truly deliver unto
yee (right honourable and the rest of our good freinds)
somewhat our opinion, or rather better judgement,
which hath observed many things, and those objected
cleare to reason, most benificiall concerning this coun-

trie. And first, we have experience, and our owne eyes witnes, how young soever we are to this place, that no countrie yealdeth goodlier corne or more manifold increase, large feildes we have as prospects houerly before us of the same, and those not many miles from our quarter (some whereof, true it is, to quitt the mischeivous Indian, and irreconsilable for his late injuries and murthering of our men, our purpose is to be masters of ere long, and to thresh it out on the flores of our barnes when the time shall serve). Next, in every boske and common hedge, and not farr from our pallisado gates, we have thousands of goodly vines running along and leaning to every tree, which yeald a plentifull grape in their kind : let me appeale, then, to knowledge, if these naturall vines were planted, dressed, and ordered by skilfull vinearoones, whether we might not make a perfect grape and fruitfull vintage in short time ? Lastly, we have made triall of our owne English seedes, kitchen hearbes, and rootes, and find them no sooner putt into the ground then to prosper as speedily and after the same quallitie as in England.

" Only let me truly acknowledge they are not an hundred or two of deboisht hands, dropt forth by yeare after yeare, with penury and leysure, ill provided for before they come, and worse governed when they are heere, men of such distempered bodies and infected mindes, whome no examples dayly before their eyes, either of goodnes or punishment, can deterr from their habituall impieties, or terrifie from a shamefull death, that must be the carpenters and workers in this so glorious a building.

" But (to delude and mock the bewsines no longer)

as a necessary quantity of provision for a yeare at
least must be carefully sent with men, so likewise must
there be the same care for men of quallitie, and paines
taking men of artes and practises, chosen out and
sent into the bewsines, and such are in dew time now
promised, sett downe in the scedule at the end of our
owne approved discource, which we have intituled ' A
true and sincere declaration of the purpose and end of
our Plantation begonn in Virginia,' &c.

" And these two, such men and such provision are
like enough to make good the ends of the ymployment
in all the waies both for re[pu]tation, search and discovery of the countrie, and the hope of the South Sea,
as also to returne by all shipps sent hither many
com[mo]dities well knowne to be heere, if meanes be
to prepare them.   W[here]upon give me leave, I beseech yee, further to make inference, th[at] since it
hath bin well thought on by yee to provide for the
gove[rnment] by chaunging the authoritie into an
absolute command (indeed . . . virtuall advancement
to these like bewsinesses and m . . . company us) of a
noble and well instructed leifet[enant] . . . . of an industrious admirall, and other knights and gen[tlemen],
and officers, each in their severall place of quallitie
and implo[yment], if the other two, as I have saide,
be taken into dew accompte . . . valewed as the sinewes
(as indeed they be) of this action (without w[hich] it
cannot possible have any faire subsisting, however
men ha[ve] belyed both it and themselves heeretofore)
then let no rumor of the poverty of the countrey (as
if in the wombe thereof there lay not those ellimentall
seedes which could produce as many goodly birthes of
plenty and increase, yea, and of better hopes as of any

f

land under the heavens unto whome the sunn is no
neerer a neighbour; I say, let no.imposture, rumor
then, nor any fame of some one or a few more
chaunceable actions interposing by the way or at
home, wave any mans faire purposes hetherward, or
wrest them to a declininge and falling of from the
bewsines.

   " For let them be assured, as of the truith itself,
these premisses considered, looke what the countrie
can afforde, which may, by the quantitie of our men,
be safely and conveniently explored, search[ed,] and
made practise of, these things shall not be omitted
for our p[art], nor will be by the lievetenant generall
to be commaunded; nor our commaunds receaved (as
in former times) with unwillingnes or falcenes, either
in our people's going forth, or in execution, being for
each one in his place, whither commaunder, overseer,
or labourer.

   " For the causes of these idle and restie untowardnes
being by the authoritie and unitie of our government
removed, all hands already sett to it; and he that knew
not the way to goodnes before, but cherisht singularitie
and faction, now can beate out a path himself of industrie and goodnes for others to trade in, such, may
I well say, is the power of exemplar vertue. Nor would
I have it conceived that we would exclude altogether
gentlemen, and such whose breeding never knew what
a daye's labour meant, for even to such, this countrie
I doubt not but will give likewise excellent satisfaction, especially to the better and stayed spirritts; for
he amongst us that cannot digg, use the square, nor
practise the ax and chissle, yet he shall find how to
imploy the force of knowledge, the exercise of counsell,

and the operation and power of his best breeding and quallitie.

"And thus, right honourable and the rest of our very good friends, assuring yee of our resolution to tarry God's mercy towards us, in continuing for our parte this plantation, I only will intreate yee to stand favourable unto us for a new supply in such matters of the two-fold phisicke, which both the soules and bodies of oure poor people heere stand much in neede of; the specialties belonging to the one, the phisitians themselves (whome I hope you will be carefull to send unto us) will bring along with them; the particularities of the other we have sent herein, inclosed unto us by Mr. Doctor Boone,[1] whose care and industrie for the preservation of our men's lives (assaulted with straunge fluxes and agues), we have just cause to commend unto your noble favours: nor let it, I beseech yee, be passed over as a motion slight and of no moment to furnish us with these things, so much importuning the strength and health of our people, since we have true experience how many men's lives these phisicke helpes have preserved since our coming in, God so blessing the practise and diligence of our doctor, whose store is nowe growne thereby to so lowe an ebb, as we have not above 3 weekes phisicall provisions, if our men continew still thus visited with the sicknesses of the countrie, of the which every season hath his particular infirmitie reighning in it, as we have it related unto us by the old inhabitants; and since our owne arrivall, have cause to feare it to be true, who have had 150 at a time much afflicted, and I am per-

---

[1] *I. e.* Bohun, mentioned hereafter in the narrative.

swaded had lost the greatest part of them, if we had not brought these helpes with us.

"And so concluding your farther troubles, with this only remembrance, that we have, with the advise of our counsell, conceived it most fitt to detaine yet a while, for all good occasions, the good shipp the Delawarr, to which we hope yee wil be no whitt gainsaying: we cease with unnecessary relations to provoke yee any farther.

James Towne, July 7th, 1610.

THO. LAWARRE. THO. GATES. FERD. WENMAN.

GEORGE PERCY.   WILLIAM STRACHEY.[1]

___

[1] A fac-simile of these signatures is given on the next page.

William Strachy

GEORGE PERCY

Thomas West

Ferdinando Wenman

THE FIRST BOOKE

OF

THE HISTORIE OF TRAVAILE INTO VIRGINIA BRITANNIA,
EXPRESSING THE COSMOGRAPHIE AND COMODITIES
OF THE COUNTRY, TOGITHER WITH THE
MANNERS AND CUSTOMES OF
THE PEOPLE :

GATHERED AND OBSERVED AS WELL BY THOSE WHO WENT
FIRST THITHER, AS COLLECTED BY

WILLIAM STRACHEY, GENT.,

THREE YEARES THITHER IMPLOYED SECRETARIE OF STATE, AND
OF COUNSAILE WITH THE RIGHT HONORABLE THE LORD
LA-WARRE, HIS MAJESTIES LORD GOVERNOR AND
CAPT. GENERALL OF THE COLONY.

PSALM CII, VER. 18.

" This shalbe written for the generation to come : and the people which
shalbe created shall praise the Lord."

To the Right Honourable SIR FRANCIS BACON, Knight, Baron of Verulam, Lord High Chancellor of England, and of His Majesties most honorable Privy Counsell.

Most worthely honor'd Lord,

Your Lordship ever approving yourself a most noble fautor of the Virginian Plantation, being from the beginning (with other lords and earles) of the principal counsell applyed to propogate and guide yt : and my poore self (bound to your observaunce, by being one of the Graies-Inne Societe) having bene there three yeares thither, imploied in place of secretarie so long there present ; and setting downe with all my wel-meaning abilities a true narration or historie of the countrie : to whome shoulde I submitt so aptly, and with so much dutye, the most humble present thereof, as to your most worthie and best-judging Lordship ? who in all vertuous and religious en-deavours have ever bene, as a supreame encourager, so an inimitable patterne and perfecter : nor shall my plaine and rude composition any thought discourage my attempt, since howsoever I should feare to appeare therein before so matchles a maister in that facultie (if any opinionate worth of mine owne worke presented me) yet as the great Composer of all things made all good with his owne goodnes, and in our only will to his imitation takes us into his act, so be his goodnes your good Lordship's in this acceptation : for which with all my poore service I shall abide ever

Your best Lordship's most humbly,

WILLIAM STRACHEY.

ÆCCLESIÆ ET REIPUB.

Wild as they are, accept them, so we're wee :
To make them civill, will our honnour bee :
And if good worcks be the effects of myndes,
Which like good angells be, let our designes,
As wee ar Angli, make us Angells too :
No better worck can state- or church-man do.

W. St.

A

PRÆMONITION TO THE READER.

Wherein (as the fowndation to all the succeeding busines) is
derived downe to our tymes, the auntyent right and clayme
which we make to this part of America, and therein both the
objections answered and doubts cleirly satisfied of such who,
through mallice, or ignorance, either have or hereafter may
call the lawfulnes of the proceeding hereof in question.

THE many mouthes of ignorance and slaunder which are ever too
apt to lett fall the venome of theire worst and most depraved
envies uppon the best and most sacred workes, and soe not afrayd
to blast both this enterprize and the devoutest laborrers therein,
wringes from me the necessity of this imperfect defence, whome yet
I have observed more in clamour (me thought) then at any tyme
in force, to cry out still upon yt, calling yt an unnationall and
unlawfull undertaking ; when lett [it] be but observed (I pray), and
soone will appeare theire mallice and petulancy to speake, as also,
what a distance there is truly sett betweene the busines and their
knowledge ; for, in a cliere judgment, if any such attaint lay uppon
the act, neither the generall peace of the tyme might not suffer yt
to goe forth with such libertie, nor the honor of such who have sett
yt forward, ymportune yt of his Majestie, nor would the consciences
(yt is knowen right well) of the chief commanders for the execution and actuall part thereof (let custome have taken away, however, that quicknes from the chargers owne insensible and seared
heart) hazard the last and setting howers of their daies in tray-
terous or ignoble prosecutions ; yet being the pious and only end
both intended by his Majestie, by the honorable Counsaile for the
busines, by the Lord Generall, Lieutenant Generall, Marshall, and

B

such like emynent officers (called forth for the dignity of so great
a cause), together with the generall adventurers, with all carefulnes,
principally to endeavour the conversion of the natives to the knowledge and worship of the true God, and the world's Redeemer,
Christ Jesus; how rotten and unsound, then, both to his Majestie
and the present faith (it is to be feared) may they be at the coare
within, that dare (except yt be as I sayd, out of ignorance, yet
cannot that excuse a factious and pragmatique tongue) quarrel
and traduce the proceedings of a whole state, and to which the.
royall authoritie, by letters made patents, both in her Majestie's
tyme, of famous memory, and nowe likewise hath ben five tymes
concurrant ?   May yt be supposed any one but luke-warme in
Christian charity would be parcell guilty herein, or make yt ques-
tionable whether should be attempted a worke of this piety uppon
a barbarous nation ?   Let the busy knowledge (to say no more) of
such a one be shrewdly suspected, and blemished.   May any lover
of his country ?   No.   Yet is [it] to be feared that he borroweth but
a counterfeyt face from Janus, to turne to the penall edict, or to
his prince (if such be his grace) : but, however, let them both
knowe the grounds of goodnes are not layd so weake, in well
weyed counsailes, that the clamour of a centurion or two can dis-
turb Numa Pompilius[1] kneelinge at the aulter.   Let them give yt
up in rumor, or more subtilly cry out, that our enemies at Sevill,
or Lishborne, at Dominica, Mevis,[2] or at the Havana, are up in
armes for us, we can yet goe on in the justifiableness of our course,
makinge only Pompilius' answere,—" And we doe   sacrifice".
Will it yet please the reader to favour me a little ?

Two sorts especially, I must conceave, of untoward (to stile
them noe worse) and ill disposed in theire wisdomes, stand much
offended with this busines, and have devysed against yt many
slaunders and calumneys, the meere ignorant (not only in *scientia
scientiæ*, as the scholman saies, but includinge grossenes and sim-

---

[1] Plutarch relates that Numa founded his hopes so strongly upon God,
that on one occasion, during the offering of a sacrifice, when he received
an announcement that his enemies were approaching, he smiled, and
made answer, "Ἐγὼ δὲ θύω,"—" And I am sacrificing".
[2] " Nevis", an island in the West Indies, discovered by Columbus.

plicytie in any knowledge) and the meere opposite in *scientia conscientiæ*, in religion ; I would to God the latter were not more dangerous, by how much
Celeberrima per loca vadet ;
and can speake amisse, out of the corrupt seedes of goodnes, and perhaps soe speaking be hearde.

And these both saye, how the undertaking cannot be lawfull. Why ? Because the King of Spayne hath a primer interest into the countrey. Next, it cannot be honest in yt self. Why ? Because injurious to the naturalls ; and which connected together, yt must then necessarily followe (saye they) that yt can be no other than a travaile of flat impiety, and displeasinge before God. Indeed, no meane objections to stumble shallowe home witts, who, whilst they looke lazely and broadly on yt, are presented with an ugly face ; but if, by a more perspective direction, we will examine how these perticularities may lie together, we shall find another modell, and an aire of that dignity and truith which aspiers to a cleane contrary comelines.

For the King of Spaine : he hath no more title nor collour of title to this place, which we by our industry and expenses have only made ours (as for the Pope's donative of all America unto him, that is sufficyently answeared ellswere, in a discourse alreddye published by a most worthy undertaker),[1] then hath any Christyan prince (or then we, or any other prince, maye have to his Mexico and Peru, or any dominions ells of any free state and kingdome) how nere soever the West Indies and Florida may joyne thereunto, and lye under the same portion of heaven ; with as great bravery maie we laye clayme to all the islands which the Seignorie of Venice nowe holdes in the Levant seas, because Ciprus was once ours, by the conquest of Richard Cour de Lion, and confines with theires, then which what more infirme and

---

1 Allusion may possibly here be made to Hieronymus Benzo, who, in his " Novæ Novi Orbis Historiæ", touching the will of Pope Alexander VI, says, " Quo jure hæc dare potuit Papa, in quæ nullum jus nunquam habuit ? Nisi fortè quia Christus cœli ac terræ hœres est, cujus bonus iste Pater vicarius est, scilicet." Or more probably, judging from the use of the word " undertaker", Hakluyt may be referred to, who treats on the subject in his " Divers Voyages", published 1582.

ridiculous pretence could be framed ? and yet is the Kinge of
Spaine's argument to our interest in Virginia just in this moode
and figure.

Noe Prince may laye claime to any more amongst these newe
discoveries (and soe it was heretofore, a just distinction being
therefore kept betweene the Kinge of Castile and Portugall) then
what his people have discovered, tooke actuall possession of, and
passed over to his right ; and noe otherwise from Columbus doth
the Kinge of Spaine hold his strength and dominions to this daye
in his golden Indies ; and noe otherwise from Soto,[1] his Adelantado,
concerninge our neighbour Florida : and soe we allow him (without any one inch of intrusion) both his longitude and latitude in
this new world, we keeping from Cape Florida norward, to Cape
Briton.   The landes, countries, and territories of this parte of
America which we call ours, and by the name of Virginia, or
Nova Britannia, being carefully laid out (of purpose) to avoid
offence unto certaine boundes, and regions, begynning from the
point of land called Cape Comfort, and so holding all along the
sea-coast to the norward two hundred myles ; and from the point
of the said Cape Comfort all along the sea-coast to the so-ward
three hundred miles ; and so only all that space and circuit of
land lying from the sea-coasts of these precincts, not coming neere
any land in his actuall possession, but rather diverting from yt
many a league ; and yet holdes he neither any chargeable forces
(to dispute his right) uppon the mayne, nor keeepes colonies
(except in Florida, at St. Augustine only), nor reckons of the
same, but that is at his best pleasure.

Within the Chesopoke Bay six leagues, which Bay the Spaniards in their cartes call Sante Maria.

But what nowe concerning this point, for the more cliering of
yt to such who stumble thereat : if we should say that our right
to the West Indies themselves (since they will needes awaken us
with pretence of title) is as firme, proper, and far more auncyent
then the Spaniards ; and before the royall spirited lady Isabella,
Princesse of Castile, layd her jewells to pawne, to Luis of St.
Angelo, the King her husband's secretary, to forward the designe,
and to prevent our King Henry VII (who was both offred, and

Vide Hack-luite's dis-coveries, lib. I.

[1] Fernando de Soto, who followed the fortunes of Pizarro, and was a
main instrument in annexing Florida to the crown of Spain.

accepted Columbus's offer, and entred into capitulations with his brother Bartholomew about them, anno 1489), sure we should not want some pregnant likelyhoodes, and those not only by our simple discoveries, but by our planting and inhabiting them with the people of our owne nation four hundred years before Columbus had notice of them by the Biscan pilot,[1] who, when he dwelt in the islands of Madera, arrived with a weather beaten caravelle, and dying in his house, bequeathed (as they say) to Columbus his card of the discription of such newe landes as he had found. True yt is, the first shippes that Columbus carryed thither were but in anno 1492, which is now since one hundred and twenty yeares ; when lett any man be but pleased to looke into the learned and industrious antiquities of Mr. Camden (the carefulnes and truth of whose searches he that will undervalew, or sclaunder, shalbe much out of love with the labours of all good men and powers of vertue), and he remembers us of Madoc, the sonne of Owen Gwineth, Prince of Nor-Wales, in the yeare 1170 (which may be four hundred and thirty-nine years since), who, leaving the land in contention betweene his two brethren, Howell and David, prepared certayne shipps with men and munition, and after many unknowne landes and straunge discoveries made (sayling within the Atlantick sea, a sowardly course, yet still into the west), at last setteled in the West Indies, as his owne relation suffers construction, which he made in his returne for newe supplies, the second and third tyme, which he transported, and after that was heard no more of ; and late observations taken in these tymes

---

[1] Many authors have attempted to mar the fame of Columbus, by asserting, in circumstantial and positive language, that he derived his notion of the existence of lands in the west, from the papers of a Biscayan pilot, named Alonzo Sanchez de Huelva, who died in his house. According to Garcilasso de la Vega, this pilot, in 1484 or thereabouts, landed on Hispaniola, and wrote an account of his voyage. These accounts, as well as, in all probability, that here hinted at by Strachey, are doubtless based upon the fallacious statement of Gomara, who abounds in such unfounded stories. There is, however, a better reason than the paucity of credit due to Gomara for refusing credence to this injurious aspersion, inasmuch as it is certain that in 1474, ten years previous to the date thus assigned to the voyage of the Biscayan pilot, Columbus communicated to Paolo Toscanelli, of Florence, his notions of a westward voyage of discovery.

may confirme the probability hereof, as first in Acuzamill (so in writing Francis Lopez de Gomera[2]) the natives when they were first found, had their crosses in their chapples, and in dedicated groves, in gardens, by woodes, springes, and fowntaines, which they did honour and fall downe before, thereto saying their usuall prayers, which must mak illustration that Christians had ben there before the coming of the Spaniard : and no ecclesiastical history comendes unto us (since Solomon's voyage to Ophir ceased), nor any recordes of other antiquities (since the fabulous drowning by Deucalion's flood, or burning by Phæton, or since the sincking of the Atlantick islands), more auncyent, or before the voyage of Madoc. Lastly, the language of the Indians admitting much and many wordes, both of places, and names of many creatures, which have the accents and Welch significations, and are yet retayned, both by the Indian, Crollos (Spaniards borne there), and Mulatoes.

Or Mestizoes.[3]

But this is materiall and punctuall to our hypothesis. King Henry VII gave his letters pattents, No. 1495, unto John Cabot, a Venetian (indenized his subject, and dwelling within the Blackfriers), and to his three sonnes, who discovered for the King the north parts of America, to Meta Incognita,[4] and annexed to the crowne of England all that great tract of lande stretching from the Cape of Florida unto those parts, mayne and islands, which we call the New-found-land, some of which were not before knowen to Columbus, nor afterwards to Nicuesa,[5] Colmenaris,[6] nor Vasquez Nunnez,[7] nor any of the Castilions ; the draught of which voyage

John Cabot discovers from Florida norward to Meta Incognita, set out by King Henry VII.

[1] The island of Cozumel, near the east coast of Yucatan, discovered by Grixalva in 1518.

[2] See Gomera's "Conquista de Mexico", Art. La Religion de Acuçamil, f°. 24. Antwerp edition, 1554. Small 8vo.

[3] This word also implies "Spaniards born in the country."

[4] An indefinite name subsequently given to the north part of America by Queen Elizabeth upon the return of Frobisher from his second voyage, "as a marke and bound hitherto utterly unknowen". See "The third Voyage of Captain Frobisher, pretended for the Discoverie of Cataia by Meta Incognita, A.D. 1578."—Hakluyt, vol. iii, f°. 74.

[5] Diego de Nicuessa, one of the early Spanish adventurers ; founder of Nombre de Dios.

[6] Rodrigo Enriquez de Colmenares, a companion of Vasquez Nuñez de Balboa. See Herrera, Dec. I, lib. ix, cap. 6.

[7] Vasquez Nuñez de Balboa, the first European who crossed the main-

is yet to be seene in his Majestie's prize gallery in his pallace at
Westminster:[1] but the tumults (say they who wrought of those
tymes) then, and preparations for warrs in Scotland, tooke away
the seconding of that enterprize, yet no whit tooke awaye (I hope)
our title, more than the King of Spayne may loose his to those
parts covered with the same heavens, which he neither fortefyes
nor planteth to this day.

Soe as we may conclude, then, at least, that as Christopher
Columbus discovered the islands and continent of the West Indies
for Spayne, John and Sebastian Cabot made discoveries no lesse of
the rest from Florida, norward, to the behouf of England, being
supported by the regall authority, and sett forth at the charge and
expence of King Henry VII ; and we hope that they will leave
unto us the same way and proprietary, both to goe unto our owne
and hold yt by, as we give them ; and if they will do so (and all
lawes of nations will assist us herein), how unjust and parciall shall
that subject be, and how ill a servant in the court of his owne
prince, that will dare to give from him and his country the right
and honor of both, gayned with the expence of the publique purse,
and with the travells and lives of the industrious subject ; as well
may such a traytor lay the crowne of his monarch uppon the
Spaniard's head, as appropriate unto him his titles, his territories,
and possessions, since so undistinguishable, and such relatives are
the prince and his principalities, as he is sayd no longer to be a
kinge that is deprived and is every way denied the title of his
kingdomes ; and if this argument be in force (he will say) only
where countryes lye neere and approximate each to other, let me,
then, ask this question : what kingdoms (I pray you) and provinces lye more disjoyned and scattered (as some famelies that
agree best when they are furthest each from other) then the
King of Spaynes ? in so much as it is only that which holdes him
to this day from not being reckoned amongst the five great

land of America, and thence obtained a view of the Pacific Ocean,—this
took place in the year 1513.

[1] This copy of Cabot's map is supposed to have perished in the fire
which destroyed that gallery in the reign of William III. See Entick's
" General History of the late War."

monarchs of the world. Let no man therefore be traduced by the
accounts which falce hearted subjects (more jelous of a forreign
prince's pride, then zealous for his Majestie's royalties, and joyous
in the felicity of his government) have heretofore made audit to
him of, here being raised to the view, though a short, yet a cliere
prospect of our right.

Her Majestie, of famous memory, so well understood her princely
right herein (derived downe from her heroik grandfather to her
self), as she graunted many large pattents and gratious commissions,
to divers gentlemen of birth and quality, to inhabite those parts,
and to keepe her title quick and panting still therein : as first, to
Sir Humfrey Gilbert (whome the light first forsooke,[1] before he
would forsake his hopes and journeis thither); and afterward, to
the some time much honored Sir W. R[alegh], knight, to whome,
and to his heires, in the 26 yeare of her raigne,[2] she confirmed, at
Westminster, a large graunt, from 33 to 40 degrees of latitude,
exemplified with many ymmunityes and priviledges ; who there-
upon sent, first, thither Captaine Amadas and Captaine Barlow
(1584), which Amadas, in memory of himself, intituled a bay at
Roanoak, to this day called Bay Amadas ; and, after them, he sent
a fleete of 7 sailes, anno 1585, comanded by Sir R. Greenvill, who,
at Wococon, likewise more to the so-ward from Roanoak, gave
name to a port which yet retaines the name of Port Greenville ;
who left a colony of 100 in the said island of Roanoak, which
remayned there one whole yeare under the charge of Sir Ralph
Lane, generall of the same, and which were afterward brought from
thence (by the neclect of due supplies growing into some wants)
by Sir Francis Drake, in his returne homewardes from the sacking
of St. Domingo, Carthagena, and St. Augustine. Yet, after this,
did Sir W. R. contynewe a third and fourth voyage, which had
their misfortunes ; and anno 1587, sent a second colony of 150,
under the command of Captaine White and 12 assistents, unto
whome he gave a charter, and encorporated them by the name of
Governour and Assistants of the Citty Raleigh, in Virginia ; all of

Capt. Ama-
das and
Capt Bar-
low disco-
ver Roan-
oak, anno
1584, at the
expence of
Sir Walter
Raleigh,
Knight.

Vide lib.
secundo.

---

[1] He was drowned at midnight of the 9th of September, 1583, having
rashly ventured, with his frigate too heavily laden, to make his homeward voyage from an enterprize in which he had taken possession of
Newfoundland.   [2] Aᵒ. 1584.

which likewise miscarried by the wretchedness of unskilful instruments (abusing therein Sir W. R.), who, falling upon other practizes, and which those tymes afforded, after the said White had been in England the second time, and was refurnished out with all things needefull for the colony, indeavoured nothing lesse then the relief of the poore planters, who afterward, as you shall read in this following discourse, came therefore to a miserable and untymely destiny.

And this fatall period had Sir W. R. his good purposes, and great charges, all which I have the more largely extracted, that yt may the more expressively appeare howe this is no newe enterprize, nor taken in hand now by a generallity (which, true yt is, before Sir W. R. his attaynder, without his leave we might not make intrusion uppon, the title being only in him), to offer cause of quarrell or offence to a peacefull confederate, or Christian neighbour prince : a purpose soe far from the undertakers, councell, or body politique, to whome the charter is graunted by his Majestie, as they shall wrest with too much streyned applicacions, the endeavours of such honourable and religious personages who would raise their country, and the fame of their soveraigne, equall with others who have enlarged their powers and their titles by the like meanes ; and to avowe unto the world, that if the Spanyard shall attempt us at any tyme with ill measure, offring either to make surreption of our ships by the way thither, or to breake into our plantations with acts of hostility (as most despightfully did Pedro Melendes, their admirall, into the French colony, 44 yeares since, in Nova Francia ; who raysed their fort, and hung up the common soldiers (Laudennier, the generall, being straungely escaped), and wrought over them disdainfull inscriptions, in Spanish, importing, " I doe not this as unto Frenchmen, but as unto Lutherans", which Spanish cruelty was yet, in the winding up, as bloudely revenged agayne, by Dominique de Gourgues, of Burdeux, who, not long after, arrived there, trussed up the selfsame Spaniards upon the boughes of the same trees whereon they hung the French, with these wordes : I doe not this as unto Spaniards, but as unto tyrants and murtherers) nowe we are sett downe here, how unjustly they shall proceede heerin, and how much they shall lay themselves, and their faithes,

c

open to the construction of all nations, and haply to our revenge, which cannot strike weakly, which strikes with the sword of justice in all quarrels, the good success of the same ever depending upon the innocency of the cause.

The second objection aunswered. Secondly, where they say yt is unhonest in yt self, because injurious to the naturalls, yt being the fulfilling of the perpetuall rule of justice, *suum cuique tribuere*—how unfitt soever that *suum* be for the possessor ; indeede, yt carryes some shewe of the right, and we culpable whilst we doe labour in the contrary, as Zenophon said, instructing the young Cyrus, when the prince, being walked forth one day into the fields, and had spied two boyes comyng towards him : a great boy, covered with a short and skant coat; and a little boy, clad in a large train'd, wyde, and long gowne ; Cyrus stript them both, and shifted them, by the exchange soe making a better proportion (as he thought) of fitnes for eyther; but, I say, his learned tutor told him, how he had not done well herein, since every one was to be maister of his owne, however yt might appeare a matter of much inequality, and the owner unworthy of so large a measure of fortune.

That mynd is to be loved well, that will not leave doubting untill it hath found out the truth ; but it must then be *veritatem quærere, non insidias st[r]uere;* indeed, this were a sufficyent argument in such a commonwealth which, governed with the well ordered powers of philosophy and all naturall knowledges, wanted not neither the supernall light, but the groundes of both these (who knowes not) doe we goe to lay amongst a simple and barbarous people ; yet had they of themselves the first, that is, the practice of all morrall pollicyes and offices of vertue, as perfect, perimptory, and exact, as the unbeleeving Grecians and infidelious Romans had ; yet, since we (as true Christians) knowe that the world never was, nor must be, only and alone governed by morality, and our charity suffers for them untill we have derived unto them the true knowledge indeed, which is the worshipp of the true God and their and our blessed Redeemer, Christ Jesus, this can be no absolute instance of the right to tye us (appeare it never so upright and full of humanity) ; for sometymes, and to the bettering of mankind, the divine politique law ytself, we see, doth put on change, and byndeth not *semper et in omne,* as in the cases of theft and adultery, etc. Let me aske this question : Doe we not goe in a busines that must result greater effects, and strive within us, beyond the powers and prescriptions of morality ? No man must denye it, that will not hoodwinck his knowledge from the end and ayme, at least, to which we lett goe all our travailes ; yet shall we no whit advaunce our early and first prosecutions against those morall duties neither, but like the best prescribers of those rules themselves (in the learned and last monarchies), and with the lovers of them nowe, we will manly proceed, and exactly observe the same, even in this worke, so as the best Christian shall not be agrieved to heare of our proceedings, when they shall reade of the same in our Decades ; most true yt is, we knowing that the offices of humanity can helpe much in the forwarding hereof.

Then if our accions must relish all of pietie (not excluding neither any one particular helpe of curtesie and manlines), how religious and manly both is yt to communicate with these simple and innocent people (unles, perhaps, you will say that it is altogether unlawfull to enter commune and traffique with salvages and infidells, so bringing to the test the rich and necessary trades into Turkey and the East Indies), kneeling when we kneele, and lifting up theire handes and eyes when we pray ; not so docyble, as willing to receive our customes, herein like raced and unblotted tables, apt to receive what forme soever shallbe first drawne theron, and who have lesse faith in religion, which maie be the more probably shaken by how much they have lesse power eyther of reason or of armes to defend yt then the Turk hath, and with whome to hold discourse of their religion carrieth not, at least, that challenge and stepping into daunger, as yt doth amongst other barbarous nations, especially with the Turkes (with whome we hold such enterchangeable curtesies), who suffer not theire divine lawe, given them in their Musaph,[2] or Alcaran, by their falce prophet Mahumet (and which

---

[1] *Mishaf* is the Arabic for a code, or book ; but when used with the Arabic article, thus, *al mishaf,* it generally refers to their sacred book, Al-Kurân, being the civil and religious code of laws of the Mohammedans. It is common for the Mohammedans to designate the Kuran by the term, " Al Mishaf el Karim", the glorious book.

makes them, as they say, the true Musselman, before the Persian),
to be subject to the disputacion of any Christian, upon the payne
of a sure death.   Where amongst these, a more easie passage lyes
open to wound the illusion of Sathan, and to gayne a poore innocent to partake in our knowledges.   We take heaven by violence,
saith the evangelist ; I am sure yt is given to men of fervent
charity *et operantibus,* and good workes, albeit they be not *con
causæ,* yet are they *con sectaria* (as the schooleman saieth) of our
faith ; though not *causa regnandi,* yet are they *via ad regnum,*—
they justifie not before God, yet they doe glorifie God in His servants ; and what more meritoryous worke can ther be then to
labour in Godes cause (let the world however brand yt for folly),
and worke them to be His, whose image they beare, and participate with us of reason, carrying in their nostrills more than the
spiritt of life, the breath of beasts, which how should we then pitty
and take religious compassion of ?   And compassion, saith Guic-
ciardine, debates not causes and reasons, but proceedes to relief, for
which the duty of a good man is said to be compounded of these
two things, the glory of his Creator, and the love of his neighbour.
And who is our neighbour, demandeth our Saviour ?   He that (as
in an inne) quartereth next lodging and doore unto us ?   No, sure,
for albeit in the old lawe, the elected Jew accompted every Jew his
neighbour only, yet, since the time of grace, we are taught to
acknowledge every man that beareth the impression of God's
stampe, to be not only our neighbour, but to be our brother, howe
farr distinguished and removed by seas or lands soever from us ;
and in that stile doe far disjoyned princes salute each the other ;
and, indeed, yt is the generall office of mankind, not only to wish
good, but to bring yt to passe, for one of the like creation.

Now, what greater good can we derive unto them then the
knowledge of the true and ever lyving God ?   And what doth
more directly and rarely minister that effect then society, and to
joyne with them in friendship ?   Since we dailye see amongst ourselves the profane and the most disordered (might I not say almost
barbarous), by keepinge company, doth light uppon somethinge
the while, which stumbles him in his hast, and makes him often
take a pawse before he proceedes, eyther shame or compunction

striving within him. Nor is this without some plea of reason; for like doth in tyme fasten and worke into like (as fier worketh wood altogeather into fier), and as the eye, if it be opposed and presented to any sensible object that excelleth, will loose his proper and naturall function, so by conversing, the tyme, or reverence and awe of the better company, or some particuler advantage, circum- staunce or other, may object that to the most sensuall which maye strike his prowd heart, so as he maye find somewhat to be amazed at, about which, whilst his imaginations busy themselves, they may beget further discourse and arguments of more and more goodnes.

O let heavy things tend to their centre; let light and ayery spiritts salute Heaven, and fly up to the circumference! That great and famous instrument of publishing the gospell and knowledge of Christ Jesus, Christopher Columbus, as also Vesputius Americus, who (five yeares after Columbus) arrived here, gave this whole country and ymmeasurable continent (which is, and maye well be called the New World for his greatnes, reaching from the one pole to the other, being devided by the streights of Magellane, where it endeth under fifty-two degrees on the south side of the equinoctiall lyne) his owne name, may teach us what progresse to make even in this glorious enterprise. The first of these opened the way to the Spaniard, who since hath fild both islands and mayne with the forme of their worship to God (I leave to saye how officious and superstitious), and the other as inflamed to doe some notable and Christian act, answeared the other (a health yet unpleadged by us unles we will now set to yt). Let the examples of these move us to advaunce (now opportunity is offred) our pro- fession and faith, as Catholique, and more purged from self inven- tions. Have we either lesse meanes, fainter spiritts, or a charity more cold, or a religion more shamefull, and afrayd to delate ytself? or is yt a lawfull worke in them, and not in us, that yt is authorized unto them even by the warrant of the Church? Here Pope Alexander VI in his bull and donation to the Kings of Castile and their successors —

"Nos itaque hujusmodi vestrum sanctum et laudabile Pro- positum, plurimum in Domino commendantes, ei cupientes ut illud ad debitum finem perducatur, et ipsum Nomen Salvatoris nostri in partibus illis inducatur, hortamus vos quamplurimum in Domino et per Sacri Lavacri susceptionem, qua mandatis Apostolicis obligati estis," etc.

Which is, " We, greatly comending this your godly and laudable purpose in our Lord, and desirous to have the same brought to a due end, and the name of our Saviour to be knowne in those parts, doe exhort you in our Lord, and by the receaving of the holy baptisme, wherby you are bound to apostolicall obedience, and earnestly require you, by the bowells of mercy of our Lord Jesus Christ, that when you intend, for the zeale of the Catholique faith, to prosecute the said expedicion to reduce the people of the foresaid landes and islands to the Christian religion, you shall spare no labours at any tyme, or be deterred with any perrylls, conceaving firme hope and assuraunce that the omnipotent God will give good successe to your goodly attempts."

It is read that Themistocles hearing of the great victory that Melciades[1] had obteyned on the playne of Marathon, said, that that report would not lett him take any rest ; and Julius Cæsar wept at the sight of Alexander's image (who had at the yeares of twenty-four obtayned the name of Great), and cryed out : " Am not I miserable, that have done nothinge worthy of memory, and yet this prince at these yeares hath executed so many notable thinges ?"   Shall these, for the smoake of momentary glory, breake out thus passionate and forward ? and shall not we, for the glory of our God, be as affectionate and ambitious ?   Shall we now, when we know most the effects and perfection of goodnes (as the sun when he is highest in the zodiack moveth slowest), be dullest in our solstice and supremest height ?   The glorious St. Augustine, in his firste booke, " De Concord. Evang.", cap. 32°. goeth so far concerning the spredding abroad and teaching of our Saviour crucified, not only to the right, but to the leaft hand, as it is in the 54 of Esau[2], as he there amply discourseth how the ghospell should be published abroad, not only by those who sincerely, with true and perfect charity, assume the function of preachers, but

---

[1] *i. e.* Miltiades.   [2] *i. e.* Isaiah.   See ch. liv, v. 1-10.

also by those that declare yt, tending to temporall endes; and surely many powerfull and divine arguments might be extracted for this place, which he there at large persecuteth, which would confirme and speak satisfaction to the most sensuall : yf so, why then besides these alleaged divine motives, politique and rationall respects, even common trade and hope of profitt might make us forward to be adventurers. Our country of Virginia hath no want of many marchandize (which we in England accomplish in Denmark, Norway, Prusia, Poland, etc.; fetch far, and buy deare) which advaunce much, and assured increase, with lesse exchaung of our owne, with as few hazardes by sea, and which would maintaine as frequent and goodly a navie as what runs the Levant stage ; and those by divers treaties, both in Lattin and English, private and publique, have ben, in their particuler names and values oftentymes expressed, especyally that which hath bene published by that true lover of vertue and great learned professor of all arts and knowledges, Mr. Hariots,[1] who lyved there in the tyme of the first colony, spake the Indian language, searcht the country, and made many proufes of the richnes of the soyle, and commodites therof, besides many planters from thence, and right worthie marchants, and those knowen to be men of much belief and credit, have witnessed as much to the world, in these latter tymes, if men will give them stoage and welcome in their good opinions, and sett aside their owne overweenings and singularity to entertaine a truith, and out of those great plenties and havings (which God hath lent them to be his stewards here) be pleased to heare themselves entreated to spare but a little, little portion to the raising and building up of a *sanctum sanctorum*, a holy howse, and a sanctuary to his blessed name, amongst infidels ; placinge those therein on whome yt hath now pleased him both to be sufficiently revenged for their forefathers' ingratitude and treasons, and to descend in mercy to lighten [them] that sate in darknes, and in the shadowe of death, and to direct their feet in the waye of peace.

But perhappes there be those who will graunt that what they

[1] Thomas Hariot, or Harriot, mathematical tutor to Sir W. Raleigh, accompanied Sir Richard Grenville's expedition to Virginia in 1585, and drew up an account of his voyage, now very rare, printed 1590. f⁰.

have read in those discourses delivered to the world may be true,
but will they say, What open and actuall injury shall we doe to the
poore and innocent inhabitaunts to intrude uppon them? I must
aske them againe, In which shall we offer them injurye? for prof-
fering them trade, or the knowledge of Christ? From one of
these two or both the injury must proceede. Why? What injury can yt be to people of any nation for Christians to come unto
their ports, havens, or territoryes, when the lawe of nations (which
is the lawe of God and man (doth priviledge all men to doe soe,
which admitts yt lawfull to trade with any manner of people, in
so much as no man is to take uppon him (that knoweth any thing)
the defence of the salvadges in this point, since the salvadges
themselves may not impugne or forbid the same, in respect of
common fellowship and community betwix man and man ; albeit
I will not deny but that the salvadges may (without peradventure)
be ignorant of as much, and (alas) of more graces beside, and
particularities of humanity, the reason whereof being, because
(poor sowles) they knowe not the good which they stand in neede
of ; but we that are Christians doe knowe howe this lawe (enrich-
ing all kingdomes) gives priviledges to ambassadours, keepes the
seas common and safe, layes open ports and havens, and allowes
free scales and liberal accesse for whosoever that will import unto
them such commodities as their countreyes have, and they want ;
or export from them some of their plentye (duties and customes
provinciall observed). Yf this be so for the first, concerning the
other yt may fully be answeared with this demaund, shall yt not
followe, if traffique be thus justifiable (which intended nothing
but transitory profitt and increase of temporall and worldly goodes)
shall not plantinge the Christian faith be much more ? Yes by
how much the divine good (not subject to change, and under no
alteracion), excells, takes an accompt, and surveyes, and surpasseth
all things, and all our actions are to bend their intentions thether-
ward ; and what waye soever we make, yet miserable and wretched
he whose every lyne he drawes, every act and thought doe not
close and meete in the center of that. Alas, would we but truly
examyne all, and the best of things, which the rownd eye of the
sun lookes uppon, what is the travell for all the pompe, the trea-

sure, the pleasure, and whatsoever belongeth to this lief, compared
to the ritches of the sowle, the excellency wherof (if there were
noe other proufe to confirme yt) ys sufficientlie sett fourth by the
rich ransome that was paid for yt, even the pretious bloud of Jesus
Christ.   O our dull ignorance, depraved wills, or imperfection of
reason, or all three, how doe yee transport us? who, when we
should labour a wane and diminution of the most imposture, the
most falce, and yet eye-pleasing objects of our carnall sences, not
soe much as makinge out (after the least of them in poore Indian
canoas), howe their godlike representations beguile us that we
neclect all good things and (like English lords) pursue these on the
streeme of delight, in swift barges ?   When let us heare the end
of all, and som of all happines, saith St. John, chapt. vii, ver. 3,
and that is, to knowe one only true God and Jesus Christ, whome
He hath sent, who being the ever blessed and only wysdome of the
Father, gives, amonge other commandments to his apostles, this,—
" Goe and baptize all nations." *Universa, enim propter semet
ipsum operatus est Dominus.*—Pro. xvi.   This worde and particle
(all) infallibly and mathumatically concluding, then, even theis
poore salvadges.

   But yet it is injurious to the naturall inhabitants, still saye ours.
Wherefore ?   It is because yt is, nowe indeede, a most doughtie
and mat[er]iall reason, a great peice of injury to bring them (to
invert our English proverb) out of the warme sun, into God's
blessing ; to bring them from bodily wants, confusion, misery, and
these outward anguishes, to the knowledg of a better practize,
and ymproving of those benefitts (to a more and ever duringe advantage, and to a civiler use) which God hath given unto them,
but envolved and hid in the bowells and womb of their land (to
them barren and unprofitable, because unknowne); nay, to exalt,
as I may saie, meere privation to the highest degree of perfection,
by bringing their wretched soules (like Cerberus, from hell) from
the chaynes of Sathan, to the armes and bosome of their Saviour :
here is a most impious piece of injury.   Let me remember what
Mr. Simondes, preacher of St. Saviour's, saith in this behalf : It
is as much, saith he, as if a father should be said to offer violence
to his child, when he beats him to bring him to goodnesse.   Had

D

not this violence and this injury bene offred to us by the Romans (as the warlike Scots did the same, likewise, in Caledonia, unto the Picts), even by Julius Cæsar himself, then by the emperour Claudius, who was therefore called Britannicus, and his captains, Aulus Plautius and Vespatian (who tooke in the Isle of Wight); and lastly, by the first lieutenant sent hither, Ostorius Scapula (as writes Tacitus in the lief of Agricola), who reduced the conquered partes of our barbarous iland into provinces, and established in them colonies of old souldiers ; building castells and townes, and in every corner teaching us even to knowe the powerfull discourse of divine reason (which makes us only men, and distinguisheth us from beasts, amongst whome we lived as naked and as beastly as they). We might yet have lyved overgrowen satyrs, rude and untutred, wandring in the woodes, dwelling in caves, and hunting for our dynners, as the wild beasts in the forrests for their praye, prostetuting our daughters to straungers, sacrificing our childrene to idolls, nay, eating our owne childrene, as did the Scots in those daies, as reciteth Tho. Cogan, bachellor of phisick, in his booke,[1] De Sanitate, cha. 137, printed 1189, and dedicated to the Earle of Hertford ; in which place he bringeth in St. Hierome himself, by way of Prosop[o]pæia, affirming soe much uppon his knowledg. His wordes, there alleged, are these : What shall I say, saieth St. Jerom, of other nations, since that, when I was a boy, I saw, in Fraunce, Scotts, a people of Britannia, eate man's flesh ; and when they found in the forrests, heardes of swine, beasts, and cattaile, they would cut off the buttocks of the boyes that kept them, and also the women's papps, and tooke that to be the most deinty and delicate meat ; and, as the reverent Beda reports (before the Britons were converted to the ghospell), murthering whole troups of men to accompanye and serve their friendes dying, in the other lief, as they did to the sondry Zemes[3] in the West Indies, at what tyme

[1] The work alluded to was published under the title of " The Haven of Health," 1589—the figure 1 being mistakenly inserted above for 5. There is a copy of the work at Oriel College, Oxford. See Wood's "Athenæ Oxonienses".

[2] See "Hieron. adversus Jovinianum", liber ii. " Epistolæ D. Hieronymi". Rom. 1565. Tom. ii, fᵒ. 50.

[3] Idols, or gods, who were pretended to foretell future events. See " Peter Martyr", Dec. i, lib. ix, and " Oviedo", lib. v.

Columbus arrived there; and as they did in Peru and Mexico, at what tyme Ferdinando Cortez reduced them to the Christianity : and as the Quiyoughquisocks (or priests) doe to the idolls of the salvadges here, albeit I hope they will not long doe soe, yf by a gentle and faire entreaty we may win them to be willing to heare and learne of us and our preachers, the more civile use of every particular in which they nowe too rudely and beastly doe amisse.

All the injury that we purpose unto them, is but the amendment of these horrible heathenismes, and the reduction of them to the aforesaid manly dutyes, and to the knowledg (which the Romans could not give us) of that God who must save both them and us, and who bought us alike with a deare sufferaunce and pretious measure of mercy.

For the apter enabling of our selfes unto which so heavenly an enterprise, who will thinck yt an unlawfull act to fortefie and strengthen our selves (as nature requires) with the best helpes, and by sitting downe with guardes and forces about us in the wast and vast unhabited growndes of their[s], amongst a world of which not one foote of a thousand doe they either use, or knowe howe to turne to any benefitt ; and therfore lyes so great a circuit vayne and idle before them ? Nor is this any injurye unto them, from whome we will not forceably take of their provision and labours, nor make rape of what they clense and manure ; but prepare and breake up newe growndes, and therby open unto them likewise a newe waye of thrift or husbandry ; for as a righteous man (according to Solomon) ought to regard the lief of his beast, so surely Christian men should not shew themselves like wolves to devoure, who cannot forget that every soule which God hath sealed for himself he hath done yt with the print of charity and compassion ; and therefore even every foote of land which we shall take unto our use, we will bargaine and buy of them, for copper, hatchetts, and such like comodityes, for which they will even sell themselves, and with which they can purchace double that quantity from their neighbours ; and thus we will commune and entreate with them, truck, and barter, our commodityes for theires, and theires for ours (of which they seeme more faine) in all love and freindship, untill, for our good purposes towards them, we shall finde them practize vio-

lence or treason against us (as they have done to our other colony
at Roanoak) : when then, I would gladly knowe (of such who pre-
sume to knowe all things), whether we maye stand upon our owne
innocency or no, or hold yt a scruple in humanitye, or any breach
of charity (to prevent our owne throats from the cutting), to drawe
our swordes, *et vim vi repellere ?*

Planting (saith Sir George Peckam,[1] writing an apologye in the
like cause) may well be divided into two sorts, when Christians,
by the good liking and willing assent of the salvadges, are admitted
by them to quiett possession ; and when Christians, being inhu-
manely repulsed, doe seeke to attayne and mayntayne the right for
which they come, in regard of establishment of Christian religion,
either of them maye be lawfully exercyzed ; for what soever God,
by the ministration of nature, hath created on earth, was, at the
beginning, common among men ; may yt not then be lawfull nowe
to attempt the possession of such lands as are voide of Christian
inhabitants, for Christ's sake ?   Harke, harke, the earth is the
Lord's, and all that is therein.

> And all the world he will call and provoke,
> Even from the east, and so forth to the west.

As it is in the 50 psalme, where David prophesieth how God will
call all nations by the gospell, and in the 12 verse :

> For all is myne that on the earth doth dwell.

And who shall bar him from his possession ?   In the second booke
of Esdras, the 6 chap., 14 ver., saieth the prophet : " And besides
this Adam, whome thow madest lord over all the workes which
thou hadst created ; of him come we all."   And in the Newe Testament, Paule, calling himself the apostle of the Gentiles, in the
11 of the Romans, 32 ver., saieth, that God hath shut up all in
unbelief, that he might have mercy on all ; yet, in another place
of the same epistle, he saieth : "And how shall they call on him

---

[1] Sir George Peckham, in an anonymous work entitled "True Reporte
of the late Discoveries and Possession taken in the right of the Crown
of Englande, of the New-found-landes, by that valiaunt and worthye
gentleman, Sir Humfrey Gilbert, Knight". By G. P.   London.   1583.
8vo.   Chap. 2.

in whome they have not beleeved, and how shall they beleeve in
him on whome they have not heard ?" and therefore, he concludeth :
" O, how beautifull are the feet of them which bring glad tidings
of peace, and bring glad tidings of good things !" and in the third
of Sophonias[1] : " The children of my dispersed " (so he calleth the
apostles) " shall bring me presents from beyond the banckes of
Æthiopia." Besides (omittinge the peregrination of Paule, and
the travells of Barnabas, into so many straunge countries, islands,
and kingdomes, of the Gentiles, laboring in this office, and reduc-
ing so many cittyes of theires to the knowledg of Christ crucified,
in Grecia, in Pisidia, Pamphilia, Perga, Attalia, in Asia, and Syria,
insomuch as Antioch was come to be called, at length, the newe
cittye, and Jerusalem of the Gentiles : as also omitting the vision
which Peter saw in Joppa, of a vessell, as it had bene a great sheet,
let downe from heaven by the four corners, in which were four
footed beasts of the earth, wilde beasts, creepinge things, and fowles
of the heaven, with the voice which accompanied yt, saying, " Arise,
Peter, slay and eate ;" and this done three tymes, forbiddinge him
to accompt those things polluted or uncleane (meaninge the Gentiles), which God had sanctified and made holy ; and let me remember, which is worth all observation, and to be bound to the palmes
of our hands, and to be written uppon the lyntells and brow posts of
all our dores, for the encouragement and comfort of us, who are im-
prest in this service ; yt is one of our daily petitions, which we are
taught by our blessed Saviour, when we pray, and of that quallity
as when we have first entreated grace to esteeme, valewe, and
honour God, according as he ought to be, both in wordes and
works, as also in our holy and Christian conversacion, for so much
signifieth " Hallowed be thy Name," we presently add, " Thy
kingdome come," which ymplieth, that it would please the great
and mercyfull God that his sacred word might have a powerfull
passage throughout the world ; yea, in such sort that all nations
might be reduced to the kingdome of grace, and made partakers
of their redemption ; nor must we ymagine that this is nowe to
be done by myracle, for which it is thus foresaid by Esay[2] in his

---

[1] Zephaniah, chap. iii, v. 10.   [2] Isaiah.

66 chap.,—" Those which shall escape out of Israell shall goe farr off to Tharsis and to the remote islands, where they shall convert many nations unto the Lord, and therefore is Christ called the salvation of nations (Gen. 4, Esay 7), there being no other name under heaven unto men whereby to be saved, but only this of Christ's" (Acts 4).   And in the Old Testament we shall read, when strange and great nations would not submitt to the yoake of this knowledge of the everlasting God by faire entreaty, they were, *ferro et flammis,* compelled thereunto.   In Josua and the Judges plentifull instances adhere to the making of this good : there is to be seene how Moses, Josua, and Gedion would send spies and discoverers for the like purposes (*misit igitur Joshue filius Nun de Setim duos viros exploratores in abscondito, et dixit eis, Ite et considerate terram urbemque Jericho.*—Jos. 2) into kingdoms, nations, and provinces, and thereafter beseiged their townes and strong howldes ; and when the Gentiles would not call for mercy, they would lay waste and burne their chief citties : so fell Jericho, and so was Ai surprised, the inhabitants slayne, and their kinge hanged up.   Read the 12 chapter, and you shall find a catalogue of 31 kings and great princes of the hethen put to the edge of the sword, whilst the Gibionites, intreating by ambassadours, were taken into proteccion, and admitted into the colonye of the Israelites, and yet made their servants, and fetch-waters.

And thus these few and unskilfull scænes, but scænes of truith, brought to this act, they shall suffice to begett a setteled opinion of goodnes, and of the right of this busines, in any who hath heretofore doubted, appealing to impartiall judgments wheather the Kinge of Spaine hath priority of title to this part of America before the English ; nay, whether he hath any coulour of title by this at all ? or whether this enterprize be an unchristian acte, or injury to the naturalls ? and if neither, whether their Epiphonema[1] deserves just showt and applause, whoe declare yt unlawfull, and an unnaturall busines, and to God displeasinge.

[1] Outcry.

FINIS.

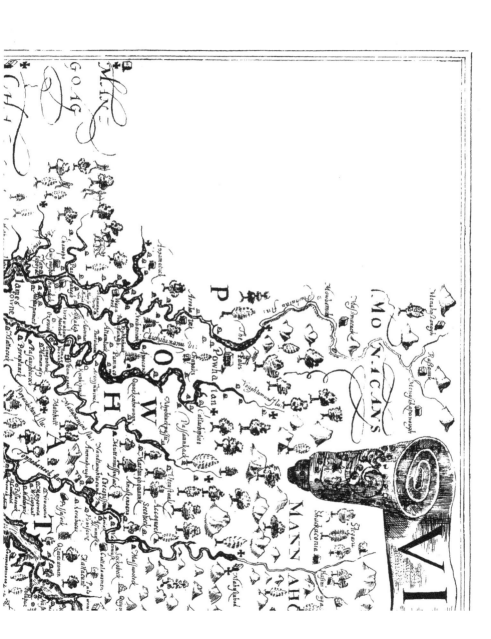

Discovered and Described by Captayn John Smith
Grauen By William Hole

and halfe

Leagues

Leagues

39

40

WD
OOKS

✝ Rushwamak

TOCWOGH

Ozinies ✝ Royal Palace

Tockwogh flu:

Chaketoin

Bolus flu:

KVSAR

Slaies flu:

Smiths Iles
Willowbyes flu:

Tesinkes mount

Sasquesahanoughs

Sasquesahanough flu:

Atquack

Quadroque

SASQVE
SAHANOVGH

Ozinies

Attaock

Vtchow

Moyoones

Moraughtacund

Menapucunt

Werowcomoco

Cinquoateck

SCALE

Macocks

Attaock

Willoughbyes flu:

ATQV
ANACK

Aquintanacksak

Aquiscack

LYKES

T. Burton Sculp: Reyxall 41 Lih 1647.

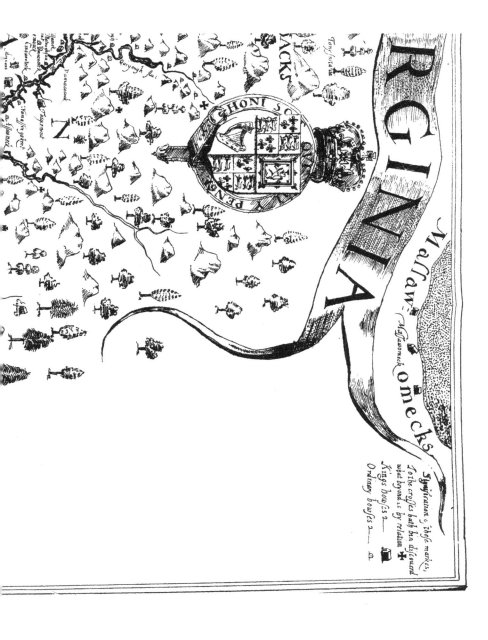

HISTORIE OF TRAVAILE

INTO

VIRGINIA BRITANNIA.

CAPUT I.

The Cosmographie of Virginia ; latitude and bounds ; extention upon a right lyne ; first division—the quality of the mountaynes, and description of the high land ; subdivided ; her temperature, wynds, soyle, valies, plaines, marishes, etc.

VIRGINIA BRITANNIA is a country in America; yt lyeth ^{Virginia} betweene the degrees of 30 and 44 of the north latitude; ^{how bounded.} the bowndes whereof may well be thus layd : on the east runneth the great ocean, or mayne Atlantique Sea ; on the south side, Florida; on the north, Nova Francia; as for the west, the lymitts thereof are unknowne, only it is supposed there maye be found the discent into the South Sea, by the Spaniards called Mar del zur, so meeting with the doubtfull north-west passage, which leades into the east, to China, Cathay, Giapan, the Moluccaes, etc., now ymagined to be discovered by our countryman Hudson, and therefore, for the more certainty therof, the search anew this presente yeare,[1] undertaken by Capt. Button, Capt. Nelson, and Capt. [2]: albeit, there be who affirme that if there should be a third land-locked sea, which hath no enter-

[1] 1612.

[2] The omitted name is Ingram. Captain Ingram commanded the Discovery, in company with Captain Button. Nelson was master of the Resolution, Captain Button's ship.

course at all with the ocean (like the Mare Caspium, and
Mare Mortuum in Palestina), yt lieth upon the north-west
of America; when yet againe Gemma Frisius recordeth[1] three
brethren that went this passage, and left a name unto the
Anian the
north-
western
streict in
the height of
supposed to
joyne Asia
and America
together. Streights of Anian, where the sea striketh sowth into Mar-
del-zur, beyond America, whereby that streict is nowe
called *Fretum trium fratrum :* we doe reade, likewise, of a
Portugal that passed this streict, of whom Sir Martin Fur-
bisher speaketh, that was imprisoned therefore many yeares
in Lishbon, likewise Anordaneta,[2] a frier of Mexico, came
out of Mar del zur this way into Germany, whose card hath
ben seene by gentlemen of good credit.

How
Virginia
extendeth
upon a
right lyne. It is a spatious and ample tract of land; from north to
south, upon a right lyne, yt maye be seven hundred myles ;
from east to west (in the narrowest place) supposed some
three hundred myles, and in other places one thousand; a
sufficient space, and ground ynough to satisfie the most
covetous and wide affection of him whoe frames to himself
any other end, then the only true one, of this plantation.

Her
division. Of all this country (in due place) we purpose to speake,
though more particularly of that parte which was begun to
be planted by the English in the yeare of our Lord God,
1606, and which may lye under the degrees of 37, 38, and
39, and which part devided may well suffer (with Germany)
Country—
high, low. the appellation of the High and Low Country, from the
mouthe of the Chesapeak Bay up to the head of the rivers,
all of which I call Virginia, as the high land about the falls
(as yet undiscovered), beinge the mayne continent, I call
Britania ; nor doe I holde this partition lesse proper, or

---

[1] See "Hakluyt", vol. iii, p. 26, (Ed. 1600), from which this passage is
copied, with very slight alterations. Reinier Gemma was a learned Dutch
mathematician and astronomer, born in 1508, at Doccum, in Friesland,
whence his cognomen of Frisius. The record alluded to, is his " Universal
Mappe".

[2] *i. e.*, Andrew Urdaneta.

more impertinent unto this kingdome, then England, Scotland, and Wales is to Great Britany; or Aquitania, Celtica, and Belgia to France; or to Spayne and Portugal, Castile and Arragon.

Concerning the high-land little can we say as yet, because thereof little have we discovered; only some Indians' relations and some fewe daies' marches into the Monocan country of our owne, have instructed us thus far.

This high land, or Britannia, then, say we, is the mayne and firme continent, which extendeth, we wot not how far, beyond that cataract or fall of water, which the Indians call Paquachowng,[1] from whence one daie's jorney into the Monocan country. Our elder planters (at their first comyng) proclaymed His Majestie king of the country at Mohominge (a neighbour village), and sett up a crosse there with His Majestie's name inscribed thereon, the said falls being one hundred and fifty myles up from the mouth of the bay, and where the current there at his head falleth, with an easye discent, three or foure fathome downe into the low contry. *Description of the high land about the falls.*

From the falls our men have heretofore marched (as the river led them) about forty or fifty miles, and fownd the high land woody, little champion,[2] with rising hills, rockey and mountanous, and so all along from the north, by a sowth-west lyne, in so much as the more so-ward the further off from the bay are those mountaynes; from them fall certaine brooks, which after come to be five principall navigable rivers,[3] these run from the nor-west into the so-est, and so into the west side of the bay, as hastinge themselves to emptye into the bay, to paye their tribute to the ocean. *The fall of every river is within 20 or 15 miles one of another.*

The mountaines here at the head are of divers natures, for *The mountaynes.*

1 The falls at Richmond, about one hundred and ten miles from the mouth of the James River.

2 Champaign.

3 Now called James River, York River, Rappahannock, Potomac, and Patuxent Rivers.

E

the rocks are of a constitution like milstones; some of a
blew metallyne coulour, some of marble, etc.; and many
pieces of scattered cristall we find, as throwne downe by
water from the mountaines; for in wynter these mountaines
are covered with snow, and when yt dissolveth, the waters
fall with such violence that they cawse great inundacions in
the narrowe vallies, which yet is scarse perceaved, being oute
in the rivers. These waters wash from the rocks such glis-
tening tinctures, that the grownd in some places seemeth as
gilded, where both the rocks and the earth are so splendant
to behold, that very good judgments would perhapps be perswaded they conteyned more then probabilities. Sure it is
that some mineralls have ben there found.

This high land is, in all likelyhoodes, a pleasant tract, and
the mowld fruictfull, especially what may lye to the so-ward;
where, at Peccarecamek and Ochanahoen, by the relation of
Machumps,[1] the people have howses built with stone walles,
and one story above another, so taught them by those
Englishe whoe escaped the slaughter at Roanoak, at what
tyme this our colony, under the conduct of Capt. Newport,[2]

Howses of stone, tame turkyes and monkyes, supposed at Peccart-canick.

landed within the Chesapeake Bay, where the people breed
up tame turkeis about their howses, and take apes in the
mountaines, and where, at Ritanoe, the Weroance Eyanoco[3]
preserved seven of the English alive—fower men, two boyes,
and one yonge mayde (who escaped and fled up the river of
Chanoke), to beat his copper, of which he hath certaine
mynes at the said Ritanoe, as also at Pamawauk are said to
be store of salt stones.

Pokotawes, which the West Indians (our neighbours) call
maiz, their kind of wheat, is here said to be in more plentye

[1] An Indian subsequently mentioned.

[2] In 1607, Captain Newport sailed in command of a squadron of three
vessels, with one hundred and ten settlers, and reached Chesapeake Bay
in April of that year. He founded James's Town,—the oldest settlement,
with the exception of St. Augustine, in the United States.

[3] Commander, or governor, as hereafter described.

then below, and the low country fruicts grow here. It is supposed that the low land hath more fish and fowle, and the high land more number of beasts. The people differ not much in nature, habit, or condicion, only they are more daring uppon us; and before we erected our forts amongst them, there was ever enmity, and open warrs, betweene the high and lowe country, going by the names of Monocans and Powhatans.

To the norward of the Falls, and bending to the noreast, lieth the skirt of this high land country, from whence the aforesaid five great navigable rivers take their heads, which run through the low land (as is before mencyoned) into the Chesapeack Bay; this quarter is altogither unknowen to us as yet, only herein are seated (say the Indians) those people whom Powhatan calls the Bocootawwonaukes, who (he saith) The Bocoo-towwon-doe likewise melt copper and other mettalls; how true we ocks melt copper. must leave to further discovery.

To the nor-ward againe of this, in the height of 44, lyeth the country called Panaquid, the kingdome wherein our Panaquid in the westerne colony, uppon the river of Sachadehock,[1] was some- height of 44. tyme planted, which is a high land, and noe lesse fruictfull then these other parts, save only the extremity of the winter's coldness makes yt lesse pleasant; yet did our men, in their yll built and bleake cottages, endure one whole wynter there, without any great losse or danger; nor is it more cold then the winter in Scotland; and therefore, though that colonye be now discontynued, yet is not yt the reason, but rather the death of the honorable gentleman, Sir John Popham, knight, late lord chief justice, chief patron of the same.

Now concerning the low land, or Virginia, which bordereth Division of the low west and nor-west, uppon the Falls, and the country of the country. Monacans and north uppon the Bocootawwanaukes, east uppon the sea, and south uppon Florida, yt may well enough be

---

[1] The Kennebeck River, where a plantation, named St. George, was founded in 1607, under the presidency of Raleigh Gilbert and George Popham, brother of Sir John, the Lord Chief Justice. Both of these brothers died in the year 1607.

devided into South Virginia and North Virginia, the Chesa-poack Bay and Powhatan River parting these twoo.

Cape Henry. The cape of this bay, on the south side, we call Cape Henry, in honour of that our most royall deceased prince, where the land shewes white hilly sand, like unto the Downes, and all along the shoare growe great plenty of pines and firrs.

Cape Charles. The north foreland of this bay, which the Indians terme Accowmack, we call Cape Charles, in honor of our now prince, at that time Duke of York : within these lyes our country, and only by the mouthe of this goodly bay the entrance there-unto.

South Virginia. South Virginia is a very low, sandy soyle, without rocks, or any stones at all; yt is thick sett with woodes of divers kindes, and in all things resembleth North Virginia, excepted the lownesse of the land and want of stones; yt hath divers rivers in yt, but none navigable to our knowledge; yt hath many islands, which lie into the sea before the firme land, but the water is not deepe for shippinge betweene them and the mayne. Yt is said to have of the same silke whereof the Chynoes make their damaske, called by the Portugalls[1] *sone del cherua,* in great aboundaunce, and sondry apothecary druggs, which are nowe found likewise as frequent in our north parte; it is a fruitfull countrey, and not much subject to cold; in this country it was that Sir Walter Raleigh planted his two colonies, in the islande aforesaid, called Roanoack.

Ronoak not under the commaund of Powha-tan : vide lib. 2. No parte of this sowth country is supposed to be under Powhatan, but under an absolute Weroance, as powerfull and great as Powhatan. It shall not fall in here so well at large to particulate the bowndes, estate, customes, and comodityes

[1] These words are not Portuguese; nor, as the " del " might at first lead us to suppose, are they Spanish. The best conjecture the editor can make is, that as allusion is doubtless made to the silk-grass of the country, the word " cherua " is a mis-spelling for " yerba", Spanish ; or " erba", Portuguese : the word "sone" is to him utterly unintelligible. The same words, without any alteration, occur in the duplicate MS. in the Ashmolean collection at Oxford.

of this south parte, since yt shal be exemplified in his due place in the second booke of this Decade, as yt is already sett forth and expressed to publike viewe, both in English and Latyn, by Theodorus de Bry[1] and Mr. Harriotts, who was a planter there one whole yeare; albeyt I must acknowledg the coleraunce of both the countryes is such, as the relation of the one maie suffice to give understanding of the condicion and quality of both.

North Virginia lyeth on the north side of Powhatan, or the first river within the Chesapeak Bay (which we have called the King's River),[2] up to the Falls,[3] and from thence by the skirt of the high land, by the heades of the rivers, even to our mayne sea, upon the northerne shoare of the which said King's River (as London upon the Thames) are seated as yet our principall townes and forts, which are in chief commaunded by their great kinge Powhatan, and are comprehended under the denomination of Tsenacommacoh, of which we maye the more by experience speak, yt being the place wherein our aboad and habitation hath now (well neere) 11[4] yeares consisted. *North Virginia Britania.*

The sommer here is hot as in Spaine, the winter cold as in Fraunce or England; the heate of the sommer is in June, July, and August, but comonly the cool breeses asswage the vehemency of the heat; the chief of winter is half December, January, February, and half March. *The temperature.*

The temperature of this country doth well agree with the English constitucions, being sometymes seasoned in the same, *Not under, or too near, the Tropicks.*

---

[1] A celebrated engraver, born at Liege in 1561, died in 1623. He is especially known for his famous collection of "Grands et Petits Voyages", Frankfort-on-the-Main, 1590-1634; 25 parts, folio, with valuable plates, some of which are used by Hariot to illustrate his "Briefe and true Report of the new found land of Virginia".

[2] James River.   [4] Falls at Richmond.

[3] In the manuscript, the word "six" was originally written, but has been crossed out, and two strokes, thus "11", inserted, in a darker coloured ink.

which hath appeared unto us by this, that albeyt, by many occasions, ill lodging at the first (the poorer on the bare ground, and the best in such miserable cotages at the best, as through which the fervent piercing heat of the sun, which there (it is true) is the first cause, creating such sommer fevers amongst them, found never resistaunce) hard fare, and their owne judgments and saffeties instructing them to worke hard in the faint tyme of sommer, (the better to be accomodated and fitted for the wynter,) they have fallen sick, yet have they recovered agayne, by very small meanes, without helpe of fresh diet, or comfort of wholsome phisique, there being at the first but few phisique helpes, or skilfull surgeons, who knew how to apply the right medecine in a new country, or to search the quality and constitucion of the patient, and his distemper, or that knew how to councell, when to lett blood, or not, or in necessity to use a launce in that office at all.

In the year 1607 was an extraordinary frost in most of Europe, and this frost was found as extreme in Virginia; but the next yeare following, and so ever since hitherto, for 8 or 10 dayes of ill weather, we have comonly 14 daies of faire and somerly weather.

The wyndes here are variable: from the so-west come the greatest gusts, with thunder and heat; the nor-west wind is commonly coole, and bringeth faire weather with it: from the north is the greatest cold; and from the east and south-east (as from the Bermudas) foggs and raines; some-tymes there are great droughts, other tymes much rayne; yet we see not but that all the variety of needfull fruits and vegetables, which we transport from hence and plant there, thrive and prosper well, of which husbandry and thrift we have made many experiments, and they stand us nowe in noe little use, having plentye of them; there is not that seed or hearb which our country here, by manuring and culture, bring forth, but doe there growe likewise quickly, and to no change-able tast from their nature,—nay, to better then in England,

The wyndes. [margin note]

Our English fruites and seedes prosper in Virginia. [margin note]

—as parsenips, carrotts, turnips, pumpions, mellons, cowcumbers, etc., and many of our English garden seedes—parsley, endiff, socory, etc.[1] There hath bene brought from the West Indies the plants of orange trees, which, put into the ground carelesly and neclected, have yet prospered; as also the vines of Fraunce, tobacco-seed from Trinidado, cotton, wool, and potatoes, we have committed to the triall of our soyle, and they yerely come to good passe; the rootes of the delicious Indian pina, sett in a sandy place, thrived, and contynued life, without respect had of yt, untill the cold wynter and the weedes choaked yt; yet is this fruict said to be daintye, nice, and of that nature, that noe art or industry hath be found out hitherto that could preserve yt in any clymate but in the West Indie Islands only. For the likelyhood of growing of sugar-canes, we have some probable hopes, by reason of the greatnes and sweetnes of the stalke of the country wheat, and the soile being aromaticall, as I may speake, by the *saxafras, galbanum mechoacon,* otherwise called *rubarbum album,* of which Dr. Bohun made triall in cold and moist bodies, for the purginge of fleame and superfluous matter; as also a whit bole, which Dr. Bohun calls *Terra alba Virginensis,* both aromaticall, and cordiall, and diapharetick, in pestilent and malignant feavers; and some other druggs; it can be but some litle tyme industriously spent to make tryall of this soe rich comoditye.

Tobacco, cotton wool, potatoes, pinas, oranges, French vynes.

Hope of the growth of sugar canes.

The vesture of the earth, in most places, doth manifestly prove the nature of the soyle, in most places, to be lusty and very rich; the coulor of the earth, we find, in dyvers places, resembleth bole armoniack, fullers' earth, marle, and that earth which we suppose of the like quality with the Lemnian *terra sigillata,* soe pricefull and marchantable in Turkey; as, likewise, there is a clay which the Indians call *assesqueth,*[2]

The soyle.

[1] Chicory.

[2] This is probably the same clay as that now called *Catlinite,* from the celebrated traveller, George Catlin, who presented the only three pieces known in this country, to the British Museum.

whereof they make their tobacco pipes, which is more smooth
and fyne then I have ellswhere seene any. But generally
the earth upon the upper crust, is a black fatt mould ; next,
under that, is a gray sandy marle, which, in dyvers places, is
a redd sand, and in other places, a hard clay ; in some places,
a fatt slimye clay ; but the best ground is knowne by burthen which it beareth, as by the greatness of trees or aboundaunce of weedes.

The val-
leyes. This part is not mountanous ; we sometyme meet with
Playnes. pleasant plaines, small risinge hills, and firtile vallies, one
Marishes. crossing another, and all watered conveniently with brookes
and springs. By the rivers are many plaine marishes, conteyning, some twenty, some one hundred, some two hundred
acres, some more, some lesse ; other playnes there are few,
but only where the salvages inhabite, but all overgrowne
with trees and woodes, being a plaine wildernes, as God first
ordeyned yt.

A digres-
sion, giving
likelihoods
that Vir-
ginia be-
neath the
falls to have
binn sea
heretofore. All the low land of South and North Virginia is conjec-
tured to have bene naturally gayned out of the sea ; for the
sea, through his impetuous and vast revolution (who knowes
not), savinge upon every coast, in some places wyns, and in
other places looseth ; and we find within the shoares of our
rivers, whole bancks of oysters and scallopps, which lye un-
opened and thick together, as if there had bene their naturall
bedd before the sea left them ; likewise, the fashion of the
earth is in smale risinge mounts, which may well be supposed
that the violence of the wynd hath cawsed, by dryving the
light sand togither ; moreover, the mould and sword of the
earth is not two foot deepe all along neare the sea ; and that
which is, comes only by the grasse, and leaves of trees, and
such rubbish, rotting upon it in contynuance of time ; for in
digging but a fathome or two, we commonly find quick sand.
Againe, under the crust of the surfage, we find not any
stones nor rocks (except neere the high land), naie, in most
places to soward, not so much as a pebble-stone, which must

proceed through want of tyme, that no duration hath there ben wrought; besides, the water ebbs and flowes well nigh unto the heades of all the rivers (I meane to the falls, unto the high land), and the natives which now people with us, on this side beneath the said falls, are conceaved not to have inhabited here belowe much more than three hundred years. But all which we cannot but truly conjecture, that the upland countrye is a faier and goodly country, more sweet and wholsome in respect of ayre, and more rich in soyle, and fraighted with better comodyties, and those more necessary, besides the assurance of mineralls, concerninge which we doe already heare the Indians talke both of allam mines and copper, to the soward, where hath bene sufficyent tyme for digestion. All which we must submitt to more cleire discoveryes.

CAPUT II.

Description of the five principall rivers within the Chesapeak Bay, together with such by-streames which fall into them; a description of the Sasquesahanougs of Cape La Warre; the falling with our coast; the fitness of Cape Comfort to fortefie at.

ON the west side of the bay, we said were five faire and delightfull navigable rivers, of which we will now proceede to report. The first of these rivers, and the next to the mouthe of the bay, hath his course from the west and by north. The name of this river we call the King's River;[1] they call Powhatan, according to the name of a principall country that lyeth upon the head of yt; the mouthe of this river is neere three myles in breadth, yet doe the shoells force the channell so neere the land, that a sacre[2] will overshoot yt

1st River.

The river Powhatan, which wee call the King's River.

---

[1] Now James River.
[2] Falco sacer; Anglicè "Sacre", or "saker", a bold and active species of falcon.

at point blanck.   This river hath a channell, for a hundred
and forty miles, of depth betwixt seven and fifteen fathome,
holding in breadth, for the most parte, two or three miles;
and in which are many isles, both great and small. Yt falleth
from rocks far west, in a country inhabited by a nation, as
aforesaid, that they call Monacan; but where yt cometh into
our discovery, yt is Powhatan.   In the furthest place that
hath been diligently observed, are falls,[1] rocks, showlds, etc.,
which makes yt past navigation any higher; albeit, forty
miles above the said falls, yt hath two branches, or other
rivers,[2] that fall into yt : the head of the northermost comes
from certaine steepe mountaines, that are said to be impass-
able; the head of the other comes from high hills afar of,
within the land, from the topps of which hills, the people
saie they see another sea, and that the water is there salt;
and the journey to this sea, from the falls, by their accompt,
should be about ten daies, allowing, according to a march,
some fourteen or sixteen miles a day.[3]   In the runing downe-
ward, the river is enriched with many goodly brooks, which
are maynteyned by an infinite number of small rundells and
pleasant springs, that disperse themselves for best service, as
doe the vaines of a man's body.

From the south side there falls into this river, first, the

[1] The falls at Richmond.

[2] The Appomatox and Chicamohominia rivers.

[3] This delusion seems to have been entertained for many years ; for in
a work entitled the "The Discovery of New Brittaine", published by
John Stephenson, London, 1651, is a map in which " the Sea of China
and the Indies" is brought close under the Alleghany mountains, with
the following information attached ;—" Sir Francis Drake was on this sea
and landed in anno 1577, in 37 degrees, where hee tooke possession in
the name of Queen Eliza : calling it New Albion, whose happy shoers
(in ten dayes march, with fifty foote and thirty horsemen, from the head
of Jeames River, over those hills and through the rich adjacent valleyes,
beautyfied with as proffitable rivers which necessarily must run into that
peacefull Indian sea) may be discovered to the exceeding benefit of Great
Brittaine, and joye of all true English."

pleasant river of Appamatuck; next (more to the east) are
the two rivers of Quiyoughcohanock;[1] a little further is a
bay,[2] wherein falleth three or four pretty brookes and creeks,
that half entrench the inhabitants of Warraskoyack; then
the river of Nandsamund,[3] and lastly, the brooke of Chesapeak.[4]

From the north side is the river of Chickahamania, the
black river of James Towne; another by the Cedar Isle,
wherein are great stoore of goodly oysters; then a convenient harbour for crayes,[5] frygatts, or fisher-boates, at Kecoughtan, the which By-Rill so conveniently turneth yt self
into baies, coves, and creeks, that the place is made very
pleasant thereby to inhabite, the corne fields being circled
therein in manner as so many peninsulaes. The most of
these by-rivers are inhabited by severall nations, or rather
families, taking theire names from those rivers, and wherein
a severall governour or weroance comaundeth.

The first, and next the river's mouthe, are the Kecoughtans, then the Paspaheghes, the Arrohatecks, and the place
called Powhatan. On the south side of this river are the
Appamatucks, the Quiyoughcohanocks, the Warraskoyacks,
the Nandsamunds, the Chesapeaks; of this last place, the
bay beareth his name.

Fourteene miles norward from the river Powhatan, is the
river Pamunck,[6] which we call the Prince's River, navigable
sixty or seventy miles with shippes of good burthen; but
with catches and small barkes, thirty or forty miles further. At the ordinary flowing of the salt water, yt devideth
yt self, at Cinquoteck, into two gallant braunches: on the
south braunch enhabite the people of Youghtamund; on the

---

[1] Chipoak Creek.   [2] Cobham Bay.
[3] Which still bears the same name.
[4] Probably Elizabeth river.
[5] Craiera ?—Old Romance. A hoy or smack.—*Bailey.*
[6] York river.

Youghta-
mund Mal-
tapanient,
braunches
of Pa-
muncke
river.
north braunch, Mattapament. On the north syde of this river
is Werowocomoco, where theire great kinge inhabited when
we came first into the country.   Ten or twelve miles lower,
on the south side of this river, is Kiskiak; these, as also
Appamatuck, Orapaks, Arrohatack, and Powhatan, are their
great king's inheritance, chief alliance, and inhabitaunce.
Upon Youghtamund is the seat of Powhatan's three brethren,
whome, we learne, are successively to govern after Powhatan,
in the same dominions which Powhatan, by right of birth, as
the elder brother, now holdes.   The rest of the countryes
under his comand, are (as they report) his conquests.

Before we come to the third river, that falleth from the
mountaines, there is another river, which takes not his birth
or head so high, but is only some thirty miles navigable, and
yssueth from out the riffs and breaches from the inland; the
river is called Payankatank, the inhabitants whereof are but
few (not now above forty or fifty), and are the remayne of
the conquered Kecoughtans, whome he transported thither;
for in the yeare 1608, Powhatan surprised the naturall inhabitaunce of Payankatank, his neighbours and subjects.   The
occasion was to us unknowne; but the manner was thus performed.   First, he sent divers of his men to lodge amongst
them one night, pretending a generall hunt, who were to
give the allarum unto an ambuscado of a greater company
within the woodes, who, upon the signe, given at the hower
appointed, environed all the howses, and fell to the execution.
Twenty-four men they kild outright (the rest escaping by
fortune and their swift footmanship) ; and the long haire of
the one side of their heads, with the skin cased off with shells
or reedes, they brought away to Powhatan.   They surprised
also the women and childrene and the Weroance, all whome
they presented to Powhatan.   The lockes of haire, with their
skynnes, they hanged on a lyne betweene two trees; and of
these Powhatan made ostentation, as of a greate triumphe, at
Werowocomoco, not longe after, shewing them to such the

English as came unto him at his appointment, to trade with him for corne, thincking to have terrified them with this spectacle, and, in the midst of their amazement, to have seased them; but, God be praysed, yt wrought not feare but courage in our people, and awaked their discreations to stand upon their guard the more cautulously; and, by that meanes, they came off agayne from him, contrary to his purpose. And let me truly saie, how they never killed man of ours, but by our men's owne folly and indiscretion, suffering themselves to be beguiled and enticed up into their howses, without their armes; when then (indeed) they have fallen uppon them, and knockt out their braynes, or stuck them full of arrowes (no force) for their credulity. But of so many men which the common report, out of ignoraunce, gives out here to have been slayed by those Indians, I would but knowe if they can name me three men that they ever killed of ours in skirmish, fort or field, but by this kind of subtilty in them and weakness in ours; and whome the sword of justice would have cut off (had they escaped the Indians), for adventuring so amongst them, either against discipline and the charge given them, or, indeed, against common sense and duty unto their owne lyves.

How our people miscarie amongst the Indians.

The third navigable river by the Naturalls of old was called Opiscatumeck, of late Toppahanock, and we the Queen's River;[3] this is navigable some one hundred and thirty miles. At the top of yt inhabite the people called Mannahoacks, amongst the mountaynes, but they are above the place described in Captain Smithe's mappe. Upon this river, on the north side, are seated a people called Cuttatawomen, with thirty fighting men; higher on the river are the Moraughtacunds, with thirty able men; beyond them Toppahanock, with one hundred men; far above is another Cuttatawomen, with twenty men; on the south, far within the river, is Nandtaughtacund, having one hundred and fifty men; this river

3rd river. Toppahanock or the Queen's river.

The inhabitants.

---

[1] Now called Rappahannock river.

also, as the former, hath her burthen extraordinary both of fish and fowle.

4th river. Patawo- meck or Elizabeth's river. The fourth river is called Patawomeck,[1] and we call Elizabeth River, and is six or seven miles in breadth; yt is navigable one hundred and twenty miles, and fed, as the rest, with many sweet rivers and springs, which fall from the bordering hills; many of them are planted, and yeld noe lesse plentye and variety of fruict then the other rivers; yt exceedeth with aboundance of fish, and is inhabited on both sides: first, on the south side, at the very entrance, is Wighcocomoco, and The inhabitants. which hath some one hundred and thirty fighting men; beyond that is Cekakawwon, with thirty men; then Onawmanient, with one hundred men; then Satawomeck, with one hundred and sixty able men: here doth the river devide ytself into three or four convenient rivers; the greatest of the least is called Quiyough, tending nor-west, but the river ytself turneth nor-east, and is still a navigable streme. On the westerne side of this bought[2] is Taxenent, with forty able men; somewhat further is Potapoco, with twenty men. In the east parte of the bought of the river is Pamacocack, with sixty men; after Moyoones, with one hundred men; and lastly, Nacothtank, with eighty able men. The river, ten miles above this place, maketh his passage downe a low pleasand valley, overshadowed in many places with high rocky mountaines, from whence distill innumerable sweet and pleasant springs.

Captain Samuell Argolls discovery in Patawomeck river. Within this river Captain Samuell Argoll, in a small river which the Indians call Oeniho, anno 1610, trading in a bark called the *Discovery*, for corne, with the great king of Potawomeck, from him obteyned well neere four hundred bushells of wheat, pease, and beanes, beside many kind of furrs, for nyne pounds of copper, four bunches of leads, eight dozen of hatchetts, five dozen of knives, four bunches of bells, one dozen of cizers, all not much more than 40s. English; as also

---

[1] The Potomac.   [2] The same as "bight", a bend or indentation.

from the said king's brother Iopassous, king of a place called Pastanzo, recovered an English boy, called Henry Spilman, who had lived amongst them one whole yeare, and despayring of ever seeing his native country, his father's howse, (for he was discended of a gentill family), or Christians any more; likewise here Captain Argoll found a myne of antimonye (which seldome goes unaccompanyed with quicksilver), as also a kind of hevy black sand upon the bancks, which, being washed, weyed massy with lead.

An English boy recovered from the King of Pastanzo.

A myne of antimony and another of leade.

The fifte river is called Pawtuxunt, and is of a lesse proportion then the rest, but the channell is sixteen or eighteen fathome deepe in some places; here are infinite sculls of divers kynds of fish more than elsewhere. Upon this river dwell the people called Acquintanacsuck, Pawtuxunt, and Mattapament; two hundred men was the greatest strength that could be there perceaved by our discoveries, but they inhabite togither, and not so dispersed as the rest; these, of all other, were found the most civile to give entertainment, and therefore from them we received great curtesie and much good cheare.

5th river. Pawtuxant or the Duke's river.

The inhabitants.

Thirtye leagues norward is a river not inhabited,[1] yet navigable, by reason of the red earth or clay resembling bolearmoniack; the discoverers called yt Bolus. At the end of the bay (where is six or seven miles in breadth) there fall into yt four small rivers, three of them yssuyng from divers boggs, envyroned with divers mountaines. Uppon the river inhabite a people called the Sasquesahanougs; they are seated two dayes higher then was passage for the discoverers' barge; howbeyt, sixty of the Sasquesahanougs came to the discoverers with skynns, bowes, arrowes, targetts, swords, beades, and tobacco-pipes for presents. Such great and well-proportioned men are seldome seene, for they seemed like giants to the English,—yea, and to the neighbours,—yett seemed of an honest and simple disposicion, with much adoe restrayned

We now call it Howard river.

The description of the Sasquesahanonges.

---

[1] The Susquehannah river.

from adoring the discoverers as gods. These are the most
straung people of all those countryes, both in language and
attire ; for their language yt may well beseeme their propor-
tions, sounding from them as yt were a great voice in a vault
or cave, as an eccoe : their attire is the skyns of beares and
woulves ; some have cassocks made of beares' hides and skyns,
that a man's neck goeth through the skynn's neck, and the
eares of the beare are fastened to his shoulders behind, the
nose and teeth hanging downe his brest, and at the end of
the nose hangs a bear's paw ; the half sleeves cominge to the
elboe were the necks of beares, and the armes through the
mouth, with pawes hanging in a chaine for a jewell ; his to-
bacco-pipe three quarters of a yard long, prittely carved with
a bird, a deare, or with some such devise, at the great end,
sufficient to beat out the braynes of an horse. Likewise their
bowes, and arrowes, and clubbs, are sutable to their greatnes ;
these are scarse knowne to Powhatan. They can make well
neare 600 able and mightie men, and are pallisadode in their
townes to defend them from the Massawomecks, their mortall
enemyes. Five of these chief Weroances came abourd the
discoverers, and crossed the bay with them in their barge: the
picture of the greatest of them is here portrayed [*See plate*] :
the calf of whose leg was three quarters of a yard about, and
all the rest of his lymes so answerable to that proportion, that
he seemed the goodliest man they ever sawe ; his haire the
one syde was long, the other shorne close, with a ridge over
his crowne like a coxcomb; his arrowes were five quarters
long, headed with flints or splinters of stones, in forme like a
heart, an ince broad, and an ynch and a half or more long ;
these he wore in a woolve's skyn on his back for his quiver,
his bow in the one hand and his club in the other.

Tockwogh,
which we
call Sydney
river.   On the east side of the bay, is the river of Tockwough,[1] and
uppon yt a people that can make a hundred men, seated
some seven miles within the river, where they have a fort

[1] Chester river.

From De Bry.

Etched by Sarah E. Major.

A SUSQUEHANNAH CHIEF.

very well pallisadode, and mantelled with the bark of trees; next to them are the Ozinies, with sixty men; more to the south of that east side of the bay, is the river of Kuscara-woak,[1] upon which is seated a people with two hundred men; after that, is the river of Wicocomaco,[2] and on it a people with one hundred men. The people of these rivers are of a little stature, and of another language from the rest, and very rude; but they on the river of Accohanock,[3] with forty men, and they on the river of Accomack, with eighty men, doe equallize any of the territories of Powhatan, and speak his language, who, over all those, doth rule as kinge.

Accowmack flu. Rapaha-nock, flu. Kuscara-woak flu. Wighcow-maw flu.

Southward, they went to some parts of Chawonock and the Mangoangs, to search them there left by Sir Walter Raleigh; which parts, to the towne of Chesapeack, hath formerly bene discovered by Mr. Harriotts and Sir Ralph Lane.[4] Amongst those people, are thus many severall nations, of sondry languages, which environ Powhatan's territories : the Chawonocks, the Mangoangs, the Monacans, the Mannacans, the Mannahocks, the Sasquesahanougs, the Acquanachuks, the Tockwoghes, and the Nuskarawaoks. Of all these, not any one understandeth another, but by interpreters; their severall habitations are more plainly described by the annexed mappe, set forth by Captain Smith, of whose paines taken herein, I leave to the censure of the reader to judge. Sure I am there will not returne from thence, in hast, any one who hath bene more industrious, or who hath had (Captain Geo. Percie excepted[5]) greater experience amongst them, however misconstruction maye traduce here at home, where is not

Chawonock, Mangogues.

Severall nations, severall languages.

A dew re-membrance of Capt. Smyth, vide lib. iii, cap.

Capt. Georg Percy.

---

[1] Choptank river. [2] This river still bears the same name.

[3] This river still bears the same name.

[4] He accompanied Sir Richard Grenville as Lieutenant-master in his voyage of 1585.

[5] Captain George Percy held the temporary presidency of the colony on two occasions, viz., on the departure of Captain John Smith in 1609, and on the return of Lord Delawarr to England, on account of ill health, in 1611.

G

easily seene the mixed sufferaunces, both of body and mynd, which is there daylie, and with no few hazards and hearty griefes undergon.

The mappe will likewise present to the eye the way of the mountaynes, and current of the rivers, with their severall turnings, bayes, shoulders, isles, inletts, and creekes, the breadth of the waters, the distances of places, and such like. In which mappe, observe this, that, as far as you see the little crosses, either rivers, mountaines, or other places, have discovered; the rest was had by informacion of the salvadges, and are set downe accordinge to their instruccions.

Likewise, from the north point of our bay, which (as aforesaid) the Indians call Accowmack, and we Cape Charles, hath the coast all along bene discovered, even to the river of Sachadehoc ; for Captain Argoll, in his returne from the search of the Bermudas, anno 1610, after he had lost Sir George Somers, 28 July, in a dangerous fogg, well beaten to and fro, fell with the mayne, standinge for Cape Cod, and made good, from 44 degrees, what Captayne Bartho. Gosnoll[1] and Captayne Waymouth[2] wanted in their discoveries, observing all along the coast, and drawing the plotts thereof, as he steered homewardes, unto our bay ; and divers tymes went ashore, offering acquaintaunce and trade unto the people: and in the latitude of 39 discovered another goodly bay,[3]

---

[1] In 1602 Captain Gosnold sailed with thirty-two men direct across the ocean and came upon the coast of Massachusetts, and after sailing onward some time, reached a bold promontory, which, from the great quantity of fish caught in the vicinity, he named Cape Cod ; thence, "trending the coast southerly," he entered Buzzard's Bay, adjoining Rhode island, which he named " Gosnold's Hope." See "A briefe and true relation of the discoverie of the north part of Virginia made this present year." By J. Brereton. 1602, 4to.

[2] See a narrative of this voyage, in a work entitled " A true relation of the most prosperous voyage made this present yeare 1605, by Captain George Waymouth in the discovery of the land of Virginia. Written by J. Rosier, a gentleman employed in the voyage. Londini, impensis Geo. Bishop. 1605, 4to.   [3] Delaware Bay.

into which fell many tayles of faire and large rivers, and which might make promise of some westerly passage; the cape whereof, in 38½, he called Cape Lawar,[1] from which, not far off, lay a faier banck into the sea, as upon the Newfoundland, where he hawled excellent fish, both hollibut, cod, and ling, of which he brought an essay and tast of two hundred couple into the colony; an excellent fish, and of such a kind that will keepe a whole yeare in shipp's hold, with little care, a triall whereof his lordshippe likewise brought with him into England; and uppon the shoares, in divers places, he killed great store of seales.

Concerninge the falling with our owne coast, yt is true Our coaste
bould to fall
with. that there cannot be a bolder shoare to come in, withall, in any country in the world; for, first, before we come in sight of yt thirty leagues, we smell a sweet savour, as is usually from off Cape Vincent, the south cape of Spayne (if the wynd come from the shoare); besides, we have chaunge of water, and sounding at twenty-five fathoms, twenty leagues off.

The coast of South Virginia, from Cape Henry, lieth south The coaste
of South
Virginia. and north, next hand some seven leagues, where there goeth in a river[2] (as is neerest gessed by the Chawonocks and Mangoangs), but it is not navigable far; all along this coast, for seven leagues, we have seven and eight fathome of water, within one league of the shoare, one not farre. More to the southward of this in-lett river, is a cape of an island called Croatoan, which cape is that which we call the South Cape of Virginia; beyond which cape, so-ward and no-west of this cape, or Croatoan, lye certayne smale islands (as before remembred), that front the coast of the mayne; but the sea betweene the mayne and them, is not for any shipping to passe. Into this shallow sea, there falls divers rivers from the mayne, which the salvadges have discribed unto us, and plentye of people thereon.

If we come in with the Chesapeak Bay open, our sound-

1 Now Cape Henlopen.   2 Currituck Inlet.

The depth of our bay and channell.

ings are fifteene fathome to five; but if we hit the channell, we have no lesse than seven or eight fathome; soe yt is all over bold inough, having neither ledges of rocks, no barres, no sandy shelfes, but the bottom even and plaine.

How our two Capes do beare.

Our two capes, Cape Henry and Cape Charles, doe lye no-east and by east, and so-west; and they be distant each from other, in breadth (where the sea runs in betweene both lands, so making our bay, and only entrance into our country), as broad as may be betweene Quinborowgh and Lee.

Point Comfort convenient and necessary to fortefy.

When we come in with Cape Henry, we have six, seven, and eight fathome, to the point at the bottome of the bay and mouthe of King's River, into which all shippes that will enter, must borrowe soe much of the shoare, as to come within little lesse then musquett shott of the point, by reason of the showldes lying uppon the sotherne shoare; by which may be observed howe convenient and necessary a pointe that is for a substanciall fortificacion to be raised, to secure all the other forts and townes upon this river from what enemies soever.

CAPUT III.

Of the begynning and originall of the people; the great King Powhatan, his description, and sale of his birthright to the English.

Paucæ civitates novint originem.

IT were, perhappes, to curious a thing to demand, how these people might come first, and from whome, and whence, to inhabite these so far remote, westerly parts of the world, having no intercourse with Africa, Asia, or Europe? And, considering the whole world, so many yeares (by all knowledg received) was supposed to be only conteyned and circumscribed in the discovered and knowne travayled bounds of those three, according to that old conclusion in the scholes: *Quicquid præter Africam et Europam est, Asia est,*—whatsoever land doth neither apperteyne unto Africk nor to Europe, is part of Asia. As also to question how that it should be, that they (if descended from the people of the first creation) should maintayne so generall and grosse a defection from the true knowledg of God, with one kind, as it were, of rude and savadge lief, customes, manners, and religion, it being to be graunted that (with us), infallably they had one and the same discent and begynninge from the universall deluge, in the scattering of Noah, his children, and nephewes,[1] with their families (as little colonies), some to one, some to other borders of the earth, to dwell; as in Egypt (so writing Berosus[2]), Esenius and his household tooke up their inhabitation; in Libia and Cyrene, Tritanes; and in all the rest of Africa, Jupetus Priscus; Attalaas in the east Asia; Ganges, with some of Comerus Gallus' childrene, in Arabia Felix, within the confines of Sabea, called the frankincense-bearer; Canaan in Damascus, unto the utmost bounds of Palestine.

But it is observed, that Cham[3] and his famely were the only far travellers and straglers into divers and unknowne countryes, searching, exploring, and sitting downe in the same; as also it is said of his famely, that what countrye soever the childrene of Cham happened to possesse, there beganne both the ignoraunce of true godliness, and a kind of bondage and slavery to be taxed one upon another; and that noe inhabited countries cast forth greater multitudes to range and stray into divers remote regions, then that parte of Arabia in which Cham himself (constrayned to flye, with wief and childrene, by reason of the mocking he had done to

[1] *i.e.* grandsons.

[2] Berosus, a Chaldæan, astronomer, and historian, and priest of Belus, lived, it is thought, about the time of Alexander. Some consider the astronomer and historian different persons. In 1545, Annius of Viterbo, published a history, in five books, under the name of Berosus, the falsity of which was soon discovered. It is from this spurious publication that Strachey derives his learning on the subject of the dispersion of the descendants of Noah. See said work, under the division, 'Genealogia primorum ducum post diluvium."

[3] Ham.

his father) tooke into possession; so great a misery (saieth
Boem of Auba[1]) brought to mankind the unsatisfied wandering of that one man; for, first from him, the ignorance of
the true worship of God tooke beginninge, the inventions of
heathenisme, and adoration of falce gods, and the devill; for
he himself, not applying him to learne from his father the
knowledg and prescribed worship of the eternall God, the
God of his fathers; yet, by a fearefull and superstitious in-
stinct of nature, carryed to ascribe unto some supernaturall
power a kind of honour and reverence not divout, to knowe
the essence and quality of that power, taught his successours
newe and devised manner of God's sacrifices and ceremonies,
and which he might the easier impresse into the childrene,
by reason they were carryed with him so yong awaye from
the elders, not instructed nor seasoned first in theire true
customes and religion.   Insomuch as then we may conclude
that, from Cham and his tooke birth and beginninge the first
universall confusion and diversity which ensewed afterwards
throughout the whole world, especially in divine and sacred
matters; whilst it is said againe of the childrene of Sem and
Japhet, how they, being taught by their elders, and content
with their owne lymitts and confines, not travelling beyond
them into new countries, as the other, retayned still, untill
the comynge of the Messias, the only knowledge of the eternall and never-changeable Trinity.

By all which, it is very probable, likewise, that both in the
travailes and idolatry of the famely of Cham, this portion of
the world westward from Africa, upon the Atlantique sea,
became both peopled and instructed in the forme of the pro-
phane worship, and of an unknowen deity.   Nor is yt to be
wondered at, where the abused Trinity of religion is suffered

[1] Johannes Bohemius Aubanus, so named from his birth-place, Aub
or Auw, a town situated on the Gollach in Bavaria. See his work as
translated by Lucio Fauno into Italian, "Gli Costumi, le Leggi et Usanze
di tutte le Genti." Venice, 1560. Lib. i, cap. 1.

to perish, if men, in their owne inventions and lives, become so grosse and barbarous, as (by reading the processe of this history will hardly be perceaved) what difference maye be betweene them and brute beasts, sometymes worshipping brute beasts, naie, things more vile, and abhorring the in-bredd motions of nature it self, with such headlong and bloudye ceremonies of will and act.

But how the vagabond race of Cham might discend into this newe world without furniture (as maye be questioned) of shipping, and meanes to tempt the seas, togither how this great continent, devided from the other three, should become stoared with beasts, and some fowle, of one and the same kind with the other parts, especially with lions, beares, deare, wolves, and such like, as from the first creation tooke begin-ninge in their kind, and after the generall flood were not anewe created, nor have their begynning or generation (as some other) *ex putredine et sole,* by corruption and heat, let me referre the reader to the search of Açosta, in his i. booke, cap. 20, 21, of his morrall and naturall history of the West Indies; who hath so officyously laboured herein, as he should but bring owles to Athens, who should study for more strayned or newe authority concerning the same.

Thus much, then, maie, in brief, be said and allowed con-cerning their originall or first begynning in generall, and which maye well reach even downe unto the particular inha-bitants of this particuler region by us discovered, who cannot be any other then parcell of the same and first mankynd.

Concerning themselves more especyally, and their division, as we find them in these provinces where we are, we maye well say how this tract or portion of land, which we call Vir-ginia Britannia,—by the inhabitants, as aforesaid, Isenacom-macah,—is governed, in chief, by a great kinge, by them called by sondry names, according to his divers places, qua-lities, or honours by himself obteyned amongst them, either for his valour, his government, or some such like goodnes,

Virginia Britania called Isenacom-macah by the natur-alls.

which they use to admire and comend to succeeding tymes with memorable titles, and so comonly they of greatest merritt amongst them aspire to many names.

Powhatan, the great king, when borne and how discended into so many severall provinces. The great emperour at this time amongst them, we comondly call Powhatan, for by that name, true yt is, he was made knowne unto us when we arrived in the country first, and so, indeed, he was generally called when he was a yong man, as taking his denomination from the country Powhatan, wherin he was borne, which is above the Falls, as before mentioned, right over aneinst the islands, at the head of our river, Powhatan sells his birth-right to the English anno 1609. and which place, or birth-right of his, he sold, anno 1609, about September, unto Captain Francys West, our lord generall's brother, who therefore erected there a fort, calling yt West's Fort, and sate himself down there with one hundred and twenty English; the inhabitants themselves, especially his frontier neighbour prince, call him still Powhatan; his owne people sometimes call him Ottaniack, sometyme Mamanatowick, which last signifies "great king"; but his proper right name, which they salute him with (himself in presence), is Wahunsenacawh.

The bownds of the great King's empire. The greatnes and boundes of whose empire, by reason of his powerfulnes and ambition in his youth, hath larger lymitts then ever had any of his predicessors in former tymes, for he seemes to comaund south and north from the Mangoages and Chawonoaks bordering upon Roanoake, and the Old Virginia, to Tockwogh, a towne pallisadode, standing at the north end of the bay, in forty degrees or thereabouts; south-west to Anoeg (not expressed in the mappe), whose howses are built as ours, ten daies distant from us, from whence those Weroances sent unto him of their comodityes; as Weinock, a servant, in whom Powhatan reposed much trust, would tell our elder planters, and could repeat many wordes of their language he had learned among them in his ymployment thither for his kinge, and whence he often returned, full of presents, to Powhatan, west to Monahassanugh, which stands at the foote of the mountaines; nor-west to the borders of Massa-womeck and Bocootawwonough, his enemyes; nor-east and by east to Accohanock, Accowmack, and some other petty nations, lying on the east side of our bay.

He hath divers seates or howses; his chief, when we came into the country, was upon Pamunky River, on the north side or Pembrook side, called Werowocomoco, which, by interpre-tacion, signifies kinges'-howse; howbeit, not liking to neigh-bour so neere us, that house being within some fifteen or six-teen miles where he saw we purposed to hold ourselves, and from whence, in six or seven howers, we were able to visite him, he removed, and ever since hath most what kept at a place in the desarts called Orapaks, at the top of the river Chickahamania,¹ betweene Youghtamund and Powhatan. He is a goodly old man, not yet shrincking, though well beaten with many cold and stormye winters, in which he hath bene patient of many necessityes and attempts of his fortune to make his name and famely great. He is supposed to be little lesse than eighty yeares old, I dare not saye how much more; others saye he is of a tall stature and cleane lymbes, of a sad aspect, rownd fatt visaged, with graie haires, but plaine and thin, hanging upon his broad showlders; some few haires upon his chin, and so on his upper lippe: he hath bene a strong and able salvadge, synowye, and of a daring spirit, vigilant, ambi-tious, subtile to enlarge his dominions: for, but the coun-tryes Powhatan, Arrohatock, Appamatuck, Panunky, Yought-amund, and Mattapamient, which are said to come unto him by inheritance, all the rest of the territories before named and expressed in the mappe, and which are all adjoyning to that river whereon we are seated, they report (as is likewise before remembred) to have been eyther by force subdued unto him, or through feare yeilded: cruell he hath bene, and quar-rellous as well with his owne weroancces for triffles, and that to strike a terrour and awe into them of his power and con-

Werowoco-macow, Powhatan's chief seat, when we first landed.

Removed from thence, and his reason.

Powhatan's description.

¹ Chicamahominia.

H

dicion, as also with his neighbours in his yonger days, though now delighted in security and pleasure, and therefore stands upon reasonable condicions of peace with all the great and absolute weroances about him, and is likewise more quietly settled amongst his owne.

His feare of us.

Watchfull he is over us, and keepes good espyall upon our proceedings, concerning which he hath his sentinells, that at what tyme soever any of our boats, pinacies, or shippes, come in, fall downe, or make up the river, give the alarum, and take it quickly one from the other, untill it reach and come even to the court or hunting howse, wheresoever he and his cronoccoes, that is, councellours, and priests are, and then he calls to advise, and gives out direccions what is to be done, as more fearing then harmed, at any tyme, with the danger and mischief which he saith we intend unto him, by taking awaye his land from him and conspiring to surprize him, which we never yet ymagined nor attempted, and yet, albeit, the con-

His subteltie.

ceipt of as much strongly possesseth him : he doth often send unto us to temporize with us, awayting perhapps a fit opportunity (inflamed by his furious and bloudy priests) to offer us a tast of the same cuppe which he made our poore countrymen drinck of at Ronoak,[1] not yet seeming willing to hold any open quarrell or hostility with us ; but in all advantages which he sometymes takes against our credulous and beguiled people, he hath yet alwaies so carried as, uppon our complaint to him, yt is rather layed uppon some of his worst and unruly people of which he tells us ; even our King James (commaunding so many divers men) must have some irreguler and unruly people, or ells uppon some of his pettie weroances, whome, peradventure, we have attempted (saieth he) with offences of the like nature, then that yt is any act of his, or done by his commaund, or according to his will, often flattering us that he will take order that it shall be no more soe, but that the Tassantasses, that is, the stranger King James his people, and his people shalbe all one, bro-

[1] The colony planted by Sir Walter Raleigh, which Powhatan destroyed.

thers and friends; and thus he served us, at what time he wrought the Chickahamines (a nation, as we have learned before the cominge in of us, so far from being his subjects, as they were ever his enemies) into a hatred of us (being a mighty people and our neighbours), and us into the suspition of them, by urging them to betray such of our men as traded with them for corne, three whereof (yt is true) they slew without cause or offence given, and had done as much for the rest, had not their owne feare and cowardize withheld them, and this he wholly laid uppon them, excusing himself to us by their nomber and unrulines, yea, soe far he will goe herein sometyme, that when some of his people have done us wrong, and by his provoking too, he will not faile underhand, after the fact, to tell us the authers of our wrong, giving us leave, and bidding us revendge us upon them, of such subtile understanding and pollitique carriage is he.

In all his ancyent inheritances he hath howses built after their manner, and at every howse provision for his entertainment according to the tyme. About his person ordinarily attendeth a guard of forty or fifty of the tallest men his country doe affourd. Every night, upon the four quarters of his howse, are four centinells drawen forth, each standing from other a flight shott; and at every half houre, one from the *corps du guard* doth hallowe, unto whome every sentinell returnes answere round from his stand; yf any fayle, an officer is presentlye sent forth that beateth him extreamlye. *His attendaunce and guarde.*

The word weroance, which we call and conster for a king, is a comon word, whereby they call all comaunders, for they have but fewe words in their language, and but few occasions to use any officers more then one comaunder, which comonly they call weroance. *The meaning of the word weroaunce.*

It is strange to see with what great feare and adoration all this people doe obey this Powhatan, for at his feete they present whatsoever he comaundeth, and at the least frowne of his brow the greatest will tremble, yt may be, because he is *The dutie and reverence which the petty kings and people beare unto this Powhatan.*

very terrible, and inexorable in punishing such as offend
him; for example, he caused certaine malefactors, at what
tyme Captain Smith was prisoner with him, (and to the sight
whereof Captain Smith, for some purpose, was brought,) to
be bound hand and foote, when certaine officers appointed
therunto, having from many fiers gathered great store of
burning coales, raked the coales rounde in forme of a cock-
pitt, and in the middst they cast the offenders to broyle to
death. Some tymes he causeth the headds of them that offend
to be layd upon the aulter or sacrificing stone, and one or
two, with clubbs, beat out their braynes. When he would
punish any notorious enemye or trespasser, he causeth him
to be tyed to a tree, and with muscle-shells or reedes the
executioner cutteth off his joints one after another, ever casting what is cutt of into the fier; then doth he proceede with
shells and reedes to case the skyn from his head and face;
after which they rip up his belly, teare out his bowells, and
so burne him with the tree and all. Thus themselves reported, that they executed an Englishman, one George Caw-
son, whom the women enticed up from the barge unto their
howses, at a place called Appocant. Howbeit, his ordinary
correction is to have an offender, whome he will only punish
and not put to death, to be beatten with cudgells as the Turks
doe. We have seene a man kneeling on his knees, and, at
Powhatan's commaund, two men have beaten him on the
bare skyn till the skyn have ben all bollen and blistered, and
all on a goare blood, and till he hath fallen senceles in a
swound, and yet never cryed, complayned, nor seemed to ask
pardon, for that they seldom doe.

And sure yt is to be wondred at, how such a barbarous and
uncivill prince should take unto him (adorned and sett forth
with no greater outward ornament and munificence) a forme
and ostentation of such maiestie as he expresseth, which oftentymes strikes awe and sufficyent wonder in our people presenting themselves before him, but such is (I believe) the

POWHATAN SURROUNDED BY HIS WIVES.

impression of the Divine nature, and however these (as other
heathens forsaken by the true light) have not that porcion of
the knowing blessed Christian spiritt, yet I am perswaded
there is an infused kind of divinities and extraordinary (appointed that it shall be so by the King of kings) to such who
are his ymedyate instruments on earth (how wretched soever
otherwise under the curse of misbelief and infidelity), as it is
in the psalme, *Dixi vos sicut Dij estis,* to governe and dwell
in the eyes and countenances of princes. Somewhat maye
this catagraph or portrature following serve to expresse the
presentment of this great king Powhatan.[1]

According to the order and custome of sensuall heathenisme, in the allowance of poligamie, he may have as many
women as he will, and hath (as is supposed) many more then
one hundred, all which he doth not keepe, yet as the Turk,
in one seraglia or howse, but hath an appointed number, which
reside still in every their severall places, amongst whome,
when he lyeth on his bedd, one sittith at his head and another
at his feet; but when he sitteth at meat, or in presenting
himself to any straungers, one sitteth on his right hand, and
another on his leaft, as is here expressed [*See plate*].

Of his women, there are said to be aboute some dozen at
this present, in whose company he takes more delight then
in the rest, being for the most parte very young women, and
these commonly remove with him from howse to howse,
eyther in his tyme of hunting, or visitacion of his severall
howses. I obteyned their names from one Kemps, an Indian,
who died the last yeare of the surveye at Jamestowne, after
he had dwelt with us almost one whole yeare, much made of
by our lord generall, and who could speake a pretty deale of
our English, and came orderly to church every day to prayers,
and observed with us the keeping of the Sabbothe, both by
ceassing from labour and repairing to church. The names of
the women I have not thought altogither amisse to sett downe
as he gave them unto me, and as they stood formost in his

His multi-plicity of weomen.

1 The portrait is not given.

king's affection, for they observe certaine degrees of greatnes
according to the neerenes they stand in their prince's love
and amorous entertainment.

The names
of some of
his weomen.

Winganuske.	Attosomiske.	Ortoughnoiske.
Ashetoiske.	Ponnoiske.	Oweroughwough.
Amopotoiske.	Appomosiscut.	Ottermiske.
Ottopomtacke.	Appimmoiske.	Memeoughquiske.

His
children.

He was reported by the said Kemps, as also by the Indian
Machumps, who was sometyme in England, and comes to and
fro amongst us as he dares, and as Powhatan gives him leave,
for yt is not otherwise safe for him, no more then yt was for
one Amarice, who had his braynes knockt out for selling but
a baskett of corne, and lying in the English fort two or three
daies without Powhatan's leave; I say they often reported

Twenty
sonns, ten
daughters.

unto us that Powhatan had then lyving twenty sonnes and
ten daughters, besyde a young one by Winganuske, Machumps his sister, and a great darling of the king's; and besides, younge Pocohunta, a daughter of his, using sometyme
to our fort in tymes past, nowe married to a private captaine,
called Kocoum, some two yeares since.

Upon his
best deserv-
stoweth his
cast women,
as doth the
Turk.

As he is weary of his women, he bestoweth them on those
that best deserve them at his hands. When he dineth or
suppeth, one of his women, before and after meat, bringeth
him water, in a woodden platter, to wash his hands; another
waiting, with a bunch of feathers, to wipe them instead of a
towell; and the feathers, when he hath wiped, are washed
and dryed again.

At Oropaks
lies his
riches.

A mile from Oropaks, in a thickett of wood, he hath a
principall howse, in which he keepeth his kind of treasure, as
skynnes, copper, perle, and beades, which he storeth upp
against the tyme of his death and buryall; here is also his
store of red paint for oyntment, and bowes, and arrowes.
This howse is fifty or sixty yards in length, frequented only
by priests. At the four corners of this howse stand four
images, not as Atlants or Telamones, supporters to beare up

pillers, posts, or somewhat ells in the stately building; nor, as in the auncient tymes, the images and pedegrees of the whole stock or family were wont to be sett in portches or the first entrance into howses, with a porter of specyall trust, who had the chardge of keeping and looking unto them, called Atrienses; but these are meerely sett as carefull sentinells (for sooth) to defend and protect the howse (for soe they be-lieve of them); one is like a dragon; another like a beare; the third like a leopard; and the fourth a giant-like man, all made evill favoured ynough according to their best workman-shippe.

CAPUT IV.

A catalogue of the severall weroances' names, with the name of the parti-culer province wherein they govern, togither with what forces for the present they are able to furnish their great king, Powhatan, in his warrs.

THE great king Powhatan hath devided his countrey into many provinces or shiers (as yt were), and over every one placed a severall absolute weroance or comaunder, to him contributary to governe the people, ther to inhabite; and his petty weroances, in all, may be in number about three or fower and thirty, all which have theire precincts and bowndes, proper and comodiously appointed out, that no one intrude uppon the other of severall forces; and for the ground wherein each one soweth his corne, plante his apoke[1] and gardeine fruicts, he tithes to the great king of all the comodityes growing in the same, or of what ells his shiere brings forth apperteyning to the lands or rivers, corne, beasts, perle, fowle, fish, hides, furrs, copper, beades, by what meanes soever ob-teyned, a peremptory rate sett downe as shal be mencioned in the sixth chapter; nor have I thought yt altogether amisse

The country devided into many shyres, and a wero-aunce or lord govern-ing in every shyre.

[1] *i. e.* tobacco. See glossary at the end of this volume.

to remember here, and offer to consideracion (for all after occasions), a cathologue of the several weroances' names, with the denominatyon of the particuler shier (as aforesaid) wherein they governe togither, with what forces, for the present, they are able to send unto the warrs. Upon Powhatan, or the King's river, are seated as followeth :—

1. Parahunt, one of Powhatan's sonnes, whome we therefore call Tanxpowatan, which is as much to say Little Powhatan, and is weroance of the country which hath his owne name, called Powhatan, lying (as before mencioned) close under the Falls, bordering the Monacans, and he maye at the present be furnished with fifty fighting and ready men.

2. Ashuaquid, weroance of Arrohateck, sixty men.

3. Coquonasum, weroance of Appamatuck, one hundred men.

4. Opussoquionuske, sister to Coquonasum, a weroancqua, or queene of a little muscaram or small village of Appamatuck, not unlike an ancyent Episcata Villatica,[1] and she was of power to have spared, uppon comaund, some twenty able fighting men. Howbeyt, her towne we burnt, and killed some of her people, herself miscarieng with small shott in pursuit in the woods in wynter 1610, for a treacherous massacre which she practized upon fourteen of our men, whome she caused her people to invite up into her towne, to feast and make merry, entreating our men before hand to leave their armes in their boate, because they said how their women would be afrayd ells of their peeces.

5. Kaquothocun, weroance of Weanock, one hundred men.

6. Oholasc, queene of Coiacohanauke, which we comonly (though corruptly) call Tapahanock, and is the same which Captain Smith, in his mappe, calls Quiyoughcohanock, on the south shoare, or Salisbury syde, whose sonne, being yet younge, shal be, by Powhatan's appointment, weroance of the said Quiyoughcohanock : his name is Tatahcoope. The wero-

[1] This (to the editor unintelligible) word is repeated in the duplicate copy of the MS. in the Ashmolean museum at Oxford.

ance Pepiscummah (whome by construction as well the Indians as we call Pipisco) was somtyme possessed in right of
this part, as by birth and possession discended the true and
lawfull weroance of the same, but upon a displeasure which
Powhatan conceaved against him, in that the said Pipisco,
and that not many yeares synce, had stollen away a chief
woman from Opechankeno (one of Powhatan's brothers), he
was deposed from that regiment, and the aforesaid Tatacope
(a supposed sonne of Powhatan's, by this said Queene Oholasc) made weroance, who, being yet young (as is said), is
for the most part in the governement of Chopoke, at Cha-
wopo, one of Pipiscoe's brothers; yet is Pipisco suffered to
retaine in this his country a little small kaasun, or village,
uppon the rivadge of the streame, with some few people about
him, keeping the said woman still, whome he makes his best
beloved, and she travells with him upon any remove, in hunting tyme, or in his visitacion of us, by which meanes, twice
or thrice in a sommer, she hath come unto our towne; nor is
so handsome a savadge woman as I have seene amongst them,
yet, with a kind of pride, can take upon her a shewe of greatnes; for we have seene her forbeare to come out of her quin-
tan or boat through the water, as the other, both mayds and
married women, usually doe, unles she were carryed forth
betweene two of her servants. I was once early at her howse
(yt being sommer tyme), when she was layed without dores,
under the shadowe of a broad-leaved tree, upon a pallett of
osiers, spred over with four or five fyne grey matts, herself
covered with a faire white drest deare skynne or two; and
when she rose, she had a mayd who fetcht her a frontall of
white currall, and pendants of great but imperfect couloured
and worse drilled pearles, which she put into her eares, and
a chayne, with long lyncks of copper, which they call Ta-
poantaminais, and which came twice or thrice about her neck,
and they accompt a jolly ornament; and sure thus attired,
with some variety of feathers and flowers stuck in their haires,

I

they seeme as *debonaire*, quaynt, and well pleased as (I wis) a daughter of the howse of Austria behune[1] with all her jewells; likewise her mayd fetcht her a mantell, which they call puttawus, which is like a side cloake, made of blew feathers, so arteficyally and thick sowed togither, that it seemed like a deepe purple satten, and is very smooth and sleeke; and after she brought her water for her hands, and then a braunch or twoo of fresh greene asshen leaves, as for a towell to dry them. I offend in this digression the willinger, since these were ceremonyes which I did little looke for, carrying so much presentement of civility, and which are not ordinarily perfourmed to any other amongst them, and the Quiyoughco-hanocks may be able to make for the wars sixty fighting men.

8. Tackonekintaco, an old weroance of Warraskoyack, whome Captain Newport brought prisoner with his sonne Tangoit, about   [2] 1610, to our lord generall, lying then at Point Comfort, and whome againe his lordship released upon promises and a sollemne contract, made by the old man, to exchange with his lordship, after he should have gathered in his harvest, in August following, five hundred bushells of wheate, beanes, and pease, for copper, beades, and hatchetts; and for the better coulour (carrying away his sonne) and left a nephew (as he said) of his with his lordshippe, as a pawne or hostage, untill the perfourmaunce; howbeit, the imposture nephew, privie before hand to the falcehood of the old man, watchinge his opportunity, leapt over bord one night (being kept in the Delawarr); and to be more sure of him at that tyme, fettered both leggs togither, and a sea gowne uppon him, yet he adventured to get clier by swiming, and either to recover the south shoare, or to sinck in the attempt. Which of either was his fortune we knowe not, only (if he miscarried) we never found his body nor gowne, and the Indians of War-raskoyack would often tymes afterward mock us, and call to

---

[1] Decked.   [2] A similar gap in the original.

us for him, and at length make a great laughter, and tell us
he was come home; how true or false is no great matter; but
indeed the old kinge, after that tyme, refused to performe
the former bargaine, for which his lordshipp, to give them to
understand how he would not be soe dealt with all, sent forth
two companyes, the   of   [1] his lordshipp's owne company, under the comaund of Captaine Brewster, and some
seamen, under Captaine Argoll, who fell uppon twoo townes
of his, and burnt them to the grownd, with all their goodly
furniture of matts and dishes, woodden potts and platters, for
of this sort is all their goodly epitrapezia or vessells belonging to their use for the table, or what ells, and these Warraskoyacks maie make sixty men.

9. Weyhohomo, a great weroance of Nansamund.

10. Amapetough, another lesse weroance of Nansamund.

11. Weyingopo, a third weroance of Nansamund.

12. Tirchtough, a fourth weroance of Nansamund, and
these fower togither may make of sturdy and bold salvadges
two hundred.

13. Wowinchopunck, weroance of Paspahegh, whome, the
9th of February, 1610, whilst he, with a company of his people,
were attempting some practize uppon our old blockhouse at
Jamestowne, and had bene for the same skulking about there
some two or three dayes and nights, Captaine Georg Percy,
governour of the towne, sent forth Ensigne Powell and Ensigne Waller to make surprize of him, yf they could possibly,
and bring him alive into the towne; but they not finding
him at any such advantage, yet loath to loose him, or let him
escape altogither, sett uppon him, (he being one of the
mightiest and strongest salvages that Powhatan had under
him, and was therefore one of his champions, and one who
had killed trecherously many of our men, as he could beguile
them, or as he, at any tyme, found them by chaunce single
in the woods, strayed beyond the comaund of the block-

[1] A similar gap in the original MS.

howse), and Powell runing uppon him, thrust him twice
through the body with an arming sword; howbeit, his people
came in soe fast, and shoat their arrowes so thick, as our men
being unarmed (in their dublets and hose only) and without
peices, were faine to retire whilst the Indians recovered the
weroance's body, and carried yt awaye with a mightye quicknes and speed of foot, and with a horrible yell and howling;
howbeit, the liuetenant of the blockhowse, one Puttock, followed hard and overreached one of the cronockoes or chief
men, and, closing with him, overthrew him, and, with his
dagger, sent him to accompanye his master in the other world;
and the Paspaheghes may make in nomber for the warrs,
forty.

14. Pochins, one of Powhatan's sonns at Kecoughtan, and
was the young weroance there at the same tyme when Sir
Thomas Gates, liuetenant-general, took possession of yt. Yt
is an ample and faire countrie indeed, an admirable porcion
of land, comparatively high, wholsome, and fruictfull; the
seat sometyme of a thowsand Indians and three hundred
Indian howses, and those Indians, as it may well appeare,
better husbands[1] then in any parte ells that we have observed,
which is the reason that so much ground is there cliered and
opened, enough, with little labour, alreddy prepared, to receave corne, or make viniards of twoo or three thowsand
acres; and where, beside, we find many fruict-trees, a kind
of goosbery, cherries, and other plombes, the maricock[2] aple,
and many prettie copsies or boskes (as it weere) of mulberye
trees, and is (indeed) a delicate and necessary seat for a citty
or chief fortificacion, being so neere (within three miles by
water) the mouth of our bay, and is well appointed a fitt seat
for one of our chiefe comaunders, since Point Comfort being

---

[1] i. e. husbandmen.

[2] The maracock is the passion flower, which though it bears no fruit in
this country, does so in the West Indies. The fruit is of the size and
colour of a pomegranate. See appendix to Gerard's Herbal.

(out of all dispute) to be fortefied to secure our townes above, to keepe open the mouth of our river, by which our shippinge maye be lett in, yt will require the faith and judgement of a worthy comaunder to be there alwayes present; besides, there wil be good fishing, and upon one of the Capes maie be placed a garrison to attend the furnasses and boyling potts for the making of salt, which without question there (as in the Bermudas) maye be made for all occasions to serve the colony, and the fishinge voyages for the same likewise upon Point Comfort. A great quantity of one kind of silke grasse growes there, as yet disorderly, which, having the grownd prepared and fitted for yt, would retribute a comodytie worthie the paines, yf not going beyond the expectacion of the good which is hooped of yt. Our lord generall and liuetenant generall have erected here two forts, as is before remembred, the one called Fort Henry, the other Charles Fort, as the river which runs in and serves both his lordship hath called Southampton river. Uppon the death of an old weroance of this place, some fifteen or sixteen yeares since (being too powerfull neighbours to side the great Powhatan), yt is said Powhatan, taking the advantage, subtilly stepped in and conquered the people, killing the chief and most of them, and the reserved he transported over the river, craftely chaunging their seat and quartering them amongst his owne people, untill nowe at length the remayne of those living have with much suit obteyned of him Payankatanck, which he not long since (as you have heard likewise) dispeopled. They might have made of able men for the warrs, thirty.

15. Upon the river of Chickahamania, some eight or twelve miles from Jamestowne, which falls from the north side unto our King's river the Chechahamias, being a warlike and free people; albeit, they paye certaine duyties to Powhatan, and for copper wil be waged to serve and help him in his warrs, yet they will not admitt of any weroances from him to governe over them, but suffer themselves to be regulated and

guided by their priests, with the assistance of their elders, whome they call Cawcawwassoughes, and they may make three hundred men.

Upon Panunky or the Prince's River

16. Opechanckeno,
17. Kequotaugh,
18. Taughaiten,

{ all three Powhatan's brethrene, and are the triumviri, as yt were, or three kings of a country called Opechanekeno, upon the head of Panunky river, and these may make three hundred men.

19. Ottahotin, weroance of Kiskiack, fifty.

At Werowacomoco, Powhatan himself hath a principall residence, and there maye be of able men, forty.

20. Ohonnamo, weroance of Cantaunkack, one hundred.

21. Ottondeacommoc, weroance of Mummapacune, one hundred.

22. Essenataugh, weroance of Pataunck, one hundred.

23. Vropaack, weroance of Ochahannanke, forty.

24. Keyghanghton, weroance of Cassapecock, one hundred.

25. Weyamat, weroance of Kaposecocke, four hundred.

26. Attasquintan, weroance of Pamareke, four hundred.

27. Nansuapunck, weroance of Shamapa, one hundred.

28. At Orapaks, Powhatan himself comaunds with fifty.

29. Opopohcumunck, weroance of Chepecho, three hundred.

30. Attossomunck, a Taux weroance of Paraconos, ten.

31. Pomiscatuck, weroance of Youghtamund, seventy.

32. Werowough, weroance of Mattapanient, one hundred and forty.

And thus yt may appeare, howe they are a people who have their severall divisions, provinces, and princes to live in, and to comaund over, and to differ likewise (as amongst Christians) both in stature, language, and condicion; some being great people, as the Susquesahanoughs; some very litle, as the Wighcocomocos; some speaking, likewise, more articulate and plaine, and some more inward and hollowe, as ys before remembred; some curteous and more civile; others cruell and bloudy; Powhatan having large territoryes and many petty kings under him, as some have fewer.

CAPUT V.

A true description of the people, of their cullour, attire, ornaments, constitutions, dispositions, etc.

THEY are generally of a cullour browne or rather tawny, which Their collour. they cast themselves into with a kind of arsenick stone, like red patise or orpement, or rather red tempered oyntments of earth, and the juyce of certaine scrused rootes, when they come unto certaine yeares, and this they doe (keeping themselves still so smudged and besmeered) eyther for the custome of the countrye, or the better to defend them (since they goe most what naked) from the stinging of muskitoes, kinds of flies or biting gnatts, such as the Greekes called scynipes, as yet in great swarmes within the arches,[1] and which heere breed aboundantly amongst the marish whorts and fenne berries, and of the same hue are their women; howbeit, yt is supposed neither of them naturally borne so discouloured; for Captain Smith (lyving somtymes amongst them) affirmeth how they are from the womb indifferent white, but as the men, so doe the women, dye and disguise themselves into this tawny cowler, esteeming yt the best beauty to be neerest such a kynd of murrey as a sodden quince is of (to liken yt to the neerest coulor I can), for which they daily anoint both face and bodyes all over with such a kind of fucus[2] or unguent as can cast them into that stayne, as is said of the Greek women how they coulored their faces

---

1 The sailors' term for the Archipelago.
2 Lat. a red dye, generally understood for alkanet, or rouge.

with certain rootes called Brenthina,[1] and as the Britaynes
died themselves red with woad ;[2] howbeit, he or she that hath
obteyned the perfectest art in the tempering of this collour
with any better kind of earth, yearb, or root, preserves yt not
yet so secrett and pretious unto her self as doe our great
ladyes their oyle of talchum,[3] or other painting white and
redd, but they frindly comunicate the secret, and teach yt
one another; after their anoynting (which is daylie) they
dry in the sun, and thereby make their skynns (besides the
coulor) more black and spotted, which the sun kissing oft
and hard, adds to their painting the more rough and rugged.

Their heads and shoulders they paint oftennest, and those
red, with the roote pochone,[4] brayed to powder, mixed with
oyle of the walnutt, or bear's grease; this they hold in sommer doth check the heat, and in winter armes them in some
measure against the cold.   Manie other formes of payntings
they use; but he is the most gallant who is the most mon-
strous and uglie to behold.

Their hayre, their no beardes. Their haire is black, grosse, long, and thick; the men
have no beardes; their noses are broad, flatt, and full at the
end, great bigg lippes, and wyde mouthes, yet nothing so
unsightly as the Moores; they are generally tall of stature,
and streight, of comely proportion, and the women have
handsome lymbes, sclender armes, and pretty hands, and
when they sing they have a pleasaunt tange in their voices.

Their attyre. For their apparrell they are sometymes covered with the

[1] The editor has only met with the word in this form in Hesychius.
It is evidently derived from Βρένθιον, of which Julius Pollux speaks, in
his " Onomasticon", lib. vi, cap. 19, as one of the μῦρα coming from Lydia.
[2] The dye of woad is not red, but blue.
[3] Talc itself enters largely into the composition of rouge ; but the so
called "oil of talc" was produced by dissolving flowers of zinc in vinegar,
and was formerly extolled as possessing vast power in many imaginary
operations, and amongst the rest, of being a sovereign remedy for all
diseases.
[4] See dictionary at the end of this volume.

From De Bry.   Etched by Sarah E. Major.

AN INDIAN FEMALE.

skynns of wyld beasts, which in winter are dressed with the haire, but in the sommer without, the better sort use large mantells of deeres' skynns, not much differing from the Irish falings,[1] some embroidered with white beads, some with copper, other painted after their manner, but the common sort have scarse wherewithall to cover their nakednes, but stick long blades of grasse, the leaves of trees, or such like, under broad baudricks of leather, which covers them behind and before.

The better sort of women cover themselves (for the most part) all over with skin mantells, finely drest, shagged and fringed at the skyrt, carved and couloured with some pretty work, or the proportion of beasts, fowle, tortayses, or other such like imagry, as shall best please or expresse the fancy of the᷍ wearer; their younger women goe not shadowed amongst their owne companie until they be nigh eleaven or twelve returnes of the leafe old (for soe they accompt and bring about the yeare, calling the fall of the leafe taquitock); nor are they much ashamed thereof, and therefore would the before remembered Pochahuntas, a well featured, but wanton yong girle, Powhatan's daughter, sometymes resorting to our fort, of the age then of eleven or twelve yeares, get the boyes forth with her into the markett place, and make them wheele, falling on their hands, turning up their heeles upwards, whome she would followe and wheele so her self, naked as she was, all the fort over; but being once twelve yeares, they put on a kind of semecinctum lethern apron (as doe our artificers or handycrafts men) before their bellies, and are very shamefac't to be seene bare. We have seene some use mantells made both of Turkey feathers and other fowle, so prettily wrought and woven with threeds, that nothing could be discerned but the feathers, which were exceeding warme and very handsome. *Nuda mulier erat pulchra* (saith Plautus) *quam purpurata pulchrior?* indeed the or-

A difference in the garments of the better sort of weomen.

---

[1] Fallaing or falluing, Celtic for a cloak or mantle.

nament of that sexe, who receave an addition of delicacy by
their garments.   True yt is sometymes in cold weather, or
when they goe a hunting, or seeking the fruits of the woods,
or gathering bents for their matts, both men and women (to
defend them from the bushes and shrubs) put on a kynd of
leather breeches and stockings, all fastened togither, made
of deere skynns, which they tye and wrappe about the loynes,
after the fashion of the Turkes or Irish trouses.

Their
ornaments. They adorne themselves most with copper beades and
paintings.   Of the men, there be some whoe will paint their
bodyes black, and some yellowe, and being oyled over, they
will sticke therein the soft downe of sundry couloured birdes
of blew birds, white herne shewes, and the feathers of the
carnation birde, which they call Ashshawcutteis, as if so many
variety of laces were stitched to their skinns, which makes a
wondrous shew ; then, being angry and prepared to fight,
paint and crosse their foreheadds, cheekes, and the right side
of their heades diversly, either with *terra sigillata* or with
their roote pochone.

The women have their armes, breasts, thighes, shoulders,
and faces, cuningly ymbrodered with divers workes, for pounc-
ing or searing their skyns with a kind of instrument heated
in the fier.   They figure therin flowers and fruits of sondry
lively kinds, as also snakes, serpents, eftes, &c., and this they
doe by dropping uppon the seared flesh sondry coulers, which,
rub'd into the stampe, will never be taken awaye agayne,
because yt will not only be dryed into the flesh, but growe
therein.

The fashion
of wearing
their hayre:
the women
play the
barbers. The men shave their haire on the right side very close,
keeping a ridge comonly on the toppe or crowne like a coxcomb ; for their women, with two shells, will grate away the
haire into any fashion they please.   On the left side they
weare theire haire at full length, with a lock of an ell long,
which they annoint often with walnut oyle, whereby it is very
sleeke, and shynes like a raven's winge.   Sometymes they

tye up their lock with an arteficyall and well-laboured knott
(just in the same fashion as I have seene the Carrazzais[1] of
Scio and Pera), stuck with many coulored gew-gawes, as the
cast-head or brow-antle of a deare, the hand of their enemie
dryed, croisetts of bright and shyning copper, like the newe
moone. Many weare the whole skyne of a hauke stuffed
with the wings abroad, and buzzards' or other fowles' whole
wings, and to the feathers they will fasten a little rattle,
about the bignes of the chape[2] of a rapier, which they take
from the tayle of a snake, and sometymes divers kinds of
shells, hanging loose by small purfleets or threeds, that, being
shaken as they move, they might make a certaine murmuring
or whisteling noise by gathering wynd, in which they seeme
to take great jollity, and hold yt a kind of bravery.

Their eares they boare with wyde holes, comonly two or
three, and in the same they doe hang chaines of stayned
pearle braceletts, of white bone or shreeds of copper, beaten
thinne and bright, and wound up hollowe, and with a greate
pride, certaine fowles' leggs, eagles, hawkes, turkeys, etc.,
with beasts' clawes, beares, arrahacounes, squirrells, etc. The
clawes thrust through they let hang upon the cheeke to the
full view, and some of their men there be who will weare in
these holes a small greene and yellow-couloured live snake,
neere half a yard in length, which crawling and lapping himself about his neck oftentymes familiarly, he suffereth to kisse
his lippes. Others weare a dead ratt tyed by the tayle, and
such like conundrums.

Their eare-rings.

The women are in themselves so modest as in the tyme of
their sicknes they have great care to be seene abroad, at what
tyme they goe apart, and keepe from the men in a severall
roome, which they have for themselves as a kynd of gynæ-

The modesty of the weomen at som tymes.

---

[1] He probably means κορῆτσαι, or, more corruptly, κορῆτσαις, Romaic
for "girls".

[2] From "chapa,", Spanish, the steel or silver tip or case that strengthens
the end of the scabbard of a sword.

ceum, nor will the men, at such a tyme, presse into the nur-
cery where they are.

The men are very strong, of able bodyes, and full of agility,
accustoming themselves to endure hardnes, to lye in the
woods, under a tree, by a small fier, in the worst of wynter,
in frost and snowe, or in the weeds and grasse, as in ambuscado, to accomplish their purposes in the sommer.

They are inconstant in everything but what feare con-
straineth them to keepe; crafty, tymerous, quick of apprehension, ingenious enough in their owne workes, as maye
testifie their weares in which they take their fish, which are
certaine inclosures made of reedes, and framed in the fashion
of a laborinth or maze sett a fathome deepe in the water, with
divers chambers or bedds, out of which the entangled fish
cannot returne or gett out, being once in. Well maye a
great one, by chaunce, breake the reedes and so escape, otherwise he remaines a pray to the fishermen the next lowe water,
which they fish with a nett at the end of a pole, as likewise
maye speake for them their netts, their arteficyall dressing of
leather, theire cordage, which they make of their naturall
hempe and flax togither, with their cuning dressing of that,
and preserving the whole yeare great litches or bundells of
the same, to be used upon any occasyon, and of their girdles
which they make of silke grasse, much like St. Frauncys cor-
don,[1] their cloaks of feathers, their bowes and bow-strings,
their arrowes, their crownetts, which their weroances weare,
and their queene's *fasciæ crinales*, borders or frontalls of white
beades, currall and copper; especyally their boats, which they
call quintans, and are very shapefull, made of one piece of
timber, like the auncyent *monoxylum navigium*,[2] theire matts
and all their houshold implements, and such like.

[1] The girdle used by the monks of the Franciscan order is of twisted
cord, and knotted.

[2] Μονόξυλα πλοῖα, vessels hollowed out of one piece of wood are men-
by Xenophon, Hippocrates, Aristotle, and Polybius.

Some of them are of disposition fearefull (as I said) and not easily wrought, therefore, to trust us or come unto our forts; others, againe, of them are so bold and audacyous, as they dare come unto our forts, truck and trade with us, and looke us in the face, crying all freinds when they have but new done us a mischief, and when they intend presently againe, yf it lye in their power, to doe the like. They are generally covetous of our comodityes, as copper, white beades for their women, hatchetts, of which we make them poore ones, of iron howes to pare their corne grownd, knives, and such like.

They are soone moved to anger, and so malitious that they seldome forgett an injury; they are very thievish, and will as closely as they can convey any thing away from us; howebe yt, they seldome steale one from another, lest their connivres should revele yt, and so they be pursued and punished. That they are thus feared yt is certaine, nor lett any man doubt that the divell cannot reveile an offence actually comitted.

CAPUT VI.

The manner of the Virginian government, their townes, their howses, dyett, fowling, and hunting, their gaming, musique, dauncing.

ALTHOUGH the country people are very barbarous, yet have they amongst them such governement as that their magistrates for good comaunding, and their people for due subjection and obeying, excell many places that would be counted civill. The forme of their comon wealth, by what hath already bene declared, you maye well gather to be a monarcall governement, where one as emperour ruleth over many kings; their chief ruler likewise for the presente you have heard before how named, and from whence; as also you heard the nomber of his weroances, their forces, and his owne discrip-

tion; you shall nowe understand how his kingdome descend-
eth not to his sonns or children, but first to his brethren,
whereof he hath (as you have heard) three, and after their
decease, to his sisters; first to his eldest sister, then to the
rest, and after them to the heires-male and female of the
eldest sister, but never to the heires-male.

He nor any of his people understand how to expresse theire
mynds by any kynds of letters, to wryte or reade, in barkes
of trees, or any other kynd of waye, which necessitye or invention might have instructed them in, as do other barba-
rians, and some even in these new discoveries; nor have they
posetive lawes, only the lawe whereby he ruleth is custome;
yet when he pleaseth, his will is a lawe, and must be obeyed,
not only as a king, but as half a god, his people esteeme him
soe; his inferiour kings are tyed likewise to rule by like customes, and have permitted them power of life and death over
theire people, as theire comaund in that nature.

Theire habitations or townes are for the most part by the
rivers, or not far distant from fresh springs, comonly upon a
rice of a hill, that they may overlooke the river, and take
every small thing into view which sturrs upon the same.
Their howses are not many in one towne, and those that are
stand dissite[1] and scattered without forme of a street, farr
and wyde asunder.

As for their howses, who knoweth one of them knoweth
them all, even the chief kyng's house yt selfe, for they be all
alike builded one to the other. They are like garden arbours,
at best like our sheppards' cotages, made yet handsomely
enough, though without strength or gaynes[s], of such yong
plants as they can pluck up, bow, and make the greene
toppes meete togither, in fashion of a round roofe, which they
thatch with matts throwne over. The walles are made of
barkes of trees, but then those be principall howses, for so
many barkes which goe to the making up of a howse are long

1 Dispersed.

tyme of purchasing. In the midst of the howse there is a louer,[1] out of which the smoake issueth, the fier being kept right under. Every house comonly hath twoo dores, one before and a posterne. The doores be hung with matts, never locked nor bolted, but only those matts be to turne upp, or lett fall at pleasure; and their howses are so comonly placed under covert of trees, that the violence of fowle weather, snowe, or raine, cannot assalt them, nor the sun in sommer annoye them; and the roofe being covered, as I say, the wynd is easily kept out, insomuch as they are as warme as stoves, albeit very smoakye. Wyndowes they have none, but the light comes in at the doore and at the louer; for should they have broad and open wyndowes in the quarters of their howses, they know not well how, upon any occasion, to make them close and let in the light too, for glasse they knowe not (though the country wants not salsodiack enough to make glasse of, and of which we have made some stoore in a goodly howse sett up for the same purpose, with all offices and furnases thereto belonging, a litle without the island, where James town stands); nor have they lynnen cloth, (albeit they want not neither naturally the materyalls for that,) paper, or such like, to dipe in oyle, to conveye in as a diaphænick body the light, or to keepe out the weather.

By theire howses they have sometymes a scæna, or high stage, raised like a scaffold, of small spelts, reedes, or dried osiers, covered with matts, which both gives a shadowe and is a shelter, and serves for such a covered place where men used in old tyme to sitt and talke for recreation or pleasure, which they called præstega, and where, on a loft of hurdells, they laye forth their corne and fish to dry. They eate, sleepe, and dresse theire meate all under one roofe, and in one chamber, as it were.

Rownd about the house on both sides are theire bedstedes,

[1] Luidhier, Celtic for a chimney or vent, the pronunciation of which somewhat resembles the English pronunciation of " louer", or "looer".

which are thick short posts stalkt into the ground, a foot
high and somewhat more, and for the sydes small poles
layed along, with a hurdle of reeds cast over, wherein they
rowle downe a fyne white matte or twoo (as for a bedd)
when they goe to sleepe, and the which they rowle up againe
in the morning when they rise, as we doe our palletts, and
upon these, rownd about the howse, they lye, heads and
points, one by the other, especially making a fier before
them in the midst of the howse, as they doe usually every
night, and some one of them by agreement maynteynes the
fier for all that night long; some of them, when they lye
downe to sleepe, cover them with matts, some with skinns,
and some lye stark naked on the grownd, from six to twentie
in a house, as doe the Irish.

About their howses they have commonly square plotts of
cleered grownd, which serve them for gardens, some one
hundred, some two hundred foote square, wherein they sowe
their tobacco, pumpons, and a fruit like unto a musk million,
but lesse and worse, which they call macock gourds, and
such like, which fruicts increase exceedingly, and ripen in
the beginning of July, and contynue until September; they
plant also the field apple, the maracock, a wyld fruit like a
kind of pomegranett, which increaseth infinitlye, and ripens
in August, contynuing untill the end of October, when all
the other fruicts be gathered, but they sowe nether herb,
flower, nor any other kynd of fruict.

They neither ympale for deare, nor breed cattell, nor
bring up tame poultry, albeit they have great stoore of
turkies, nor keepe birdes, squirrells, nor tame partridges,
swan, duck, nor goose. In March and Aprill they live much
upon their weeres, and feed on fish, turkies, and squirrells,
and then, as also sometymes in May, they plant their fields
and sett their corne, and live after those monthes most of
acrons, walnutts, chesnutts, chechinquarnins,[1] and fish; but,

---

[1] A kind of grain. See glossary.

to mend their dyett, some disperse themselves in small companyes, and live uppon such beasts as they can kyll with
their bow and arrowes, upon crabbs, oysters, land-tortoyses,
strawberryes, mulberries, and such like. In June, July, and
August they feed upon rootes of tockohow, berries, grownd
nutts, fish, and greene wheate, and sometyme uppon a greene
serpent, or greene snake, of which our people likewise use
to eate.

It is straung to see how their bodies alter with their dyett;
even as the deare and wild beasts they seeme fatt and leane,
strong and weake. Powhatan and some others that are pro-
vident, roast their fish and flesh upon hurdells, and reserve
of the same untill the scarse tymes; commonly the fish and
flesh they boyle, either very tenderly, or broyle yt long on
hurdells over the fier, or ells (after the Spanish fashion) putt
yt on a spitt and turne first the one side, then the other, till
yt be as dry as their jerkin beef in the West Indies, and so
they maye keepe yt a monethe or more without putrifying;
the broath of fish or flesh they suppe up as ordinarily as
they eat the meate.

Their corne they eat in the eares greene, roasted, and
sometyme brusing yt in a morter of wood with a little pestle;
they lap yt in rowlls within the leaves of the corne, and so
boyle yt for a deyntie; they also reserve that corne late
planted that will not ripe, by roasting yt in hott ashes, the
which in wynter (being boyled with beanes) they esteeme for
a rare dish, calling yt pausarawmena: their old wheat they
firste steepe a night in hot water, and in the morning pound-
ing yt in a morter, they use a small baskett for the boulter
or searser,[1] and when they have syfted fourth the finest, they
pound againe the great, and so separating yt by dashing their
hand in the baskett, receave the flower in a platter of wood,
which, blending with water, they make into flatt, broad cakes

[1] Searse, a fine sieve made of lawn, etc., from the French "sas"—Bailey's
Dictionary.

L

(much like the sacrificing bread which the Grecians offred to
their gods, called popanum), and these they call appones,
which covering with ashes till they be baked (as was the ancyent escharitos[1] panis raked within the embers), and then
washing them in faire water, they let dry with their own heate,
or ells boyle them with water, eating the broath with the
bread, which they call ponepopi. The growtes and broken
pieces of the corne remayning, they likewise preserve, and by
fannyng away the branne or huskes in a platter or in the
wynd, they lett boyle in an earthen pott three or four howres,
and therof make a straung thick pottage, which they call
Vsketehamun, and is their kind of frumentry, and indeed is
like our kind of ptisane, husked barley sodden in water. Yt
maye be not much unlike that homely *jus nigrum*, which the
Lacidemonians used to eate, and which Dionisius could not
abide to tast of; albeit he brought a cooke from thence only
to make him that broath, for which the cooke told him he
must have a Lacedemonian stomach, indeed to eate of the
Lacedemonian dyett;[2] and some of them, more thriftye then
cleanly, doe burne the coare of the eare to powder, which they
call pungnough, mingling that in their meale, but yt never
tasted well in bread or broath.

Their drinck is, as the Turkes, cliere water; for albeit they
have grapes, and those good store, yet they have not falne
upon the use of them, nor advised how to presse them into
wyne. Peares and apples they have none to make syder or
perry of, nor honye to make meath, nor licoris to seeth in
their water. They call all things which have a spicy tast
wassacan, which leaves a supposition that they maie have
some kind of spice trees, though not perhapps such as ellswhere.

The men bestow their tymes in fishing, hunting, warres,
and such manlike exercises, without the dores, scorninge to

[1] It should be Εσχαριτης, *i. e.* baked on the hearth.
[2] See Plutarch's Επιτηδεύματα λακωνικά.

be seene in any effemynate labour, which is the cause that the women be very painfull and the men often idle.

Their fishing is much in boats. These they call quintans, as the West Indians call their canoas. They make them with one tree, by burning and scraping awaye the coales with stones and shells, tyll they have made them in forme of a trough. Some of them are an ell deepe, and forty or fifty foote in length, and some will transport forty men; but the most ordinary are smaller, and will ferry ten or twenty, with some luggage, over their broadest rivers. Instead of oares, they use paddles and sticks, which they will rowe faster then we in our barges.

They have netts for fishing, for the quantity as formerly brayed and mashed as our's, and these are made of barkes of certaine trees, deare synewes, for a kynd of grasse, which they call pemmenaw, of which their women, betweene their hands and thighes, spin a thredd very even and redily, and this threed serveth for many uses, as about their howsing, their mantells of feathers and their trowses, and they also with yt make lynes for angles.

Theire angles are long small rodds, at the end whereof they have a clift to the which the lyne is fastened, and at the lyne they hang a hooke, made eyther of a bone grated (as they nock their arrowes) in the forme of a crooked pynne or fis-hooke, or of the splinter of a bone, and with a threed of the lyne they tye on the bayte. They use also long arrowes tyed in a line, wherewith they shoote at fish in the rivers. Those of Accowmak use staves, like unto javelins, headed with bone; with these they dart fish, swymming in the water. They have also many arteficyall weeres (before described) in which they take aboundaunce of fishe.

In the tyme of their huntings, they leave their habitations, and gather themselves into companyes, as doe the Tartars, and goe to the most desart places with their families, where they passe the tyme with hunting and fowling up towards the mountaines, by the heads of their rivers, wher in deed there is plentye of game, for betwixt the rivers the land is not so large belowe that therein breed sufficyent to give them all content. Considering, especyally, how at all tymes and seasons they destroy them, yt maye seeme a marveyle how they can so directly passe and wander in these desarts, sometymes three or fower dayes' journyes, meeting with no habitacions, and, by reason of the woods, not having sight of the sun, wherby to direct them how to coast yt.

Theire huntinge howses are not soe laboured, substancyall, nor artyficyall as their other, but are like our soldiers' cabins, the frame sett up in too or three howers, cast over head, with matts, which the women beare after them as they carry likewise corne, acornes, morters, and all bag and baggage to use, when they come to the place where they purpose for the tyme to hunt.

In the tyme of hunting every man will strive to doe his best to shew his fortune and dexterity, for by their excelling therin they obteyne the favour of the women.

At their hunting in the desarts they are comonly two or three hundred togither. With the sun rising they call up on[e] another, and goe forth searching after the heard, which when they have found, they environ and circle with many fiers, and betwixt the fiers they place themselves, and there take up their stands, making the most terrible noise that they can. The deare being thus feared by the fires and their voices, betake them to their heeles, whome they chase so long within that circle, that many tymes they kill six, eight, ten, or fifteen in a morning. They use also to drive them into some narrow point of land, when they find that advantage, and so force them into the river, where with their boats they have ambuscades to kill them. When they have shott a deare by land, they followe him (like bloodhounds) like the blood and straine,[1] and often tymes so take him. Hares, partriges,

---

[1] Hunting term. The view or track of a deer.

turkeys, fatt or leane, young or old, in eggs, in breeding
time, or however they devour, at no time sparing any that
they can catch in their power.

On[e] savadge hunting alone useth the skyne of a deare
slitt in the one side, and so put upon his arme through the
neck, in that sort that the hand comes to the head, which is
stuffed, and the hornes, head, eyes, eares, and every part as
arteficyall counterfeited as they can devise; thus shrowding
his body in the skynne, by stalking he approacheth the
deere creeping on the ground from one tree to another; yf
the deare chaunce to find fault, or stand at gaze, he turneth
the head with the hand to the best advantage to win his
shoot; having shott him, he chaseth him by his blood and
straine till he gett him.

In these hunting and fishing exercizes they take extreame
paines, and they being their ordinary labours from their in-
fancy, they place them amongst their sports and pleasures,
and are very prowd to be expert therein, for thereby (as before
remembered) they wyn the loves of their women, who wilbe the
sooner contented to live with such a man, by the readynes and
fortune of whose bow and diligence such provision they perceave they are likely to be fedd with well, especially of fish
and flesh, as the place where they are to dwell can afford; for
(indeed) they be all of them hugh eaters, and of whome
we may saye with Plautus, *Noctes diesque estur*, for which
we ourselves doe give unto every Indian that labours with us
in our forts, doble the allowance of one of our owne men;
and these active hunters, by their continuall ranging and
travell, do know all the advantages and places most frequented and best stored with deare or other beasts, fish,
fowle, roots, fruicts, and berries.

A kynd of exercise they have often amongst them much
like that which boyes call bandy[1] in English, and maye be

[1] In the game of bandy-ball, the ball was struck with a bat called
bandy, from its being bent.

an auncient game, as yt seemeth in Virgill; for when Æneas
came into Italy at his marriage with Lavinia, King Latinus'
daughter, yt is said the Troyans taught the Latins scipping
and frisking at the ball.   Likewise they have the exercise of
football, in which they only forceably encounter with the
foot to carry the ball the one from the other, and spurned
yt to the goale with a kind of dexterity and swift footmanship, which is the honour of yt; but they never strike up
one another's heeles, as we doe, not accompting that praise-
worthie to purchase a goale by such an advantage.

Dice play, or cardes, or lotts they knowe not, how be it
they use a game upon russhes much like primero,[1] wherein
they card and discard, and lay a stake too, and so win and
loose.   They will playe at this for their bowes and arrowes,
their copper beads, hatchets, and their leather coats.

If any great comaunder arrive at the habitacion of a wero-
aunce, they spread a matt, as the Turkes do a carpett, for
him to sitt uppon; uppon another right opposite they sitt
themselves, then doe they all, with a tunable voice of showting, bid him welcome; after this doe twoo or more of the
chief men make severall orations, testifying their love, which
they doe with such vehemency, and so great earnestnes of
passion, that they sweat till they droppe, and are so out of
breath that they can scarse speake, in so much as a stranger
would take them to be exceeding angry, or starke mad.
After this verball entertaynment, they cause such victuall as

[1] Primero is reckoned among the most ancient games of cards known
to have been played in England.   Each player, we are told, had four
cards dealt to him one by one ; the seven was the highest card, in point
of number, that he could avail himself of, which counted for twenty-one ;
the six counted for sixteen, the five for fifteen, and the ace for the same ;
but the two, the three, and the four for their respective points only.   The
knave of hearts was commonly fixed upon for the quinola, which the
player might make what card or suit he thought proper ; if the cards
were of different suits the highest number was the primero ; if they were
all of one colour, he that held them won the flush.   See Strutt, taken
from the Hon. Daines Barrington on card-playing, Archæologia, vol. viii.

they have or can provide to be brought forth, with which they feast him fully and freely, and at night they bring him to the lodging appointed for him, whither, upon their departure, they send a young woman, fresh paynted red with pochone and oyle, to be his bedfellowe.

The void tyme betweene their sleepe and meate they commonly bestow in revelling, dauncing, and singing, and in their kind of musique, and have sundry instruments for the same. They have a kynd of cane on which they pipe as on a recorder, and are like the Greeke pipes, which they called *bombyces*, being hardly to be sounded without great straynyng of the breath, upon which they observe certain rude times; but their chief instruments are rattles made of small gourdes or pompion shells; of these they have base, tenor, counter tenor, meane, and treble; these myngled with their voices, sometymes twenty or thirty togither, make such a terrible howling as would rather affright then give pleasure to any man.

They have likewise their *errotica carmina*, or amorous dittyes in their language, some numerous, and some not, which they will sing tunable enough. They have contrived a kind of angry song against us, in their homely rymes, which concludeth with a kynd of petition unto their okeus,[1] and to all the host of their idolls, to plague the Tassantasses (for so they call us) and their posterities; as likewise another scorneful song they made of us the last yeare at the falls, in manner of tryumph, at what tyme they killed Capt. William West, our Lord Generall's nephew, and two or three more, and tooke one Symon Skove, a saylor, and one Cob, a boy, prisoners. That song goeth thus:—

1. Matanerew shashashewaw erawango pechecoma
   Whe Tassantassa inoshashawyehockan pocosack.
   Whe whe, yah haha nehe wittowa, wittowa.

[1] Their Indian name for their gods.

2. Matanerew shashashewaw erawango pechecoma
   Capt. Newport inoshashaw neir mhoc natian matassan
   Whe whe, etc.

3. Matanerew shashashewaw erawango pechecoma
   Thom. Newport inoshashaw neir inhoc natian moncock :
   Whe whe, etc.

4. Matanerew shashashewaw erawango pechecoma
   Pochin Simon moshashaw ningon natian monahack,
   Whe whe, etc.

Which maye signifie how they killed us for all our pocca-
sacks, that is our guns, and for all that Captain Newport
brought them copper, and could hurt Thomas Newport (a
boy whose name in deede was Thomas Savadge, who Captain
Newport leaving with Powhatan to learne the language, at
what tyme he presented the said Powhatan with a copper
crowne, and other gifts from his Majestie, said he was his
sonne) for all his monachock, that is his bright sword, and
how they could take Symon (for they seldome said our surname) prisoner for all his tamahanke, that is his hatchet,
adding, as for a burden unto their song, what lamentation
our people made when they kild him, namely, saying how
they would cry whe, whe, etc., which they mockt us for, and
cryed againe to us yah, ha, ha, Tewittawa, Tewittawa; for yt
is true they never bemoane themselves nor cry out, gyving
up so much as a groane for any death, how cruell soever and
full of torment.

As for their dauncyng, the sport seemes unto them, and
the use almost as frequent and necessary as their meat and
drynck, in which they consume much tyme, and for which
they appoint many and often meetings, and have therefore,
as yt were, set orgies or festivalls for the same pastyme, as
have yet at this daye the merry Greekes within the Arches.
At our colonies first sitting downe amongst them, when any
of our people repaired to their townes, the Indians would not
thinck they had expressed their welcome sufficyentlie enough
untill they had shewed them a daunce, the manner of which

From De Bry.

AN INDIAN DANCE.

Etched by Sarah E. Major.

is thus : One of them standeth by, with some furre or leather
thing in his leaft hand, upon which he beats with his right
hand, and sings with all as if he began the quier, and kept
unto the rest their just tyme, when upon a certaine stroak or
more (as upon his cue or tyme to come in) one riseth up and
begynns to dawnce ; after he hath daunced a while stepps
forth another, as if he came in just upon his rest ; and in
this order all of them, so many as there be, one after another, who then daunce an equall distaunce from each other
in ring, showting, howling, and stamping their feete against
the ground with such force and paine that they sweat agayne,
and with all variety of strang mymick tricks and distorted
faces, making so confused a yell and noyse as so many fran-
tique and disquieted bachanalls, and sure they will keepe
stroak just with their feete to the tyme he gives, and just
one with another, but with the hands, head, face, and body,
every one hath a severall gesture ; and who have seene the
darvises, in their holy daunces, in their moscas, upon Wendse-
dayes and Frydayes in Turkey, maye resemble these unto
them.   You shall find the manner expressed in the figure in
the second Decade, capt. [*See print to face this page*].

Every weroance knoweth his owne meeres and lymitts to
fish, fowle, or hunt in (as before said), but they hold all of
their great weroance Powhatan, unto whome they pay eight
parts of ten tribute of all the comodities which their country
yeldeth, as of wheat, pease, beanes, eight measures of ten,
(and these measured out in litle cades or basketts, which the
great king appoints) of the dying roots, eight measures of ten
of all sorts of skyns, and furrs eight of ten ; and so he robbes
the people, in effect, of all they have, even to the deare's
skyn wherewith they cover them from cold, in so much as
they dare not dresse yt and put yt on untill he have seene
yt and refused yt, for what he comaundeth they dare not dis-
obey in the lest thinge.

M

CAPUT VII.

Of the religion amongst the inhabitants,—their god, their temples, their
    opinion of the creation of the world, and of the immortalitie of the
    sowle, of their conjurations and sacrificing of children.

THERE is yet, in Virginia, no place discovered to be so savadge
and simple, in which the inhabitaunts have not a religion
and the use of bow and arrowes : all things they conceave
able to doe them hurt beyond their prevention, they adore
with their kind of divine worship, as the fier, water, lightning, thunder, our ordinaunce pieces, horses, etc. ; but their
chief god they worship is no other, indeed, then the divell,
whome they make presentments of, and shadow under the
forme of an idoll, which they entitle Okeus, and whome they
worship, as the Romans did their hurtfull god Vejovis, more
for feare of harme then for hope of any good ; they saie they
have conference with him, and fashion themselves in their
disguisments as neere to his shape as they can imagyn.

In every territory of a weroance is a temple and a priest,
peradventure two or three ; yet happie doth that weroance
accompt himself who can detayne with him a Quiyoughquisock, of the best, grave, lucky, well instructed in their mis-
teryes, and beloved of their god ; and such a one is noe lesse
honoured then was Dianae's priest at Ephesus, for whome
they have their more private temples, with oratories and
chauncells therein, according as is the dignity and reverence
of the Quiyoughquisock, which the weroance wilbe at charge
to build upon purpose, sometyme twenty foote broad and a
hundred in length, fashioned arbour wyse after their buylding, having comonly the dore opening into the east, and at
the west end a spence or chauncell from the body of the
temple, with hollow wyndings and pillers, whereon stand
divers black imagies, fashioned to the shoulders, with their
faces looking downe the church, and where within their wero-

ances, upon a kind of beere of reedes, lye buryed; and under them, apart, in a vault low in the ground (as a more secrett thing), vailed with a matt, sitts their Okeus, an image ill-favouredly carved, all black dressed, with chaynes of perle, the presentment and figure of that god (say the priests unto the laity, and who religiously believe what the priests saie) which doth them all the harme they suffer, be yt in their bodies or goods, within doores or abroad; and true yt is many of them are divers tymes (especyally offendors) shrewdly scratched as they walke alone in the woods, yt may well be by the subtyle spirit, the malitious enemy to mankind, whome, therefore, to pacefie, and worke to doe them good (at least no harme) the priests tell them they must do these and these sacrifices unto [them], of these and these things, and thus and thus often, by which meanes not only their owne children, but straungers, are sometimes sacrificed unto him : whilst the great God (the priests tell them) who governes all the world, and makes the sun to shine, creating the moone and starrs his companyons, great powers, and which dwell with him, and by whose vertues and influences the under earth is tempered, and brings forth her fruicts according to her seasons, they calling Ahone; the good and peaceable God requires no such dutyes, nor needes be sacrificed unto, for he intendeth all good unto them, and will doe noe harme, only the displeased Okeus, looking into all men's accions, and examining the same according to the severe scale of jus-tice, punisheth them with sicknesses, beats them, and strikes their ripe corne with blastings, stormes, and thunder clapps, stirrs up warre, and makes their women falce unto them. Such is the misery and thraldome under which Sathan hath bound these wretched miscreants.

Indeed their priests, being the ministers of Sathan (who is very likely or visibly conversant amongst them), feare and tremble lest the knowledg of God, and of our Saviour Jesus Christ, should be taught in those parts, doe now with the more vehemency perswade the people to hold on their wonted ceremonies, and every yeare to sacrifice still their owne children to the ancyent God of their fathers, and yt is supposed gayne doble oblations this waye, by reason they doe at all tymes so absolutely governe and direct the weroances, or lords of countries, in all their accions, and this custome he hath politiquely maynteyn'd, and doth yet universally (a few places excepted), over all the Indies. In Florida they sacrifice the first-borne male child. In Mexico they forbeare their owne, and offer up such prisoners as they take in the warrs, whome they torture with a most barbarous cruelty. That the devill hath obteyned the use of the like offring in many other parts of America, Acosta hath observed and related, in his morrall and naturall History of the West Indies; the same honour the devill obteyned from all antiquity, in effect even from the Israelites and their borderers, from the Carthagenians, Persians, and the first planters of Italy, and other nations. To have suffred still therefore, me thincks, these priests of Baal or Belzebub, were greatly offensive to the majestie of God, and most perilous for the English to inhabite within those parts; for these their Quiyoughquisocks or prophetts be they that perswade their weroances to resist our settlement, and tell them how much their Okeus wilbe offended with them, and that he will not be appeased with a sacrifice of a thowsand, nay a hecatomb of their childrene, yf they permitt a nation, dispicing the ancyent religion of their forefathers, to inhabite among them, since their owne gods have hitherto preserved them, and given them victory over their enemies, from age to age.

It is true that hitherto our colony hath consisted (as yt were) but of a handfull of men, and not stored with desired victualls fitt for such eaters as the English are; nor untill 1610 hath yt ben the best governed to undertake this service to God; but now the commodities of our owne country being thither in some good quantety transported, and those there thriving and growing daily into good increase, as kyne, goats, swyne, horses, mares, etc.; and the first ragged government nowe likewise prudentlie chaunged into an absolute comaund, and over the same many learned and juditious gentlemen of his majestie's councell (as a body politique) resident in England, and they also enlightened from the supreme understanding of his majestie's privy councell; and the lord generall now to goe againe is a very worthy, valiant noble man, and well instructed in the busines, who hath Sir Thomas Gates, liuetenant-generall (whose comendacion lieth in his name), Sir Thomas Dale, marshall, both there at this present, informing themselves of the country and people, both excellent soldiers, and well knowing all circumstances of warre and advantages of ground, yt cannot be doubted but that all things shall be soe foreseene, that the best courses shalbe taken, and the surreption of these priests more seriously thought on then heartofore, and by whose apprehension wilbe wrought the saffety of such our people as shalbe imployed herein for his majestie's honour and the enlargement of his dominion, for whose sake God will prosper all our lawfull and Christian attempts. Yet noe Spanish intention shalbe entertayned by us, neither hereby to root out the naturalls, as the Spaniards have done in Hispaniola and other parts, but only to take from them these seducers, untill when they will never knowe God nor obey the king's majestie, and by which meanes we shall by degrees chaunge their barbarous natures, make them ashamed the sooner of their savadge nakedness, informe them of the true God and of the way to their salvation, and, finally, teach them obedience to the king's majestie and to his governours in those parts, declaring (in the attempt thereof) unto the several weroances, and making the comon people likewise to understand, how that his majestie hath bene acquainted, that the men, women, and childrene of the first plantation at Roanoak were by practize and comaundement of Powhatan (he himself perswaded ther-

unto by his priests) miserably slaughtered, without any
offence given him either by the first planted (who twenty
and od yeares had peaceably lyved intermixt with those salvages, and were out of his territory) or by those who nowe
are come to inhabite some parte of his desarte lands, and to
trade with him for some comodityes of ours, which he and
his people stand in want of; notwithstanding, because his
majestie is, of all the world, the most just and the most mer-
cifull prince, he hath given order that Powhatan himself, with
the weroances and all the people, shalbe spared, and revenge
only taken upon his Quiyoughquisocks, by whose advise and
perswasions was exercised that bloudy cruelty, and only how
that Powhatan himself and the weroances must depend on
his majestie, both acknowledging him for their superiall lord;
and wherunto the inferiour weroances sure will most willingly condiscend, when yt shalbe told them, that wheras
Powhatan doth at his pleasure dispoile them both of their
lives and goods without yeilding them any reason, or alleadg-
ing or proving any just cause against them, they shall for
heareafter be delivered from his tyranny, and shall enjoye
freely the fruicts of their owne territories, so shall they the
fish and the fowle thereof, of which the most rare and delicate of the one, and the best and wholsomest of the other,
are now forbidden them, and reserved and preserved to Powhatan, and that they shalbe freed likewise from delivering up
their children for sacrifice; and the poore women's songs of
lamentation converted into rejoycings, the true God, and his
governour king James, comaunding that the childrene of men
be preserved and not slaughtered without offence given, as
the devill and his Quiyoughquisocks have ordeyned. Against
which Sathanicall invention, maye yt please his majestie to
make an ordinaunce, that the fathers of those childrene, and
all that consent unto the sacrifices hereafter, shalbe put to
death as traytors to God and his majestie. As also when they
shall understand how the tribute which they shall pay unto

his majestie shalbe far leasse then that which Powhatan
exacteth from them, who robbs them, as you have heard, of
all they have; but after such tyme as they shall submitt themselves to the king's majestie, and consent to pay him a tribute
to be agreed upon, Powhatan shall lay no more his exactions
upon them, but they shall freely enjoy all they can gather,
and have a peaceable and franck trade with the English for
the comodities they can make of their owne, exchaunging
them for ours, and that the English will take of their poorest
into their famelies, as their better sort shall by patents and
proclamations hold their lands, as free burgers and citizens
with the English, and subjects to king James, who will give
them justice, and defend them against all their enemyes;
whereas now they live in miserable slavery, and have no
assuraunce either of their lyves or of their goods, and indeed
hereby these dooble and mixt comodities will arrise, namely
the English garrisons shall not only be provided of corne,
and their storehowses of merchandizes, but the naturalls being
thus constrayned to pay duly this their trybute, will clense
dowble as much ground as they doe, wherby the country will
not only be made the more passeable both for horse and foot,
but the people themselves, who are now for the most part of
the yeare idle, and do little ells then sharpen their arrowes
against the English, shall find, by the gathering together of
their severall sorts of tribute, somewhat ells to entertayne
themselves withall; and although, peradventure, this maye
seeme a burthen at the first, untill they have acquainted
themselves with another kind of life, and perceave themselves
indeed to become thereby the more civile, as likewise to
enjoye the rest of their owne more freely then under Powhatan, they will find themselves in farr better estate then now
they are; for the cussiques or comaunders of Indian townes
in Peru, whom the Virginians call weroances, although they
paye unto the king of Spaine great tribute, yet because they
make exchaunge with the Spaniard for that remaynes, they

do not only keepe greate hospitality and are riche in their
furniture, horses, and cattell, but, as Captain Ellis avowes,
who lyved amongst them some few yeares, their dyett is
served to them in silver vessells, and many of them have
naturall Spaniards that attend them in their howses, when,
on the other side, the Spaniards were not able to make the
twentieth part of profitt which they now doe but by the helpe
of those cussiques, for they furnish out of their severall territories not so few as fifty thousand people to worke in the
mynes of Potosi, who after so many monthes' travaile are
returned to the countryes, and fifty thousand others by an
other company of cussiques provided to supply them. In
New Spaine they doe the like, for the naturall people gather
all the scuchinella[1] which the Spaniards have, and require no
more for a week's labour then so much money as will buy
them a pott of wyne to drinck drunck the Satterday night.
In Guiana, thirty of the people, with their canoa, wilbe hired
for one hatchett to rowe where they are comaunded for a
whole moneth, and sell a hundred weight of good biskett for
a threepenny knife, and if our copper had ben well ordered
in Virginia, as maye be hereafter, I am assured that lesse
then one ounce will serve to entertayne the labour of a whole
howshould for ten dayes. This being delivered in fitt termes
by some perfect interpreter, and to men that are capable
ynough of understanding yt, maye begett a faire conceipt in
them of us and our proceedings, and leave them well satisfied ; and indeed be yt beleeved, that when so just an occasion shall offer these priests of Asmodius or the devill into
the hands of the lord generall, a better tyme then that will
not be found to performe the same acceptable service to God
that Jehu, king of Israell, did, when he assembled all the
priests of Baal, and slue them, to the last man, in their owne
temple. Of this may every vulgar sence be well assured,
that seeing these monsters doe offer up unto the devill their

[1] Cochineal.

TOMB OF THE WEROANCES.

owne childrene, and being hardened against all compassion, naturall and divine, enforce their owne mothers to deliver them to the executioner with their owne hands, they will easily condiscend unto, and assist the destruction and extirpacion of all straungers, knowing or acknowledging the true God.

Within the chauncell of the temple, by the Okeus, are the cenotaphies or the monuments of their kings, whose bodyes, so soone as they be dead, they embowell, and, scraping the flesh from off the bones, they dry the same upon hurdells into ashes, which they put into litle potts (like the auncyent urnes); the annathomy of the bones they bind togither or case up in leather, hanging braceletts, or chaines of copper, beads, pearle, or such like, as they used to wear about most of their joints and neck, and so repose the body upon a litle scaffold (as upon a tomb), laying by the dead bodies' feet, all his riches in severall basketts, his apook, and pipe, and any one toy, which in his life he held most deare in his fancy : their inwards they stuff with pearle, copper, beads, and such trash, sowed in a skynne, which they overlapp againe very carefully in whit skynnes one or two, and the bodyes thus dressed lastly they rowle in matts, as for wynding sheets, and so laye them orderly one by one, as they dye in their turnes, upon an arche standing (as aforesaid) for the tomb, and thes are all the ceremonies we yet can learne that they give unto their dead. We heare of no sweet oyles or oyntments that they use to dresse or chest their dead bodies with ; albeit they want not of the pretious rozzin running out of the great cedar, wherwith in the old tyme they used to embalme dead bodies, washing them in the oyle and licoure therof. Only to the priests the care of these temples and holy interments are comitted, and these temples are to them as solitary Asseteria[1] colledges or minsters to exercise

---

[1] Possibly misspelt from Ασσύτερος quasi Ἐπασσύτερος, i. e. following in a row one after another.

themselves in contemplation, for they are seldome out of them, and therefore often lye in them and maynteyne contynuall fier in the same, upon a hearth somewhat neere the east end.

For their ordinary burialls they digg a deepe hole in the earth with sharpe stakes, and the corps being lapped in skynns and matts with their jewells, they laye uppon sticks in the ground, and soe cover them with earth : the buryall ended, the women (being painted all their faces with black coale and oyle) do sitt twenty-four howers in their howses, mourning and lamenting by turnes, with such yelling and howling as may expresse their great passions.

Their principall temple, or place of superstition, is at Vtamussack, at Pamunky. Neere unto the towne, within the woods, is a chief holie howse, proper to Powhatan, upon the top of certaine red sandy hills, and it is accompanied with two other sixty feet in length, filled with images of their kings and devills, and tombes of the predicessors. This place they count so holy as that none but the priests and kings dare come therein. In this (as the Grecian nigromancers psychomantie did use to call up spiritts) eyther the priests have conference, or consult (indeed) with the devill, and receave verball answeares, and so sayth Acosta; he spake to the $\beta o\iota\tau\eta$[1] or chaplaines of the West Indies, in their guacas or oratories, or at least these conjurers make the simple laytie so to believe, whoe, therefore (so much are the people at the priests' devotion), are ready to execute any thing, how desperate soever, which they shall commaund. The salvadges dare not goe up the river in boats by yt, but that they solemly cast some piece of copper, white beads, or pochones into the river, for feare that Okeus should be offended and revenged of them. In this place commonly are resident seven priests, the chief differing from the rest

---

[1] Query—Boῄται, from βοάω, to cry. Pape, in his "Handwörterbuch der Griechischen Sprache", gives Hippocrates as a reference for the use of the word.

in his ornament, whilst the inferior priests can hardly be knowne from the common people, save that they had not (it maye be maye not have) so many holes in their eares to hang their jewells at. The ornaments of the chief priest were, uppon his showlders a middle-sized cloke of feathers much like the old sacrificing garment which Isodorus calls cassiola, and the burlett or attire of his head was thus made; some twelve or sixteen or more snakes' sloughes or skyns were stuffed with mosse, and of weasells or other vermyn were skynns perhapps as many; all these were tyed by the tayles, so as their tayles meet in the tope of the head like a great tassell, and round about the tassell was circled a crownett (as yt were) of feathers, the skynns hanging round about his head, neck, and showlders, and in a manner covering his face. The faces of all their priests are painted so uglye as they can devise; in their hands they carry every one his rattle, for the most part as a symbole of his place and profession, some basse, some smaller. Their devotion is most in songs, which the chief priest begynns and the rest follow him; sometymes he makes invocation with broken sentences, by starts and straung passions, and at every pawse the rest of the priests give a short groane.

We have not yet hitherto perceaved that any solemne fasti, or *feriæ præcidaneæ vigilli*,[1] or any one daye more holy then other, is amongst them, but only in some great distresse of want, feare of enemyes, tymes of tryumph, and gathering togither their fruicts. The whole country—men, women, and children—come togither to their solempnities, the manner of which jolly devotion is sometymes to make a great fier in the house or fields, and all to sing and daunce about yt, in a ring like so many fayries, with rattles and showtes, four

---

[1] This unusual expression for vigils or eves is thus treated of by Aulus Gellius, lib. iv, cap 6.—" Porcam et hostias quasdam præcidaneas, sicuti dixi, appellari vulgo notum est; *ferias præcidaneas* dici, id opinor, a vulgo remotum est."

or five howers togither, sometymes fashioning themselves in twoo companies, keeping a great circuite; one company daunceth one waye and the other the contrary, all very finely painted, certaine men going before with eyther of them a rattle, other following in the midst, and the rest of the trayne of both wings in order four and four; and in the reare, certayne of the chiefest yong men, with long switches in their hands, to keepe them in their places; after all which followes the governour, or weroance himself, in a more slow or solemne measure, stopping and dauncinge, and all singing very timable.

They have also divers conjurations : one they made at what tyme they had taken Captain Smyth prisoner, to know, as they reported, if any more of his countrymen would arrive there, and what they intended; the manner of yt Captain Smyth observed to be as followeth : first, soe sone as daie was shut in, they kindled a faire great fier in a lone howse, about which assembled seven priests, takinge Captain Smyth by the hand, and appointing him his seat ; about the fier they made a kynd of enchanted circle of meale ; that done, the chiefest priest, attyred as is expressed, gravely began to sing and shake his rattle, solemly rownding and marching about the fier, the rest followed him silently untill his song was done, which they all shutt up with a groane. At the end of the first song the chief priest layd downe certaine graines of wheat, and so continuyed howling and invoking their okeus to stand firme and powerful to them in divers varieties of songs, still counting the songs by the graynes, untill they had circled the fier three tymes, then they devided the graynes by certaine number with little sticks, all the while muttering some ympious thing unto themselves, oftentymes looking upon Capt. Smyth. In this manner they contynued ten or twelve howers without any other ceremonies or intermission, with such violent stretching of their armes, and various passions, jestures, and simptoms, as might well seeme strang to him before whom they so conjured, and who every hower expected to be the hoast and one of their sacrifice. Not any meat did they eat untill yt was very late, and the night far spent. About the rising of the morning starr they seemed to have finished their work of darknes, and then drew forth such provision as was in the said howse, and feasted themselves and him with much mirth. Three or fower dayes they contynued these elvish ceremonies. Now besides these manner of conjurations thus within dores (as we read the augurers, in the old tymes of the like superstition, did ascend or goe up into the certaine towers or high places, called therefore *auguracula,* to divine of matters), so doe they goe forth, and either upon some rock standing alone, or upon some desolate promontery top, or ells into the midst of thick and solitary woodes they call upon their okeus and importune their other quioughcosughes with most impetuous and interminate clamours and howling, and with such paynes and strayned accions, as the neighbour places ecchoe againe of the same, and themselves are all in a sweat and over wearied.

They have also certaine aulter stones which they call pawcorances; but those stand from their temples, some by their howses, others in the woodes and wilderness; upon these they offer blood, deare suett, and tobacco, and that when they returne safe from the warrs, luckely from hunting, and upon many other occasions.

We understand they give great reverence to the sun; for which, both at his early rising and late sitting, they couch themselves downe, and lift up their hands and eyes, and at certayne tymes make a round circle on the ground with tobacco, into which they reverently enter, and murmure certaine unhallowed wordes with many a deformed gesture.

They have also another kind of sorcery which they use in stormes, a kynd of botanomantia[1] with herbes; when the waters are rough in the rivers and sea-coasts, their conjurers

---

[1] Soothsaying from herbs.

run to the waters sides, or, passing in their quintans, after many hellish outcryes and invocations, they cast whesican, tobacco, copper, pocones, or such trash into the water, to pacifye that god whome they thinck to be very angry in those stormes.

Before their dinners and suppers (as Heliodorus remembers the Egyptians were wont to doe when they sate to meate, or at candlelight) the better sort will doe a kind of sacrifice, taking the first bitt and castinge yt into the fier, and to yt repeat certaine wordes. I have heard Machumps, at Sir Thos. Dale's table, once or twice (upon our request) repeat the said grace as yt were, howbeit I forgot to take yt from him in writinge.

In some part of the country they have yerely a sacrifice of children; such a one was at Quiyoughcohanock, some ten miles from James Towne, as also at Kecoughtan, which Capt. Georg Percy was at, and observed. The manner of it was, fifteene of the properest yonge boyes, betweene ten and fifteene yeares of age, they paynted white; having brought them forth, the people spent the forenone in dauncing and singing about them with rattles. In the afternoone they solemly led those childrene to a certayne tree appointed for the same purpose; at the roote whereof, round about, they made the childrene to sitt downe, and by them stood the most and the ablest of the men, and some of them the fathers of the childrene, as a watchfull guard, every one having a bastinado in his hand of reedes, and these opened a lane betweene all along, through which were appointed five young men to fetch those childrene; and accordingly every one of the five tooke his turne and passed through the guard to fetch a child, the guard fiercely beating them the while with their bastinadoes, and shewing much anger and displeasure to have the children so ravisht from them; all which the young men pacyently endured, receaving the blowes and defending the children, with their naked bodies, from the unmersifull stroakes, that paid them soundly, though the children escaped. All the while sate the mothers and kinswomen afar off, looking on, weeping and crying out very passionately, and some, in pretty waymenting[1] tunes, singing (as yt were) their dirge or funeral song, provided with matts, skynnes, mosse, and dry wood by them, as things fitting their children's funeralls. After the childrene were thus forceably taken from the guard, the guard possessed (as yt were) with a vyolent fury, entred uppon the tree and tore yt downe, bowes and braunches, with such a terrible fierceness and strength, that they rent the very body of yt, and shivered yt in a hundred peeces, whereof some of them made them garlandes for their heads, and some stuck of the braunches and leaves in their haire, wreathinge them in the same, and so went up and downe as mourners, with heavy and sad downecast lookes. What ells was done with the childrene might not be seene by our people, further then that they were all cast on a heape in a valleye, where was made a great and solemne feast for all the companye; at the going whereunto, the night now approaching, the Indians desired our people that they would withdraw themselves and leave them to their further proceedings, the which they did: only some of the weroances being demanded the meaning of this sacrifice, made answeare, that the childrene did not all of them suffer death, but that the okeus did suck the blood from the leaft breast of the child whose chaunce it was to be his by lott, till he were dead, and the remaine were kept in the wilderness by the said young men till nine moones were expired, during which tyme they must not converse with any; and of these were made the priests and conjurers, to be instructed by tradition from the elder priests. These sacrifices, or catharmata, they hold to be so necessary, that if they should omitt them they suppose this okeus, and all the other quioughcosughes, which are their other gods, would

---

[1] So in MS. Probably "plaintive".

let them no deare, turkies, corne, nor fish, and yet besides he would make a great slaughter amongst them; insomuch as if ever the ancyent superstitious tymes feared the devill's *postularia fulgura,* lightnings that signified religion of sacrifices and vowes to be neglected,[1] these people are dreadfully afflicted with the terror of the like, insomuch as, I may truly saye therefore, the like thunder and lightening is seldome againe eyther seene or heard in Europe as is here.

Concerning the ymmortality of the sowle, they suppose that the common people shall not live after death ; but they thinck that their weroances and priests, indeed whom they esteeme half quioughcosughes, when their bodyes are laied in the earth, that that which is within shall goe beyond the mountaynes, and travell as farr as where the sun setts into most pleasant fields, growndes, and pastures, where yt shall doe no labour; but, stuck finely with feathers, and painted with oyle and pocones, rest in all quiet and peace, and eat delicious fruicts, and have store of copper, beades, and hatchetts; sing, daunce, and have all variety of delights and merryments till that waxe old there, as the body did on earth, and then yt shall dissolve and die, and come into a woman's womb againe, and so be a new borne unto the world; not unlike the heathen Pythagoras his opinyon, and fable of metempsychosis; nor is this opinion more ridiculous or savage then was the Epicures, long since, in tyme too of morality, who taught that the sowle of man, as of brute beasts, was nothing ells but life, or the vitall power arrisinge of the temperature and perfeccion of the body, and therefore died and extinguished togither with the body, the sowle so being a meere quality in the body, and when the body was

---

[1] The rendering here given by Strachey of "postularia fulgura" is evidently from Festus, though his quaint diction would mislead the reader as to the intention of the words. Festus gives the following definition of the term. "Fulgura quæ votorum aut sacrificiorum spretam religionem designant".

to dissolve, the sowle must likewise become nothing ; nor is it more hethenous then our Athists, who would even out of scripture prophanely conclude no ymortality of the sowle, to be wresting that of Solomon, who saieth, "The condicion of men and beasts are even as one", not acknowledging their impious reasonings by fallacies, concluding that which is in some respect soe to be simply so, as because their bodies dye alike, therefore the sowle of man must perish too. But, alas, well maye these heathen be pityed and pardoned untill they shall be taught better, neither borne under grace, nor of the seed of promise, when such as professe themselves in their great place to be our Saviour Christ's chief vicars here upon earth, dare be farr more dissolute, as yt is written of Paule the third, Pope of Rome, when he was breathing out his sowle, and ready to dye, said that now, at length, he should try and knowe three things whereof in his whole tyme he much doubted (viz.), whether there was a God; secondly, whether sowles were immortal; and lastly, whether there was any hell : and Stephanus upon Heroditus remembers us how Pope Leo X answered Cardinal Bembo, that alleadged some part of the gospell unto him,—"Lord Cardinall, what a wealth this fable of Jesus Christ hath gotten us." I say, therefore, yt may well seeme lesse straung if amonge these infidells both the knowledg of our Saviour be questioned, and the ymmortality of the sowle not rightly understood. Howbeyt, to divert them from this blindness, many of our people have used their best endeavours, chiefly with Pepis-cumah, weroance of Quiyoughcohanock, whose apprehension and good disposicion towards us hath hitherto much exceeded any in those countryes, with whom, though as yet we have not prevayled to forsake his falce gods, yet this he was wonne to saye, that he believed our God as much exceeded theirs, as our guns did their bowe and arrowes; and many tymes, upon our people's first comyng into the country, did send to the president at James Towne men with presents, entreating

O

him to pray to his God for rayne, for his gods would not
send him any; and in this lamentable ignorance doe these
poore sowles live.

I will conclude these points with opinion of the Indians
of Patawomeck River. The last yeare 1610, about Christ-
mas, when Captain Argoll was there trading with Jopassus,
the great king's brother, after many daies of acquaintaunce
with him, as the pynnace road before the towne Matcho-
pongo, Jopassus comyng abourd and sitting (the wheather
being very cold) by the fier, upon a hearth in the hold, with
the captaine, one of our men was reading of a Bible, to which
the Indian gave a very attent care, and looked with a very
wisht eye upon him, as if he desired to understand what he
read, whereupon the captayne tooke the booke, and turned
to the picture of the Creation of the World, in the begynning
of the booke, and caused a boy, one Spilman, who had lyved
a whole yere with this Indian kinge, and spake his language,
to shewe yt unto him, and to enterprete yt in his language,
which the boy did, and which the king seemed to like well
of; howbeit, he bad the boy tell the captayne if he would
heare, he would tell him the manner of their begyning, which
was a pretty fabulous tale indeed. " We have (said he) five
gods in all; our chief god appeares often unto us in the like-
nes of a mighty great hare; the other four have noe visible
shape, but are indeed the four wynds which keepe the four
corners of the earth (and then, with his hand, he seemed to
quarter out the scytuations of the world). Our god, who
takes upon him this shape of a hare, conceaved with himself
how to people this great world, and with what kinde of creatures, and yt is true (said he) that at length he devised and
made divers men and women, and made provision for them,
to be kept up yet a while in a great bag. Nowe there were
certayne spiritts, which he described to be like great giants,
which came to the hare's dwelling-place (being towards the
rising of the sun), and had perseveraunce of the men and

women which he had put into that great bagg, and they
would have had them to eat, but the godlye hare reproved
those caniball spiritts, and drove them awaye." Now if the
boy had asked him of what he made those men and women,
and what those spiritts more particularly had ben, and so had
proceeded in some order, they should have made yt hang
together the better; but the boy was unwilling to question
him so many things, least he should offend him; only the
old man went on, and said how that godlike hare made the
water, and the fish therein, and the land, and a great deare,
which should feed upon the land; at which assembled the
other four gods, envyous hereat, from the east, the west, from
the north and south, and with hunting pooles kild this great
deare, dreast him, and, after they had feasted with him,
departed againe, east, west, north, and south; at which the
other god, in despight for this their mallice to him, tooke all
the haires of the slaine deare, and spred them upon the earth,
with many powerfull words and charmes, whereby every haire
became a deare; and then he opened the great bag, wherein
the men and the women were, and placed them upon the
earth, a man and a woman in one country, and a man and a
woman in another country, and so the world tooke his first
begynning of mankind. The captaine bad the boy ask him
what he thought became of them after their death, to which
he answered somewhat like as is expressed before of the
inhabitaunts about us, how that after they are dead here,
they goe up to a top of a high tree, and there they espie a
faire plaine broad path waye, on both sides wherof doth grow
all manner of pleasant fruicts, as mulberies, straberries,
plombes, etc. In this pleasant path they rune toward the
rising of the sun, where the godly hare's howse is, and in the
midway they come to a house where a woman goddesse doth
dwell, whoe hath alwaies her doares open for hospitality, and
hath at all tymes ready drest greene vskatahomen and poka-
hichory, (which is greene corne brused and boyled, and wal-

nutts beaten small, then washed from the shells with a quantity of water, which makes a kind of milke, and which they
esteeme an extraordinary dish,) togither with all manner of
pleasant fruicts, in a readines to entertayne all such as doe
travell to the great hare's howse; and when they are well
refreshed, they run in this pleasant path to the rising of the
sun, where they fynd their forefathers lyving in great pleasure, in a goodly field, where they doe nothing but dawnce
and sing, and feed on delitious fruicts with that great hare,
who is their great god; and when they have lyved there untill
they be starke old men, they saie they dye there likewise by
turnes, and come into the world againe.

Concerning further of the religion we have not yet learned,
nor indeed shall we ever know all the certaintye eyther of
these their unhallowed misteries, or of their further orders
and policyes, untill we cann make surprize of some of their
Quiyoughquisocks.

CAPUT VIII.

Their manner of warrs, and consultations thereabout; of certain prophesies amongst them; of Powhatan's auncient enemies, and how
they maie be wrought into league with us, and turned against him,
whereby we maie bring him likewise to be in freindship with us; of
their bowes, arrowes, and swordes, targetts, drumes; of their phisick
and chirurgery.

WHEN they intend any warrs, the weroances usually advise
with their priests or conjurers, their allies and best trusted
chauncellors and freinds; but comonly the priests have the
resulting voice, and determyne therefore their resolutions.
Eyther a weroance or some lustie fellowe is appointed captaine over a nation or regiment to be led forth; and when
they would presse a number of soldiers to be ready by a day,
an officer is dispacht awaye, who comyng into the townes,
or otherwise meeting such whome he hath order to warne,

to strike them over the back a sound blow with a bastinado, and bidds them be ready to serve the great king, and tells them the randevous, from whence they dare not at any tyme appointed be absent. They seldome make warrs for lands or goods, but for women and children, and principally for revenge, so vindicative and jealous they be to be made a dirision of, and to be insulted upon by an enemy.

There be at this tyme certayne prophesies afoot amongst the people enhabiting about us, of which Powhatan ys not meanly jealous and careful to divert the construction and danger which his priests contynually put him in feare of. [It is] not long since that his priests told him how that from the Chesapeack Bay a nation should arise which should dissolve and give end to his empire, for which, not many yeares since (perplext with this divelish oracle, and divers understanding thereof), according to the ancyent and gentile customs, he destroyed and put to sword all such who might lye under any doubtful construccion of the said prophesie, as all the inhabitants, the weroance and his subjects of that province, and so remaine all the Chessiopeians at this daye, and for this cause, extinct.

Some of the inhabitants, againe, have not spared to give us to understand, how they have a second prophesie likewise amongst them, that twice they should give overthrow and dishearten the attempters, and such straungers as should invade their territories or labour to settle a plantation among them, but the third tyme they themselves should fall into their subjection, and under their conquest; and sure in the observacion of our settlement, and the manner therof hitherto, we maye well suppose that this their apprehension may fully touch at us. I leave to expresse the particulers unto another place, albeyt, let me saye here, straunge whispers (indeed) and secrett at this hower run among these people and possesse them with amazement, what may be the yssue of these straung preparations landed in their coasts, and

yearly supplyed with fresher trouppes. Every newes and
blast of rumour strykes them, to which they open their eares
wyde, and keepe their eyes waking, with good espiall upon
every thing that sturrs; the noyse of our drums, of our shrill
trumpetts and great ordinaunce, terrifies them, so as they
startle at the report of them, how far soever from the reach
of daunger. Suspicions have bredd straunge feares amongst
them, and those feares create as straung construccions, and
those construccions, therefore, begett strong watch and gard,
especially about their great kinge, who thrusts forth trusty
skowtes and carefull sentinells, as before mencyoned, which
reach even from his owne court downe almost to our palisado
gates, which answeare one another duly. Many things (whilst
they observe us) are suffred amisse among themselves, who
were wont to be so servily fearefull to trespasse against their
customes, as yt was a chief point of their religion not to
breake in any, and all this, and more then this, is thus with
them, whilst the great tyrant himself nor his priests are now
confident in their wonted courses. Judge all men whether
these maye not be the forerunners of an alteration of the
devill's empire here ? I hope they be, nay, I dare prognos-
ticate that they usher great accydents, and that we shall
effect them ; the Divine power assist us in this worke, which,
begun for heavenly ends, may have as heavenly period.

  Powhatan had many enemies, especially in the westerly
countryes, before we made our forts and habitations so neere
the Falls; but now the generall cause hath united them, and
the poore power of their mallice they contend to power upon
us. Beyond the mountaynes, and at the heads of the rivers
upon the head of the Powhatans, are the Monacans, whose
chief habitacion is at Rassawck, unto whome the Mowhemen-
chuges, the Massinnacacks, the Monahassanughes, and other
nations, pay tribute ; and the Monacans, as I said, have been
deadly enemyes ever unto Powhatan, and maye easily be
wyned frindship with by us to be so againe ; untill when we

shall ever have Powhatan at these prowd and insolent termes
at which he now stands ; and therefore yt was most consider-
ably and directly advised by one of good place, and great
knowledg, and by long experience trayned in the managing
of busines of this nature, when Sir Thomas Gates went over
sole governour, May 1609, that we should endeavour what all
envaders and planters seeke out, namely to knowe and entertayne the bordering enemye of that nation, whom we shalbe
forced by our sitting downe amongst them, out of many
offred occasions, to offend and constraine ; for who can be
ignorant, saith he, that there was never any invaysion, conquest, or far of plantation, that had successe without some
partie in the place ytself, or neere yt ? witnes all the conquests made in these our parts of the world, and all that the
Spaniards have performed in America ; yt cannot but appeare
to all men of judgment essensially necessary for our colony
to get knowledg or make friendship, as conveniently as yt
may, with as many of the weroances which border and make
warr with Powhatan, as yt can, against whome, or against
whose people, yf we should fynd cause now or hereafter to
use violence. There is no man among themselves so savage,
or not capable of so much sence, but that he will approve our
cause, when he shalbe made to understand that Powhatan
hath slaughtered so many of our nation without offence given,
and such as were seated far from him, and in the territory
of those weroances which did in no sort depend on him or
acknowledg him ; but yt hath ben Powhatan's great care to
keepe us, by all meanes, from the acquaintance of those
nations that border and confront him, for besides his knowledge how easely and willingly his enemies wilbe drawne upon
him by the least countenance and encouragement from us,
he doth, by keeping us from trading with them, monoplize
all the copper brought into Virginia by the English. And
whereas the English are now content to receave, in exchaunge,
a few measures of corne for a great deale of that mettell

(valuyng yt according to the extreame price yt beares with them, not to the estymacion yt hath with us), Powhatan doth againe vent some small quantity thereof to his neighbour nations for one hundred tyme the value, reserving, notwithstanding, for himself a plentifull quantity to leavy men withall when he shall find cause to use them against us; for the before-remembred weroance of Paspahegh did once wage fourteen or fifteen weroances to assist him in the attempt upon the fort of James towne, for one copper plate promised to each weroance.

Beyond the springs of the river Tappahanock (the second from Powhatan's) is a people called Mannahoaks; to these are contributory the Tanxsnitanians, the Shackaconias, the Outpankas, the Tegoneas, the Whonkentias, the Stogaras, the Hassinugas, and divers others, all confederates with the Monacans, though many of them different in language and very barbarous, living for the most part upon wild beasts and fruicts, and have likewise assisted the Monacans, in tymes past, against Powhatan, and maie also by us be dealt withall and taken into freindship, as opportunity and meanes shall affourd.

Beyond the mountaines, from whence is the head of the river Patawomeck, do inhabite the Massawomecks (Powhatan's yet mortall enemies) upon a great salt water, which by all likelyhoods may either be some part of Caneda, some great lake, or some inlett of some sea, that may fall into the west ocean or Mar del zur.   These Massawomecks are a great nation, and very populous, for the inhabitants of the heads of all those rivers, especyally the Patawomecks, the Pawtuxunts, the Sasquesahanoughes, the Tockwoghs, are contynually harbored and frighted by them, of whose cruelty the said people generally complained, and were very ymportunate with Captain Smyth and his company, in the tyme of their discovery, to free them from those tormentors, to which purpose they offred food, conduct, assistants, and contynuall subjection, which were motives sufficyent for Captain Smyth to promise to returne with sufficient forces to constraine the said Massawomecks; but there were in the colony at that tyme such factions and base envyes, as malice in some, in some ignorance, and cowardize in others, made that oportunity to be lost. Seven boats'-full of these Massawomecks, the discoverers before mentioned encountred at the head of the bay, whose targetts, basketts, swords, tobacco-pipes, platters, bowes and arrowes, and every thing, shewed they much exceeded them of our parts; and their dexterity in their severall boats, made of the barkes of trees sowed togither, and well luted with gum and rosin of the pine-tree, argueth that they are seated upon some great water. Of these, likewise, yt may please the lord generall againe to enforme himself, as circumstances and occasion shall serve to turne against Powhatan.

I graunt that such the new inhabitants who now people Chesapeak againe (the old extinguished, as you have heard, upon the conceipt of a prophesie), togither with the weroances of Nandsamund, Warraskoyak, and Weanock, are now at peace with him; howbeit, they maie, peradventure, be drawne from him for some rownd rewards and a plentifull promise of copper, thus much (and not unnecessarily) digressed.

Their weapons for offence are bowes and arrowes, and wodden swords; for defence, targetts. The bowes are of some young plant, eyther of the locust-tree or of weech,[1] which they bring to the forme of ours by the scraping of a shell, and give them strings of a stagg's gutt, or thong of a deare's hide twisted. Their arrowes are made some of streight young spriggs, which they head with bone, two or three inches long, and these they use to shoote at squirrells and all kind of fowle. Another sort of arrowes they use made of reedes : these are peeced with wood, headed with splinters of

---

[1] The witch hazel—" *Hamamelis Virginiana*".

cristall or some sharp stone, with the spurrs of a turkey cock, or the bill of some bird, feathered with a turkey's feather, which with a knife (made of the splinter of a reed, which he will make as sharpe as a surgeon's gamott[1]) he cutts him into forme, and with which knife, also, he will joynt a deare, or any beast, shape his sandalls, buskins, mantell, etc. To make the notch of his arrowe, he hath the tooth of a bever sett in a stick, wherewith he grateth yt by degrees; his arrowe hedd he quickly maketh with a litle bone (which he ever weareth at his bracer, and which bracer is comonly of some beast's skynne, eyther of the woolf, badger, or black fox, etc.) of any splint of a stone, or peece of a deare's bone, of an oyster shell, or of cristall, in the forme of a heart, barb'd and jagged, and these they glue to the end of their arrowes with the synewes of deare and the topps of deare's horne boyled into a jelly, of which they make a glue that will not dissolve in cold water. Forty yards will they shoot levell, or very neere the marke, and one hundred and twenty is their best at random.

Their swordes be made of a kind of heavy wood which they have, much like such wooden instruments as our English women swingle their flax withall, and which they call monococks, as the salvadges in Bariena,[2] in the West Indies, call their[s] macanas, and be alike made; but oftentymes they use for swordes the horne of a deare put through a peice of wood in forme of a pickaxe. Some use a long stone sharpened at both ends, thrust through a handle of wood in the same manner, and these last they were wont to use instead of hatchetts to fell a tree, or cut any massy thing in sonder; but now, by trucking with us, they have thowsands of our iron hatchetts, such as they be.

Targetts they have, though not many, nor every where; but those they have are made of the barkes of trees, rownd and thicke ynough to keepe out an arrowe.

[1] An incision-knife.
[2] It should be Darien. See Herrera, dec. i, lib. ix, cap. 6.

For their drums they have a great deepe platter of wood, the mouth whereof covering with a skyn, at each corner they ty a walnutt, which meeting on the back side neere the bottome, with a small cord they twitch them together untill they be so tough and stiffe, that they maye beat upon them as doe wee upon a drum, and they yield a reasonable rattling sownde.

Their chief attempts are by stratagems, surprizes, and trecheries, yet the weroances, women, or children, they put not to death, but keep them captives. They have a method in warre, and for a pleasure Powhatan would needs have yt shewed once to our people, and yt was in this manner performed at Mattapanient.

Having painted and disguised themselves in the fairest manner they could devise, they devided themselves into two companies, well neere one hundred in a company; the one company they called Monacan's, the other Powhatan's, eyther army had their captaine. These (as enemies) took their stand a muskett shott one from another, rancking themselves fifteen abreast, and each ranck from other four or five yardes, not in file, but in the opening betwixt their files, so as the reare could shoot as convenyently as the front. Having thus pitched the field, from eyther part went a messenger with condicions that whosoever were vanquished, such as escaped, upon their submission or comyng in, though two daies after, should live, but their wives and childrene should be prize for the conquerors. The messengers were no soner returned, but they approached in their orders, on each flank a serjeant, and in the reare an officer for liuetenant, all duly keeping their rancks, yet leaping and singing after their accustomed tune, which they use only in warrs. Upon the first flight of arrowes, they gave such horrible showts and scritches as so many infernall helhounds; when they had spent their arrowes they joyned togither prettily, charging and retiring, every ranck seconding other. As they gett advantage, they catched their enemies by the haire of their head, and downe he came that was taken; his enemy, with a woodden sword, seemed to beat out his braines, and still they crept to the reare to mayntayne the skyrmish. The Monocans decreasing, the Powhatans charged them in forme of a halfe moone; they, unwilling to be inclosed, fled all in a troupe to their ambuscadoes, on whome they led them very cunningly. The Monocans disperst themselves among the freshmen, whereupon the Powhatans retired themselves with all speed to their seconds, which the Monocans seeing, tooke that advantage to retire againe to their owne battaile, and so each returned to theire owne quarter. All their accion, voices, and gestures, both in chardging and retiring, were so strayned to the height of their quality and nature, that the straungness thereof made yt seeme very delightfull.

Concerning a greene wound cawsed eyther by the stroake of an axe, or sword, or such sharpe thinge, they have present remedy for, of the juyce of certayne hearbes; howbeyt a compound wound (as the surgeons call it) where, beside the opening and cutting of the flesh, any rupture is, or bone broken, such as our small shotte make upon them, they knowe not easily how to cure, and therefore languish in the misery of the payne thereof. Old ulcers likewise, and putrified hurts are seldome seene cured amongst them : howbeit, to scarrefye a swelling, or make incisyon, they have a kind of instrument of some splinted stone.

Every spring they make themselves sick with drincking the juyce of a roote which they call wighsacan and water, wherof they take soe great a quantity, that yt purgeth them in a very violent manner, so that in three or four daies after they scarse recover their former health. Sometymes they are sore trobled with dropseyes, swellings, aches, and such like deceases, by reason of their uncleanenes and fowle feeding ; for cure whereof they buyld a stove in the forme of a dove howse, with matts soe close, that a fewe coals therein, covered with a pott, will make the patient sweat extreamely.

For swelling, also, they use small pieces of touch wood in the forme of cloves, which, pricking on the grief, they burne close to the flesh, and from thence drawe the corruption with their mouthe. They have many professed phisitians, who, with their charmes and rattles, with an infernall rowt of words and accions, will seeme to suck their inward grief from their navells, or their affected places; but concerning our chirugians they are generally so conceipted of them, that they believe that their plaisters will heale any hurt.

CAPUT IX.

Of their æconomick or howshold affaires ; how they obteyne their wives ; the women's works ; and wherefore they contend for manie wives.

THEY expresse their loves to such women as they would make choise to live withall, by presenting them with the fruicts of their labours, as by fowle, fish, or wild beasts, which by their huntings, their bowes and arrowes, by weeres, or otherwise, they obteyne, which they bring unto the young women, as also of such somer fruicts and berries which their travells abroad hath made them knowe readely where to gather, and those of the best kind in their season. Yf the young may-den become once to be *sororians virgo*,[1] and live under pa-rents, the parents must allow of the sutor ; and for their good wills, the woer promiseth that the daughter shall not want of such provisions, nor of deare skynns fitly drest for to weare ; besides, he promiseth to doe his endeavour to procure her beades, perle, and copper, and for handsell gives her before them something as a kind of *arrasponsalitia*,[2] token of betroathing or contract of a further amity and acquaintance to be contynued betweene them, as so after as the likeing

[1] *i.e.* arrived at puberty. Festus says "Sororiare mammæ dicuntur puellarum, cum primum tumescunt."
[2] Earnest money in ratification of the espousals.

growes; and as soone as he hath provided her a house (if he have none before) and some platters, morters, and matts, he takes her home; and the weroances after this manner maye have as many as they can obteyne, howbeyt all the rest whome they take after their first choise are (as yt were) mercynary, hired but by covenant and condicion, for a tyme, a yeare or soe, after which they may putt them awaye; but if they keepe them longer then the tyme appointed, they must ever keepe them, how deformed, deseased, or unaccompaniable soever they may prove.

They are people most voluptious; yet are the women very carefull not to be suspected of dishonesty, without the leave of the husbands; but he giving his consent, they are like Virgill's *scrantiæ*,[1] and may embrase the acquaintance of any straunger for nothing, and it is accompted no offence; and incredible yt is, with what heat both sexes of them are given over to those intemperances, and the men to preposterous Venus, for which they are full of their countrye desease (the pox) very young; for cure of which, yet, they have both meanes of their owne, and sufficient skill, applying certaine herbes and brused roots which doe presently ease, and in tyme cure (which kind of medicines Paracelsus calleth *sedativa medicamenta*), having, beside the saxafras, one hearb which (as yt is supposed) in short tyme quencheth and mortifieth the malignant poyson of that fowle desease.

The women are said to be easily delivered of child; yet do they love childrene very dearly. To make the children hardye, in the coldest mornings they wash them in the rivers, and by paintings and oyntements so tanne their skynns that, after a yeare or twoo no weather will hurt them; as also, to practize their children in the use of ther bowes and arrowes, the mothers doe not give them their breakfast in a morning before they have hitt a marke which she appoints them to shoot at:

---

[1] We have not met with this word in Virgil. It occurs in Plautus as the epithet of a despicable woman.

and comonly so cunning they will have them, as throwing up in the ayre a piece of mosse, or some such light thinge, the boy must with his arrowe meete yt in the fall, and hit it, or ells he shall not have his breckfast.

Both men, women, and childrene have their severall names; at first according to the severall humour of their parents; and for the men children, at first, when they are young, their mothers give them a name, calling them by some affectionate title, or, perhapps observing their promising inclination give yt accordingly; and so the great King Powhatan called a young daughter of his, whome he loved well, Pochahuntas, which may signifie little wanton; howbeyt she was rightly called Amonate at more ripe yeares. When they become able to travel into the woods, and to goe forth a hunting, fowling, and fishing with their fathers, the fathers give him another name as he finds him apt and of spiritt to prove toward and valiant, or otherwise changing the mother's, which yet in the family is not so soone forgotten; and if soe be yt be by agility, strength, or any extraordinary straine of witt he performes any remarkeable or valerous exploite in open act of armes, or by stratagem, especyally in the tyme of extreamity in the warrs for the publique and common state, upon the enemie, the king, taking notice of the same, doth then not only in open view and solemnely reward him with some present of copper, or chaine of perle, and bedes, but doth then likewise (and which they take for the most emynent and supreme favour) give him a name answearable to the attempt, not much differing herein from the auncyent warlike encouragement and order of the Romans to a well deserving and gallant young spirrit.

The men fish, hunt, fowle, goe to the warrs, make the weeres, botes, and such like manly exercises and all laboures abroad. The women, as the weaker sort, be put to the easier workes, to sow their corne, to weed and cleanse the same of the orabauke, dodder, and choak weed, and such like, which

ells would wynd about the corne and hinder the growth of
yt; for, by reason of the rankness and lustines of the grownd,
such weedes spring up very easely and thick, and if not
pluckt awaie, the corne would prosper so much the worse;
for which they keepe the hillocks of theire corne, and the
passadg between (for they sett their wheat as we doe our
hoppes, an equal distance one hill from another) as neat and
cleane as we doe our gardein bedds: likewise the women
plant and attend the gardeins, dresse the meate brought
home, make their broaths and pockerchicory drinckes, make
matts and basketts, pownd their wheat, make their bread,
prepare their vessels, beare all kindes of burthens, and such
like, and to which the children sett their handes, helping
their mothers.

There are notes to be taken by which may be discerned a
marryed woman from a mayd: the maydes have the forepart
of their heads and sides shaven close, the hinder part very
long, which they wynd very prettely and ymbroyder in
playtes, letting yt hang so to the full length: the marryed
women weare their haire all of a length, shaven as the Irish
by a dish.[1]

The women have a great care to maynteyne and keepe
fier light still within their howses, and if at any time it go
out, they take yt for an evil signe, but if yt be out they kin-
dle yt againe presently, by chauffing a dry pointed stick in
a hole of a little square piece of wood; that firing ytself will
so fier mosse, leaves, or any such like thing that is apt
quickly to burne.

They make them sometimes candells of the fattest splinters of the pine or firre tree, which will give a good cliere
light, and burne strongly, though the matter will soon consume, for which they have many slivers ready cut out a foote
long, some shorter, to be ready to light a second as soone as
the first goes out; and in Shropshier, betweene the lordships

[1] i. e. a bowl.

of Oswestry and Ellesmere, the like lightes they use at this daie of the firre tree, of which yt is sayd there be infinite taken dailie out of the earth in a marish grownd, and supposed to have lyen in the moist earth ever since the generall flood, the chippes whereof they use in steed of candells, in poore howses, so fatt is the wood, as is the smell also strong and sweet.

Their corne and (indeed) their copper, hatchetts, howses, beades, perle, and most things with them of value, according to their owne estymacion, they hide, one from the knowledge of another, in the grownd within the woodes, and so keepe them all the yeare, or untill they have fitt use for them, as the Romains did their monies and treasure in certaine cellars, called, therefore, as Plinye remembers, *favissæ*; and when they take them forth, they scarse make their women privie to the storehowse.

They are much desirous of our comodityes, and therefore when any of our boates arrive before their townes, they will come downe unto us, or suffer us to come up into their howses, and demaund after copper, white beades, howes to pare their corne feilds, and hatchetts, for which they will give us of such things as they have in exchaung, as deere skins, furrs of the wild catt, black fox, beaver, otter, arachoune, fowle, fish, deare, or beare's flesh dried, deare's suet made up handsomely in cakes, their country corne, peas, beanes, and such like; and indeed (to say truith) their victuall is their chief riches.

We have observed how when they would affirme any thing by much earnestnes and truith, they use to bynd yt by a kynd of oath; either by the life of the great king, or by pointing up to the sun and clapping the right hand upon the heart, and sometymes they have bene understood to sweare by the manes of their dead father.

If they will expresse that we and they wilbe or are all one friendes or brothers, as their word is, they will joyne the

Q

indices or twoo forefingers togither of either hand, as the
Indians of Nova Francia; or ells, clasping their fingers within
ours, they will saie, so and so close joyned and neere we are
unto their loves.

The reason whie each chief patron of a familie, especially
weroances, are desirous, and indeed strive for manie wives, is,
because they would have manie children, who maie, if chaunce
be, fight for them when they are old, as also then feed and
mayntein them; yet sure, for the nomber of people inhabiting
these partes, this country hath not appeared so populous
here to us as ellswhere in the West Indies; and perhappes
their ignorance in not fynding out yet the use of many
things necessarie and beneficiall to nature, which their countrie yet plentifully and naturally affordes, their often warrs
for women (in which manie hundreds perish), and their
ymoderate use and multiplicity of women (and those often
full of fowle diseases) leave this country not so well stocked
as other parts of the maine, and as the islands have bene
found to be by the Spaniards; besides (under correction)
yt yet maie be a probleme in philosophy whether variety of
women be a furtherance or hinderer of manie birthes? yt
being cleere in these conntries where (as I said) so manie
penuries for want of knowledge yet be amongst the people,
that the tired body cannot have those sensuall helpes (as the
Turkes) to hold up the ymoderate desires, manie women
deviding the body, and the strength thereof, make yt generall
unfitt to the office of increase rather than otherwise : and so
maie the comon people especially, for the most part, for this
reason likewise be not so long lived here as ellswhere, even
amongst salvadges where greater moderacion is used, and
where they keepe a stricter ceremonie in their kind of marriages, and have not as manie women as they can buy or wyn
by force and violence from the enemyes.

CAPUT X.

Of the commodities of the country,—fruicts, trees, beasts, fowle, fish, perle, copper, and mines.

THAT yt may yet further appeare howe this country is not so naked of commoditie nor wretched of provision fitt for the sustenance of mankind, as some ygnorantly ymagine, and others have falcely reported, I will in this chapter propose (for the testimonie of the truith thereof I may appeale to many hundreds, which may convince), the relation of a discourse only for forme or assentacion delivered; nor lett any man suppose that materialls of so good a navie as maie be there framed for planckes, masts, pitch, and tarre, soapashes, turpentine, iron, cordage, mulberry trees for silke, and another kind of silke of the grasse, saxafras, and other aromaticall druggs, gums, oyle, and dyes are of noe value, or not worthy the exposure of a colonie for secondarie and politique endes to be established there, since Muscovia and Polonia doe yearlie receave manie thowsandes for pitch, tarre, sopeashes, rosin, flax, cordage, sturgeon, masts, yardes, waynscot, firrs, glasse, and such like; also Swethland[1] receaves much from us for iron and copper; France, in like manner, for wyne, canvass, and salt; Spayne as much for iron, steele, figgs, raysons, and sacks; Italy for silks and velvetts, consumes our chief commodites; Holland maynteynes yt self by fishing and trading at our own dores. All these temporize with others for necessity, but all as uncertaine as peace and warre; besides the charge, travell, and daunger in transporting them by seas, lands, stormes, and pyratts. Then how much may Virginia have the prerogative for the benefitt of our land, when as within one hundred miles all these are to be had either readie provided by nature, or ells to be prepared, were there but industrious men to labour; so as, then, here

[1] *i.e.* Sweden.

is a place, a nurse for soldiers, a practize for marriners, a
trade for marchants, a reward for the good, and, that which
is most of all, a busines most acceptable to God, to bring
poore infidells to his knowledge; and, albeit, our shipps
(some will object) now returning from thence yearly, come
freighted home only, yet with certaine pretious woods; yt is
to be remembered how that from Hispaniola, Cuba, and
Portrico the Spaniards, in their yearely daies of possessing
the Indies, made returnes a long tyme of the like, as of
cassia, fistula, ebony, guacum, lignum vitæ, etc., untill they
found out the mynes, as may wee, we doubt nothing, in the
heart and bosome of ours when we shalbe enabled truly to
dissect yt, fynding such appearances now in the suburbs of
yt, as yt were, the which to tyme, the true revealer of great
thinges, I submit, or rather to Him from whom, if our un-
thankfulness deprive us not of the blessing, we may expect a
prosperous and assured compensacion and satisfaccion to
wipe of all skores, *et in assem satisfacere,* all the chardges
and disbursements which have hitherto gone out for yt;
albeit, such is the busines, as yt should awake all charitable
Christians to follow yt according to the goodness of the
cause, and not according to the greatnes of proffitt and
commodities.   Lett Mammon perish with his gold, that
hath no other but such stubble meerely to enkindle the flame
of his zeale unto so holie a worke.

The natives have here a kinde of wheat which they call
poketawes, as the West Indians call the same maiz. The
forme of yt is of a man's tooth, somewhat thicker; for the
preparing of the ground for which, they use this manner :—
they bruise the barke of those trees which they will take
awaie neere the roote, then do they scorch the rootes with fier,
that they grow no more; the next yeare, with a crooked piece
of wood, they beat up those trees by the rootes, and in their
mowldes they plant their corne : the manner is thus, they

make a hole in the earth with a stick, and into yt they put three or five graines of wheat, and one or three of beanes: these holes they make four or five foot one from another, for the corne being set close together, one stalke would choak ells the growth of another, and so render both unprofitable. Their women and children do contynually keepe the ground with weeding, and when the corne is growne middle high, they hill yt about like a hoppeyard, and the stalke will growe a man's height, or rather more, from the ground, and every stalke commonly beareth twoo eares, some three, manie but one, and some none. Every eare groweth with a great hose or pill about yt and above yt; the stalke being greene hath a sweet juyce in yt, somewhat like a sugar-cane, which is the cause that when they gather the corne greene, they suck the stalkes, for as we gather greene peas, so do they, their corne being greene, which excelleth their old.

Peas[1] they have, which the natives call assentemmens, and are the same which in Italy they call fagioli.

Their beanes[2] are little like a French beane, and are the same which the Turks call garvances, and these kind of pulse they much esteeme for daynties.

By their dwellings are some great mulberrye[3] trees, and these in some parte of the country are found growing naturally in pretty groves: there was an assay made to make silke, and surely the wormes prospered excellently well untill the master workeman fell sick, during which tyme they were eaten with ratts, and this wilbe a commoditie not meanely profitable. Now yt is seriously considered of, and order taken that yt shalbe duly followed.

In some places we fynd chesnutts,[4] whose wild fruict I maie

[1] Probably a species of *phaseolus*, and the same as the " wild pease" of Clayton.

[2] Also probably a species of *phaseolus*.

[3] *Morus rubra*, L. A species differing from the European.

[4] The same species with the European chestnut, *castanea vesca*, Gærtn.

well saie equallize the best in Fraunce, Spaine, Germany, Italy, or those so commended in the Black sea, by Constantinople, of all which I have eaten.

They have a small fruict growing in little trees, husked like a chesnut, but the fruict most like a very small acron, this they call chechniquamins,[1] and these, with chesnutts, they boile four or five houres, of which they make both broth and bread, for their chief men, or at their greatest feasts.

They have cherries,[2] much like a damoizin, but for their tast and cullour we called them cherries; and a plomb there is, somwhat fairer then a cherrie, of the same relish, then which are seldome a better eaten.

They have a berry much like our goose-berries[3] in greatness, cullour, and tast, these they call rawcomenes, and they doe eate them rawe or boyled.

In the watry valleis groweth a berry which they call ocoughtanamins, very much like unto capers; these they gather and dry in the heat of the sun, and when they will eate them, they boyle them nere halfe a daie, for otherwise they differ not much from poison.

Nattourne groweth as our bents doe in meadowes, the seed is not much unlike to rie,[4] though much smaller; these they use for a deyntie bread, buttered with deare's suett.

They have a plomb which they call pessemmins,[5] like to a medler, in England, but of a deeper tawnie cullour; they grow on a most high tree. When they are not fully ripe, they are harsh and choakie, and furre in a man's mouth like allam,

---

[1] The "chinquapin-bush" of Catesby's "Carolina", and *castanea pumila* of Michaux.

[2] There are several native species of cherries and plums; but the description is not sufficient for their discrimination.

[3] Probably a true gooseberry; but Clayton gives the name of "gooseberries" to the *vaccinium stamineam* of Linnæus.

[4] *Leersia Virginica*, Willd.? but if so, the comparison should be with *rice*, and not with *rye*.

[5] *Diospyros Virginiana*, L. (now called *persimon*.)

howbeit, being taken fully ripe, yt is a reasonable pleasant fruict, somewhat lushious. I have seene our people put them into their baked and sodden puddings; there be whose tast allowes them to be as pretious as the English apricock; I confesse it is a good kind of horse plomb.

Here is a cherry-redd fruict both within and without (as I have seene the like in the Bermudas), which wee call the prickle peare;[1] in the Indies they are well knowne to every common marryner; they beare a broad, thick, spungeous leafe, full of kernells; they be like unto the pomegranet; the tast of this peare is verie pleasant, and the juyce cold and fresh, like the water in the West Indian nut called cocus; the juyce is sharpe and penetrable like deale-wyne,[2] prescribed powerfull against the stone.

Here is a fruict by the naturalls called a maracock;[3] this groweth generally low, and creepeth in a manner amongst the corne (albeit I have seene yt, planted in a gardein within our fort, at James Towne, to spred and rise as high as the pale); yt is of the bignes of a queen apple, and hath manie azurine or blew karnells, like as a pomegranet, and yt bloometh a most sweet and delicate flower, and yt is a good sommer cooling fruict, and in every field where the Indians plant their corne be cart-loads of them.

The macokos[4] is of the forme of our pumpeons,—I must confesse, nothing so good,—'tis of a more waterish tast; the inhabitants seeth a kind of *million*,[5] which they put into their walnut-milke, and so make a kynd of toothsome meat.

1 *Opuntia vulgaris*, Mill. The well-known Indian fig, or prickly pear.
2 *i.e.* spruce.
3 *Passiflora incarnata* of Linnæus.
4 Gerard notices "the Virginian macocks or pompion", and also "the Virginian water-melon". These are probably varieties of the common pumpkin, *cucurbita pepo*, L.; but this plant is not regarded by American botanists as indigenous, while the calabash, *lagenaria vulgaris* of Séringe, is known to have been cultivated by the Indians from the earliest period.
5 Melon.

In Aprill, Maie, and June, are great store of strawberries, raspices,[1] hurts,[2] etc., and many hearbs in the spring time are comonly dispersed throughout the woodes, good for broathes and sallotts, as violetts, purselin, sorrell, and roses, in their season, etc., besides many we used whose names we knowe not.

It would easilie raise a well-stayed judgement into wonder (as Sir Thomas Dale hath writt sometimes unto his majesty's counsell here for Virginia) to behold the goodly vines[3] burthening every neighbour bush, and clymbing the toppes of highest trees, and those full of clusters of grapes in their kind, however dreeped and shadowed soever from the sun, and though never pruned or manured. I dare saie yt, that we have eaten there, as full and lushious a grape as in the villages betweene Paris and Amiens, and I have druncke often of the rathe[4] wine, which Doctor Bohune and other of our people have made full as good, as your French British wyne.

Twenty gallons at a tyme have bene sometimes made without any other helpe then by crushing the grape with the hand, which letting to settle five or six daies, hath, in the drawing forth, proved strong and headdy. Unto what perfection might not these be brought by the art and industry of manie skilfull *vineroones*,[5] being thus naturally good? And how materiall and principall a commoditie this maie prove, either for the benefitt of such who shall inhabit there, or to be returned over hither (especially where we maie have pipe staves to make our casks of, so cheape, and at hand), I preferre yt to indifferent judgements.

---

[1] "Raspices" probably comprehended all kinds of blackberries. The true raspberry is not indigenous to the United States; but there are several closely related native species.

[2] "Hurts" are, no doubt, the fruits of a species of *vaccinium*, so called from their resemblance to the hurts, or whortleberries, of our own country.

[3] Probably *vitis vulpina* of Linnæus, the fox-grape of the southern states. The cultivated varieties of *vitis labrusca*, the fox-grape of the northern states, appear to be at present more esteemed.

[4] Early.   [5] Vignerons.

Many rootes the Indians have here likewise for food. The chief they call tockowhough,[1] and yt groweth like a flag in low muddy freshes; in one day a salvadge will gather sufficient for a weeke : these rootes are much of the greatnes and tast of potatoes. They use to rake up a great nomber of them in old leaves and ferne, and then cover all with earth or sand, in the manner of a coal-pit; on each side they contynue a great fier a daie and a night before they dare eate yt : rawe, yt is no better then poison, and being roasted (except yt be tender and the heat abated, or sliced and dryed in the sun, mixed with sorrell and meale, or such like), yt will prickle and tor- ment the throat extreamely, and yet in sommer they use this ordinarily for bread.

They have another roote which they call vighsacan; as the other feedeth the bodie, so this cureth their hurts and dis- eases, yt is a smale roote, which they bruise and applie to the wound.

Pocones[2] is a small roote that groweth in the mountaines, which, being dried and beat into powlder, turneth red, and this they use for swellings, aches, annoynting their joynts, paynting their heads and garments with yt, for which they accompt yt very pretious and of much worth.

Musquaspenne is a root of the bignes of a finger, and as red as blood; in drying, it will wither almost to nothing : with this they use to paynt their matts, targetts, and such like.

There is here great store of tobacco, which the salvages call apooke; howbeit yt is not of the best kynd, yt is but poore and weake, and of a byting tast, yt growes not fully a yard above ground, bearing a little yellowe flower, like to henne-

---

[1] *Lycoperdon solidum* of Linnæus. "Ad panem conficiendum Indi utuntur, vulgo Tuckahoo."—Clayton.

[2] *Anchusa Virginiana* of Linnæus, "Puccoon indigenis dicta, quâ se pingunt Americani."—*Plukenet.* But it appears from Clayton that the natives gave the same name to the "blood-root," *sanguinaria canadensis* of Linnæus. Perhaps one or other of these (and more probably the latter) may be indicated in the following paragraph.

bane, the leaves are short and thick, somewhat round at the upper end; whereas the best tobacco of Trynidado and the Oronoque is large, sharpe, and growing two or three yardes from the ground, bearing a flower of the bredth of our bell-flowers in England: the salvages here dry the leaves of this apooke over the fier, and sometymes in the sun, and crumble yt into poulder, stalks, leaves, and all, taking the same in pipes of earth, which very ingeniously they can make. We observe that those Indians which have one, twoo, or more women, take much,—but such as yet have no appropriate woman take little or none at all.

Here is also pellitory of Spaine, and divers other symples, which our appothecaries have geathered and found to be good and medicinable.

In the low marishes grow plotts of onions conteyning an acre of ground or more in manie places, but they are small, like the chiballs,[1] or schallions,[2] not past the bignes of the toppe of one's thumb: they eate well sod or otherwise in sallet or in bakt meats. Our people find good and whol-some relish in them; howbeit the inhabitants cannot abyde to eate of them; and these onions doe for the most part appeare in the last season of the yeare, for yt is to be under-stood how the Indians devide the yeare into five seasons,— the winter, which they call popanow, the spring, cattapeuk, the sommer, cohattayough, the earing of their corne, nepen-ough, the harvest and fall of the leafe, taquitock.

They have divers beasts fitt for provision; the chief are deare, both redd and fallow; great store in the country towards the heads of the rivers, though not so many amongst the rivers. In our island, about James Towne, are some few nothing differing from ours in England, but that of some of them the antletts of their hornes are not so manie. Our peo-ple have seene two hundred, one hundred, and fifty in a herd.

There is a beast they call arocoune, much like a badger,

---

[1] *Chives, cipolle.*   [2] *Shallots, echalottes.*

tayled like a fox, and of a mingle black and grayish cullour, and which useth to live on trees, as squirrells doe. Excellent meate we kill often of them : the greatest nomber yet we obteyne by trade.

Squirrells they have, and those in great plentie ; are very good meat ; some are as great as our smallest sort of wild rabbitts, some blackish, or black and white, like those which here are called silver hayred ; but the most are grey.

A small beast they have which the Indians call assapa- nick, not passing so big as a ratt, but we call them flying squirrells, because, spreading their leggs, from whence to either shoulder runs a flappe, or fynne, much like a batt's wing, and so stretching the largeness of their skyns, they have bene seene to make a pretty flight from one tree to another, sometymes thirty or forty yardes.

An opussum is a beast as big as a pretty beagle, of grey cullour ; yt hath a head like a swyne; eares, feet, and tayle like a ratt ; she carries her young ones under her belly, in a piece of her owne skyn, like as in a bagg, which she can open and shutt, to lett them out or take them in, as she pleaseth, and doth therein lodge, carry, and suckle her young, and eates in tast like a pig.

Muscascus[1] is a beast black in cullour, proportioned like a water ratt ; he hath a cod within him, which yieldeth a strong sent, like unto musk ; yt is a good meat if the cod be taken out, otherwise the flesh will tast most strong and ranck of the musk ; so will the broath wherein yt is sod.

Hares they have some few about James Towne ; but both in the islands and mayne, up at the falls, and below about Fort Henry and Charles Fort, great store ; howbeit they are no bigger than our conies.

Beares there be manie towardes the sea-coast, which the Indians hunt most greedily ; for indeed they love them above all other their flesh, and therefore hardly sell any of them

[1] *i.e.* Musquash.

unto us, unles upon large proffers of copper, beads, and hatchetts. We have eaten of them, and they are very toothsoome sweet venison, as good to be eaten as the flesh of a calfe of two yeares old; howbeit they are very little in comparison of those of Muscovia and Tartaria.

The beaver there is as big as an ordinary water dog, but his leggs exceeding short; his forefeet like a doggs, his hinder like a swannes, his tayle somewhat like the forme of a rackett, bare, without haire, which, to eate, the salvages esteeme a great delicate.

Otters there be manie, which, as the bevers, the Indians take with gynns and snares, and esteeme the skynns great ornaments; and of all these beasts they use to feed when they catch them.

Lyons I will not posetively affirme that the country hath, since our people never yet saw any; howbeit, in their discoveryes to the Mangoagues, they did light once upon twoo skynns, which, by all the judgements in the fort, were supposed to be lyons' skinnes; and this last yeare, myself being at the falls with Sir Thomas Dale, I found in an Indian howse certaine clawes tyed up in a string, which I brought awaie, and into England, and they are assured unto me to be lyons clawes.[1]

There is also a beast, which the Indians call votchumquoyes, in the forme of a wild catt.[2]

Their foxes are like our silver-hayred conies, of a small proporcion, and not smelling so ranck like those in England.

The doggs of the country are like their woulves, and cannot barke, but howle, and are not unlike those auncyent doggs called cracutæ, which were said to be engendred of a wolfe and a bitch, and are like the Turkish jackalls, keeping about the graves of the dead, in the common poliandrium or place of sepulture.

---

[1] There are no lions in North America. Probably the puma (*felis concolor*) is alluded to.

[2] Probably a species of lynx.

Their woulves are not much bigger then our English foxes.

Martins, polecatts, weesells, and monkeys[1] we knowe they have, because we have seene many of their skynns, though very seldome any of them alive; but one thing is worth the observing,—we could never perceave that their flies, serpents, or other vermyn, were any waie pernitious,—when, in the south part of America, they are alwaies dangerous, and often deadly.

Likewise, as they have fruicts and beasts, so have they fowle, and that great store. Of birdes, the eagle is the greatest devourer, and many of them there : there be divers sortes of hawkes, sparhawkes, laneretts,[2] goshawkes, falcons, and ospreys; I brought home from thence this yeare myself, a falcon, and a tassell, the one sent by Sir Thomas Dale to his highnes the Prince, and the other was presented to the Earle of Salsburye, faire ones. What the prowf of them maie be, I have not learned, they prey most upon fish.

Turkeys there be great store, wild in the woods, like phesants in England, forty in a company, as big as our tame here, and yt is an excellent fowle, and so passing good meat, as I maye well saie, yt is the best of any kind of flesh which I have ever yet eaten there.

Partridges there are little bigger then our quailes ! I have knowne of our men to have killed them with their small shott, sometime from off a tree five or six at a shoot.

Cranes, white and grey; herons, both grey and white; woosells, or black byrds, with redd showlders;[3] thrushes, and divers sorts of small byrdes, some carnation, some blew, and some other straunge kyndes, to us unknowne by name.

In winter there are great store of swannes, geese, brants,[4] duck, widgeon, dottrell, oxeyes, mallard, teale, sheldrakes,

[1] They have no monkeys; possibly some of the large species of squirrels, which are numerous there, may be referred to.

[2] A kind of hawk.

[3] *Agelaius Phœnicius*, or red-shouldered starling.   [4] Brent geese.

and divers diving fowles, and of all these sortes, that aboundance, as I dare avowe yt, no country in the world may have more.

Parakitoes I have seene manie in the winter, and knowne divers killed, yet be they a fowle most swift of wing, their winges and breasts are of a greenish cullour, with forked tayles, their heades, some crymsen, some yellowe, some orange-tawny, very beautifull. Some of our colonie who have seene of the East Indian parratts, affirme how they are like to that kynd,[1] which hath given us somewhat the more hope of the nerenes of the South Sea, these parratts, by all probability, like enough to come from some of the countryes upon that sea.

A kind of wood-pidgeon we see in the winter time, and of them such nombers, as I should drawe (from our homelings here, such who have seene, peradventure, scarce one more then in the markett) the creditt of my relation concerning all the other in question, yf I should expresse what extended flocks, and how manie thousands in one flock, I have seene in one daie,[2] wondering (I must confesse) at their flight, when, like so many thickned clowdes, they (having fed to the norward in the daye tyme) retourne againe more sowardly towards night to their roust ; but there be manie hundred witnesses, who maie convince this my report, yf herein yt testifieth an untruth.

To the naturall commodities which the countrye hath of fruicts, beasts, and fowle, we maie also adde the no meane commoditie of fish, of which, in March and Aprill, are great shoells of herrings.

Sturgeon, great store, commonlie in Maie if the yeare be

[1] These are of the kind called *psittacus Caroliniensis*, which belongs to quite a different subdivision from the Indian parrot.
[2] The migratory pigeon (*ectopistes migratorius*). For accounts of the prodigious number of these birds, see Wilson's and Audubon's works on the birds of North America.

forward. I have beene at the taking of some before Alger-
noone fort, and in Southampton river, in the middst of March,
and they remaine with us June, July, and August, and in
that plenty as before expressed in the chapter.

Shaddes, great store, of a yard long, and for sweetnes and
fatnes a reasonable good fish, he is only full of small bones,
like our barbells in England.

Grampus, porpois, seales, stingraies, bretts, mulletts, white
salmons, troute, soles, playse, comfish, rockfish, eeles, lam-
preys, cat-fish, perch of three sorts, shrimps, crefishes, cockles,
mushells, and more such like, like needles[s] to name, all
good fish.

There is the garfish,[1] some of which are a yard long, small
and round like an eele, and as big as a man's legg, having a
long snout full of sharp teeth.

Oysters there be in whole bancks and bedds, and those of
the best: I have seene some thirteen inches long. The salvages use to boyle oysters and mussells togither, and with
the broath they make a good spoone meat, thickned with the
flower of their wheat; and yt is a great thrift and husbandry
with them to hang the oysters upon strings (being shauld and
dried) in the smoake, thereby to preserve them all the yeare.

There be twoo sorts of sea crabbs, and the one our people
call a king crabb,[2] and they are taken in shoall waters from
off the shoare a dozen at a tyme hanging one upon another's
taile; they are of a foote in length and half a foote in bredth,
havinge manie leggs and a long tayle; the Indians seldome
eate of this kind.

There is a kind of shelfish of the proporcion of a cockle,
but far greater, yt hath a smooth shell, not ragged as our
cockles; 'tis good meat, though somwhat tough.

Tortoyses here (such as in the Bermudas) I have seene
about the entrance of our bay, but we have not taken of them,
but of the land tortoyses we take and eate dailie; the dif-

---

[1] A species of *belone*.   [2] *Limulus Polyphemus*.

ference betweene which is nothing in shape, but in cullour and bignes, those of the land are gray with a long tayle, those of the sea have black shells, speckled with yellowe, the bodyes great in compasse like a targett.

But the most straung fish is a small one,[2] so like the picture of St. George's dragon as possible can be, except the leggs and winges, and the toad fish,[3] which will swell till yt be like to burst when yt cometh into the ayre.

Thus yt appeareth, that this country affordeth manie excellent vegitables and living creatures; yet, I must saie true, of grasse, for the present, there is little or none but what groweth in low marshes, for all the country is overshadowed with trees, whose droppings contynually turneth grasse to weedes by reason of the rancknes of the grownd, which would soone be amended by good husbandry.

Howbeit, woodes yt hath, great, beautifull, fruictfull, pleasant, and profitable, the grounds cleane under them, at least passeable both for horse and foote. The oake here, for stature and tymber, may compare with any, being so tall and streight, that they will beare   [4] square of good tymber for twenty yardes long; of this wood there is twoo or three severall kyndes, the acrons of one kind, whose barke is more white then the other, is somewhat sweetish, which, being boyled halfe a daie in severall waters, at last affordes a sweet oyle, which they call monohominy: they keepe yt in gourdes to annoint their heads and joynts; the fruict they eate made in bread or otherwise.

There is also elme and ash, of which are made sopeashes. Yf the trees be very great, the ashes wilbe verry good, and melt to hard lumps being carefully burned; but if they be small, and suffered to partake too much of the smoak, they wilbe but powder, nothing so good as the other, besyde they wilbe very fowle and black.

---

[1] Perhaps the *chelydra serpentina*.   [2] A species of *hippocampus*.
[3] A species of *diodon*.   [4] A similar gap in the original.

Of walnutts there be three kindes, the black walnutt,[1] which is returned home yearly by all shipping from thence, and yields good profitt, for yt is well bought up to make waynscott tables, cubbardes, chaires, and stooles, of a delicate grayne and cullour like ebonie, and not subject to the worme: the fruict of this is little, yt is thinne shelled, and the karnell bitter. Annother kynd there is, which beares a great fruict,[2] with a hard shell, and the meat very sweet, and of these the Indians make oyle to droppe their joynts and smeere their bodies with, which do make them supple and nymble. The third sort[3] is, as this last, exceeding hard shelled, and hath a passing sweet karnell; this last kind the Indians beat into pieces with stones, and putting them, shells and all, into morters, mingling water with them, with long woodden pestells pound them so long togither untill they make a kind of mylke, or oylie liquor, which they call powcohicora.

There is a kynd of wood which we call cypres,[4] because both the wood, the fruict, and leafe, did most resemble yt; and of these trees there are some neere three fathome about at the root very streight, and fifty, sixty, or eighty foote without a braunch.

The cedars,[5] for savour and cullor, maie compare with those of Lybanon, the clymate of the one and the other differing little.

Of saxafras[6] there is plenty enough, the rootes whereof, not monie yeares since, were sold for twenty shillings per lb. and better, and if order maie yet be taken that overmuch quantety be not returned, and that which shalbe brought be

---

[1] *Juglans nigra* of Linnæus.

[2] Probably the *juglans cinerea*, L., the "white walnutt" of the settlers.

[3] Probably the hiccory, *juglans alba*, L.

[4] *Cupressus disticha* of Linnæus. The "swamp cedar" of the Southern States.

[5] *Juniperus Virginiana* of Linnæus, which is not a cedar, but produces the wood so called, of which pencils are made.

[6] *Laurus sassafras*, L.

kept in one hand, all Europe maie be served thereof at good
rates. The cedars and saxafras yeild a kynd of gomme in a
small proporcion of themselves; there have bene conclusions
tryed to extract yt out of the wood, but nature affourded
greater quantety then art could produce.

There are pines infinite, especially by the sea coast, and
manie other sortes, the use of which are commodious for
shipping, pipe-staves, clapbourd,[1] yardes and masts for shipping, and those here are so faire and large, as a ship of three-
hundred tonne burthen, called the Starre (sent thither the
last yeare upon purpose fitted and prepared with scupper-
holes to take in masts), was not able to stowe forty of the
fower score, unles they should have cut them shorter, which
is a commoditie, rightly understood, of such moment for this
kingdome (all the easterly countryes from whence we have
hitherto had them, so ympoverished and wasted as they are
not able to furnish his majesty's navie, witnes how hardly
were obteyned those which we had last from thence, and those
upon his majesty's private and particular letter to the king of
Denmark) as were ynough (yt may be boldly sayd) to make
good the whole charge of our plantation.

By the dwellings of the salvages are bay-trees,[2] wild roses,
and a kynd of low[3] tree, which beares a cod like to the peas,
but nothing so big : we take yt to be locust.[4]

Crabb trees[5] there be, but the fruict small and bitter, howbeit, being graffed upon, soone might we have of our owne
apples of any kind, peares, and what ells.

Besides these fruict-trees, there is a white poplar,[6] and
another tree[7] like unto yt, that yieldeth a verye cleere and

---

[1] Board ready cut for the cooper's use.

[2] Probably *laurus Caroliniensis* of Catesby.

[3] *Robinia pseudacacia* of Linnæus, the acacia of our plantations is
probably the tree meant.

[4] *Pyrus coronaria* of Linnæus, a tree differing slightly from the European crab.   [5] *Populus heterophylla* of Linnæus.

[6] *Populus balsamifera* of Linnæus.

odoriferous gumme like turpentine, which I have heard Doctor Bohune, and some of our surgeons there, saie, maie well be reckoned a kynd of balsome, and will heale any greene wound.

There groweth in the island of James Towne a small tree, of leaves, armes, and fruict, like the mirtle tree, the fruict thereof hath a tast with the mirtle, but much more bynding; these trees growe in great plentie, round about a standing pond of fresh water in the middle of the island, the pill or rind whereof is of a great force against inveterate dissentericall fluxes, of which Doctor Bohune made open experiment in manie of our men labouring with such diseases, and therefore wisheth all such phisitians as shall goe thither to make use thereof.

For mineralls we will promise nothing; but the hope of which, seeing the low grownd, yieldes manie faire shewes; the mountaines cannot be doubted but that in them manie sortes will be found : and our people, in their first discovery into the Monocan country discovered two mynes, the one within six miles of the head of the falls, which takes the name of Namantack, the fynder of yt: which is conceaved wilbe worth the exploring, and with little charge; the other lyes in the myd-waie betweene twoo townes of Monocan, the neerest called Mowhemincke, the furthest, Massinnacock, distant one from another fourteen miles, of whose goodnes there is no doubt, since the sparre only taken no further then two or three foote into the earth affourdes mettall worth the labour. And concerning a silver-myne, not far from the same place, an Helvetian, one William Henrick Faldoe, assured our Lord Generall, and therefore made his provision for the search thereof; and having bene in England, made earnest suit unto our threasourer and his Majestie's counsaile resident for Virginia, with whome he contracted, and entred into condicions for one yeare and a halfe for the full performaunce of this worke ; but his lordship being not at that time enabled with sufficient companie to make good that search,

by raising forts and planting so far into the country (which
only must have secured the workemen), yt hath pleased God,
since that tyme, that the said Helvetian hath died of a burning fever, and with him the knowledge of that myne, which,
in his life-time, he would not be drawn to reveyle unto any
one ells of the colonie : and there is extant an old plott,
which his Lordship hath shewed me, wherein, by a Portugall,
our seat is layd out, and in the same, two silver mynes
pricked downe; and at the head of the said falls, the Indians
there inhabiting tip their arrowes with cristall, and we fynd
manie pieces scattered in the gritt and sand of the same,
where, likewise, on Pembrook side, Sir Thomas Dale hath
mentioned, in his lettres to the lordships of the Counsaile,
of a goodlie iron myne; and Capt. Newport hath brought
home of that mettell so sufficient a triall, as there hath bene
made sixteen or seventeen tonne of iron so good, as the East
Indian marchants bought yt of the Virginian Companie, pre-
ferring yt before any other iron of what country soever; and
for copper, the hills to the norwest have that store, as the
people themselves, remembred in the first chapter, called the
Bocootauwanaukes, are said to part the solide mettall from
the stone without fire, bellowes, or additamant, and beat it
into plates, the like whereof is hardly found in any other
parte of the world : likewise Capt. Argoll (as his Lordship
beares record in his printed narration), in the river Potawomeck, found a myne of antimony, which, as aforesaid, never
dwells single, but holds assured legue with quicksilver, as likewise a myne of lead ; and we heare the Indians make manie
particular discriptions of allam mynes to the southward.

    Lastly, that the lakes have perles yt cannot be doubted,
for we ourselves have seen manie chaynes and braceletts
worne by the people, and wee have found plentie of them in
the sepulchres of their kings, though discoloured by burning
the oysters in the fier, and deformed by the grosse boring.
And thus (to conclude), we maie well saie how these poore

people have manie morrall goodes, such as are by accidens plentifull ynough amongst them : and as much (poore sowles) as they come short of those *bona moralia* which are *per se*, for the countrie (who sees not by what hath bene sayd?) is not so barren, ill destyned, and wretched, under an unhappy constellation, but that yt hath (even beside necessary helpes and commodities for life) apparent proufes of many naturall riches, and which are all *bona fortunæ*. Again, they are healthie, which is *bonum corporis* : nor is nature a stepdame unto them concerninge their *aptas membrorum compositiones*; only (God wot) I must graunt, that *bonum morale*, as afore-said, which is *per se*, they have not *in medio*, which is *in virtute*; and then, how can they ever obtayne yt *in ultimo*, which is *in fælicitate?* To teach them both, which is the end of our planting amongst them; to lett them knowe what vertue and goodnes is, and the reward of both; to teach them religion, and the crowne of the righteous; to acquaint them with grace, that they maie participate with glorie; which God graunt in mercye unto them.

FINIS LIB. I. DECAD. PRIMI.

THE SECOND BOOK

OF

THE FIRST DECADE OF THE HISTORIE OF TRAVAILE INTO VIRGINIA
BRITANNIA, ENTREATING OF THE FIRST DISCOVERIES OF THE
COUNTRY, AND OF THE FIRST COLONIE, TRANSPORTED BY
SIR RICHARD GREENVILE, KNIGHT, UPON THE ISLAND
OF ROANOAK, AT THE EXPENCE AND CHARGE OF
SIR WALTER RALEIGH, KNIGHT.

AS ALSO OF THE NORTHERN COLONIE, SEATED UPON THE RIVER OF
SACHADEHOC, TRANSPORTED ANNO 1585, AT THE CHARGE
OF SIR JOHN POPHAM, KNIGHT, LATE LORD CHIEFE
JUSTICE OF ENGLAND, GATHERED BY

WILLIAM STRACHEY, GENT.

PSALM CII, VER. 18.

" This shalbe written for the generation to come : and the people which
shalbe created shall praise the Lord."

BOOK THE SECOND.

CAPUT I.

Of the first discoverie in generall of America, being certain islands belonging to the mayne, by Columbus, anno 1492 ; of the discoverie of the mayne, or continent to the so-ward, by Vesputius Americus, anno 1497, who gave it to name America ; of Cabot his discoverie from Florida norward, for the behoof of King Henry VII, anno 1495.

WHETHER that ever famous Genoese, Christopher Columbus, were sufficiently learned, that by reading of divine allegories, named *Timæus*, of Plato, whose subject is of the universall nature and frame of the whole world, under the person of a subtile and misterious priest, old Cricia, of Egypt, discoursing to Solon, an auncient and superannuat history of an island, in tyme of great antiquity, called Athlantides,[1] lying to the west, by which Columbus might instruct his laboring understanding with a greater cliernes, that more then probable yt was the sun and moone, and all ye faier eyes of heaven, did not looke downe from above, nor shedd their influence uppon the things put under the beames of the wandring and lowest plannett confyned only to Europe, Asia, and Africa, running thereby half their courses without proffitt and in vaine, shyning upon the solitary waters and desolate places empty and desolate of man and other living creatures ; or whether Columbus, being a great cosmographer, did well observe, that Asia, Europe, and Africk, concerning the longitude of the world, did conteyn in them but 180 visible degrees, and therefore did conceave yt to be most likely, that in the other 180

---

[1] Critias. Plato gives the name of Critias to one of his dialogues, and introduces him also in the *Timæus*. In both of these dialogues occur allusions to the fabled Atlantis.

(which filleth up the whole course of the sun to the nomber
of 360 degrees, as well observe our moderne writers intreating
de America sive orbe novo) God would not suffer the waters
only to possesse all, but would leave a place for the habitation
of men, beasts, flying, and creeping creatures ; or whether

Whose
name was
not left to
posterity, to
the end so
great a
worck, & of
such import-
ance, should
not be attri-
buted to any
other author
then to God.
Acosta, lib.
i, cap. 19 of
his Naturall
and Morall
Histories.

As left for
payment of
his lodging;
so sayth
Acosta, lib.
i, cap. 19.
Columbus, by his entertaynment of a Biscan pilot (as the
Spaniards, ambitious of their countryes fame, will have yt),
arrising (after many stowers and stormes in an old carravell,
brused and weather-beaten) in the island of Madera, for his
hospitallity and friendly curtesyes, had bequeathed unto him
by that dying pilott, all his cardes and sea instruments, by
which he was therby first moved to seek the lands of anti-
podes and the rich island of Cipango (whereof Marcus Pawlus
writeth, and Peter Martir, before his decades of the ocean,
remembreth the same); or whether yt nowe pleased the
Eternall Wisdome, in His due and appointed tyme, that those
misteries and secrets of His goodly workmanship of His,
should to His utmost bounds be extended, reveyled, and laied
open, and those goodly nations and ample regions discovered,
which He had seated even beneath the pole starre, and under
the equinoctiall lyne (which left our philosophers and poetts
noe belief, that they might possebly be habitable); or whether
all these joyntly concurring (for which how much are we
bound to that mighty and mercyfull Providence, who, in our
tymes, would vouchsafe to lett us see these so many riches,
wonders, and salvation of nations, the testimony of His great
love unto us, which He had, with strong barrs as yt were, shut
up from our forefathers) to make good the prophesy of rever-
end Seneca:—

> Venient annis
> Secula seris ; quibus oceanus
> Vincula rerum laxet, et ingens
> Pateat Tellus, Typhisque novos
> Détegat orbes,
> Nec sit terris ultima Thyle.

Thus in English :—

> That age shall come, albeit, in latter tymes,
>   When as the sea shall ope her lockt-up bownds,
> And mighty lands appeare : new heavens, new clymes
>   Shall Typhis bring to knowledg, and new grownds,
>   New worlds display: then shall not Thule be
>   The farthest nor-west isle our eyes shall see.

Whether of these, or whither all these I saye, have brought these discoveries to passe, which have found out this straung and new half world, true yt is, we find that Columbus, with three shippes and two hundred and twenty Spaniards, in the yeare of Christ [1492] sett forward on his voyage, about the kalends of September,[1] from the islands of Gadez, uppon the mouth of Gibralter, and after sondry casualties, and the chaunces of sea, at length fell upon the islands Dominica, Cuba, etc., which since have bene called by the names of the West Indye Islands.

And five yeares after him was Vesputius Americus set out by the same king of Castile to discover the continent, who, likewise, as Columbus, happely perfourming the same, gave unto yt his owne name, which it ever since hath retayned, namely, America.

The consideracion of both these voyages, so famous and notorious in those dayes, moved the royall heart of king Henry VII (after yt had much repented him for rejecting the first profer of Columbus, who would have made him lord and king of those golden islands, and for which no prince was better fitted, having at that tyme the goodliest navye of any kinge in Christendome), who, therefore, furnished forth a skilfull and expert navigator, one John Cabot, a Venetian, howbeit, endenized an English subject, and at that tyme, governour of the companye of the marchants of Cathay in the citty of London, to make discovery of what was left untoucht at, or unsurveyed by Columbus and Americus, upon

---

[1] He sailed on the third of August, 1492.

those new and unknowne lands for his behoofe, in Anno
1495 sett forth, fell to the soward of America (to that part
afterwards called Florida, by Johannes Pontius, of Leon,[1]
because by him, on Palme-sonday, discovered, 1512, which the
Spaniards call Pasca Florida), and from thence layde open and
annexed to the crowne of England all the coast of Meta Incognita.   So as true yt is, that this portion of America, which
we call ours, and whereunto both Sir W. R[alegh], twenty
yeares since, and upward, and we have nowe for these six
yeares addressed our divers forces and severall colonyes for
plantation, by a princely godmother, her renowned late
majesty, of famous memory, in witnes of her owne well-
chosen vertues, baptized by the name of Virginia, concludinge
(indeed) under that denomination (as the auncyent poetts
did all Italy by the name of Latium) all the bounds and
regions, both to the south and norward, from 30 to 44 degrees,
togithere with the manie islands adjacent thereunto, is no
other then the same first continent and tract of land, which
the said Venetian, old John Cabot, the father, discovered,
from whom only, indeed, we laye our earliest clayme and interest (as we maye right well) to this country.

And sure, albeit from the tyme, after that first discovery (during some yll destined few yeares, wherein our home
occasions importuned the residence within our owne ports,
both of our men and shipps), our voyages hither for a while
might seeme to lye slumbering, yet our tytle could not thereby out-sleepe ytself, nor were our English spiritts so sunck
with the tyme, and many shippes which tempt the wide seas
in the like new searches, as that we abandoned our hopes and
fortunes thither.

[1] The reader will easily recognize the name of Juan Ponce de Leon,
the discoverer of Florida.

[2] Upon the comparative agency of John and Sebastian Cabot, see
learned dissertations by Biddle,—"Memoir of Sebastian Cabot," chap. 5,—
and by Fraser Tytler, in opposition, in the appendix to his " Progress of
Discovery on the Northern Coasts of America".

We shall find, however, the far famous king Henry VIII
(full of many impatient and personall, as well domestick
troubles, as warrs abroad) could not attend the seconding
his royall father in his enterprize, any other then giving
leave to a voluntary fryer or twoo in a shipp called the *Deus
Nobiscum*, to run upon new searches;[1] yet his noble sonne,
prince Edward VI, entred into so serious consultations of the
same, as he gave, therefore, to Sebastian Cabot, borne at
Bristoll, sonne to the father John Cabot, a large pencion
out of his treasury, and constituted him in the Trinity-howse,
graund pilot of England, in the second yeare of his raigne,
and in the yeare of grace 1548, to undertake againe a new
search of these straung lands; and had not that towardly
yong prince too unhappely ben cutt of by an untymely des-
tine, he had prosecuted both what the too too affecting Roome
(the otherwise faultles) qveene Mary neglected, (though perhapps not with out some princely and economick colour of
reason), by contracte to the Spanish Phillipp, whose pretence
of right might well debarr the proceedings in any such practize then, when our Spanishe harts and Romish Catholiques
dare yet to make good his title unto all this fourth quarter
of the world, by the donation of a Pope (though against all
the rules of justice, prescription, or equality), as also what
our never enough admired late soveraigne, queene Elizabeth,
did anew revive, and gave a fresh birth and spiritt unto, sometyme under the discharge of one, sometyme of another, untill
at length yt discended unto and settled in Sir Walter Rawley,
unto whome and his heires, her majesty, in the twenty-six
yeare of her reigne, and anno 1584, at Westminster, gave a

[1] Biddle, in the ninth chapter of his "Memoir of Cabot", brings a
variety of evidence to shew that the two ships which sailed to the west
from England in 1527 (one of which was reported by Hakluyt to have
been named the "Dominus Nobiscum") were named the "Samson," and
the "Mary of Guildford," and that the name "Dominus Nobiscum" was
mistakenly recorded. That the name was a pure invention, seems, however, very improbable.

large patent, from 33 to 40 degrees of latitude, who, therefore, the same yeare, in April, sent out Capt. Phillip Amadas and Capt. Arthur [Barlow] Florida norward, the whole coast of Cape Britton, so called of the people of St. Malo, who first found and fell with it, and the 4th of July following, they arrived upon the coast in a harborow called Hatorask, in the height of 36 and one 3d, and the 13th put out their small boates, and rowing seven leagues from that harborough, came to an island called Roanoak, where they landed and tooke possession of the country in right of the queene's majestie, and after delivered the same over againe to the use of Sir W. Ralegh.

CAPUT II.

Of the discovery, more in perticuler, of the country of Wingandecoa and the isle of Roanoak, by Capt. Amadas and Capt. Barlow, for the behoofe of Sir W. Raleigh, who, presenting their travailes therein, and the cart of the coast to her Majestie, baptized the country by the name of Virginia.

WHEN they first had sight of this country, some thought the first land they saw to be the continent; but after they had entred the haven, they saw before them another mighty long sea, for there lyeth along the coast a tract of islands two hundred miles in length, adjoyning to the ocean sea, and betweene the islands two or three entraunces. When they were entred betweene them (these islands being very narrow for the most parte, as in most places six miles broad, and in some places lesse, in some more), then there appeared the other great sea, conteyning in breadth in some places forty, and in some fifty, in some twenty miles over, before the continent be come unto, which continent the Indians call Wingandacoa; and in this inclosed sea there are about one hundred islands of divers bignes, whereof the aforesaid Roanoak, fifteen to sixteen miles long; a pleasaunt and fertill grownd, full of sedars, saxafras, currants, flax, vines,

deare, conies, hares, and the tree that beareth the rind of
black synamon, of which like Capt. Winter brought from the
Streights of Magellaun, and manie other commodityes and
riches, the particulars whereof are more at large to be seene
in Mr. Hariott's discourse.

The chief king's name, governing at that tyme, they fownde
to be Wingina, his brother, Quangimino, whose wife and
daughter came abourd our discoverers' barkes, who were
about their forehedd a band of white corall, and earings of
pearle.

The river before Roanoak,[1] and which runneth from thence
up to the citty Skicoak, they call Occam; upon which likewise standeth the towne of Pameik, six dayes' journey from
the aforesaid graet citty, called Skicoak, to the so-ward.

And in this river Occam falleth too other great rivers; the
one called Cipo, wherein are great store of the perle muscles,
the other called Nomopana, upon which standeth Chawa-
nooke, not subject to the king of Wingandagoa, but is a
free state, under a lord, at that time, called Pooneno; beyond
which province is another absolute king likewise, called
Menatonon; and these three kings were then in league.

From Hattorask, to the so-ward four daies journey, they
discovered Socoto, the last towne southwardly of the bounds
of Wingandacoa, neere unto which, twenty yeares before
these tymes, a shipp was cast away; some of the people
whereof, in an out island called Wococon, saved themselves;
and after three weekes aboard there, fastened two Indian
canoas togither, and, with their shirts for sailes, made out,
but were soone cast away, and the boats found wreckt upon
the out islands.

And with thus much knowledg of the country, and some
commodityes from the salvadges obteyned, as chamoyse,

---

[1] By the river before Roanoak he would appear to mean Albemarle
Sound; but according to De Bry's map, Skicoak stands on Nandsamund
river, which falls into the Chesapeake.

buffe, and deare skyns; twenty skynes, worth twenty nobles, for a tyn dish, and of other skyns, fifty, worth fifty crownes, for a copper kettle, and a bracelett of pearle, as bigg as pease, brought home and delivered to Sir W. Raleigh, the discoverers returned, and about the midst of September following, arrived in the west of England with two of the native people, one Wanchese, and the other Manteo, brought along with them.

CAPUT III.

Sir Richard Grenvile, generall of the first colonie of one hundred howse-houlders.

AFTER the relation of this discovery up unto Sir W. Raleigh by the said captaines, that part of the country about Roan-oack (beyond which lieth the maine land) was conceaved to be an apt and likely place, both for seat and riches, for a colony to be transported unto; whereupon, the next yeare following, anno 1585, Sir W. Raleigh prepared a fleete of seven sailes, with one hundred howsholders, and many things necessary to begin a new State, which in Aprill departed from Plymouth; Sir Richard Greenvile generall[1] of the same, accompanied with many choyse and principall gentlemen,— Mr. Ralph Lane, Mr. Thomas Candish, Mr. John Arundell, Mr. Reymond, Mr. Stukely, Mr. Bremige, Mr. Vincent, Mr. John Clark, and divers others, some captaines, and other assistents, for councell and good discretions in the voyage, all and every of which, in their severall places, refused no travaile of body, nor carefulnes of mynd, to lay the founda-cion and beat the path to that great and goodly worke which God, I hope by us, in His appointed tyme, will nowe finishe to His owne glory, to the salvation of poore seduced infidells,

[1] It must not be understood from this expression that Sir Richard Grenville was governor of the colony, but simply commander of the expedition. The governorship was committed to Mr. Ralph Lane.

and to the never dying fame and honour of those noble and praise worthy spiritts who shall personally travell in the same.

The most of this fleete by the twentieth of June fell with the maine of Florida, and keeping by the coast, were in some daunger the twenty-fifth of a general wrack on a beach called the Cape of Feare; but the twenty-sixth ancored safe at Wocokon, by Secota, four daies' journey short of Hatorask, where the Admirall, through the unskilfulnes of the master, stroak on grownd, as she was to be brought into the harbour, and sunk, and from whence the generall sent to Wingina, the K[ing] at Roanoak, to advertize of his arrivall, as likewise he sent to the maine Mr. Arundell, with Manteo the salvadge, and Capt. Aubry, and Capt. Boniten, to Croatoan, where they fownd two of their men left there, with thirty other, by Capt. Raymond, who fell with that place certayne dayes before.

Lykewyse from hence the generall, well accompanied in his tilt boat with divers of the gentlemen aforesaid; and Mr. Harriott, with twenty others, following in a pynnace: Capt. Amadas and Capt. Clerk, with ten others, in a shipp boat; Frauncys Brooke aud John White in another shipp boat, passed over the water to the maine land, victualled for eight daies. In which voyage they discovered the townes of Pomeioke, Aquascogoke, and Secotan, and the great lake called by the salvages Paquippe, and so returned, and the twenty-seventh of July ancored the fleet at Hatorask, and there rested; from whence he landed all his planters, and those which were to remayne in the country, in the aforesaid island of Roanoak, togither with such provisions as were to be left for their use, after which, having setteled some orders amongst the principall commaunders, and constituted Mr. Ralph Lane governour of the colony, advising with him in many necessary businesses to be perfourmed, the twenty-fifth of August he sett saile againe for England, and the eighteenth

U

of October followinge, with a prize, a Spanish shipp of three hundred tonne, arrived in Plynmouth.

The partycularyties of such businesses as were performed by Mr. Ralph Lane, the captaines and gentlemen, and the rest of the colony, to the nomber (as aforesaid) seene in the booke of the discoveries.[1]

Of the hope-
full river of
Maratico,
& the myn
of copper
therein. Only I cannot but remember and mencyone the river of Maratock,[2] up which the Mangoags have traffique, and which river openeth into the broad sound of Weapemeiock, running with a violent current from the west and sowest, as broad as the Thames betweene Greenewich and the Isle of Doggs, and as London-bridge upon a vale water; the head being thirty daies from Roanoak, which head springeth out of a mayne rock in that aboundance, that forthwith yt maketh a most violent streame, and which rock standeth soe neere unto a sea, that manye tymes in stormes, the wind arrising outwardly from the sea, the waves thereof are beaten into the said fresh streame, soe that the fresh water, for a certaine space, groweth salt and brackish, and which Maratock, by Mr. Harriott's opynion, either arriseth out from the Bay of Mexico,[3] or ells from very neere unto the same, that openeth out of the South Sea.

This river maketh promise of great things, for up the same the Mangoags have recourse and traffique in a province called Claunis Temoatan,[4] where there is a marvellous and most straunge minerall, to the Chawanooks, and all the people to the westward, most notorious; the minerall they call wassa-dor, which is copper, but they call by the name of wassador every mettell whatsoever: they saie yt is of the cullour of our copper, but our copper (saie they) is better then theirs, and

[1] He doubtless refers to Hakluyt.

[2] The river now called Roanoke.

[3] The river Roanoke rises in the Alleghanies, Montgomery county, Virginia.

[4] Whether this spelling, or that used by the author a few lines lower down, be the correct one, the editor has been unable to decide.

the reason is because yt is redder and harder, whereas that of Chanius Temoalan is very soft and pale. The manner of taking of which mettell out of the river, I referr to the discourse at lardg, and of many things ells therein conteyned, especyally of the treachery of many of the savage weroances, to the rooting out and cutting off the whole colony, as of Pemipan, of Roanoak, Okisco, king of Weopmeiock, with the Mandongs, and the Chesapeians, with seven hundred uppon the mayne of Dasamanquepeio ; as also how Mr. Lane acquitted himself of their conspiracie, as not altogither necessary for this place, I overpasse.

Only be yt remembred how, that after the colony had laboured herein many searches, and acquired many knowledges, eleaven monthes expecting the returne of their generall with a franck and new supplye out of England, and being in some wants for necessarye and fresh victualls, had dispersed themselves into sondry parts of the countrye, the better to be fitted and accommodated with the provisions thereof, Capt. Stafford lyving then, with twenty in his company, in Croatan, my lord admirall's island, about the beginning of June, had escried a great fleet of many shippes uppon the coasts, standing in, as he conceaved, for Hatorask, of which he gave speedy intelligence unto the fort at Roanoak, who were not a little amazed with the nomber of the shippes, not conceaving what they might be; in the midst of which doubtfulnes of theires, the whole fleet arrived in the road of the bad harborow of Hatoraske, and was soone found to be Sir Fraunces Drake and his company, returning home this way from the sacking of St. Domingo, Carthagena, and St. Augustine, who, sending his boats off to Roanoak, and having intelligence from the governour, of the condicion of which the colony then stood, of their many wants, and daylie expectance of supply from England (the generall, by promise, appointing to have bene there by the first of the spring), Sir Fraunces Drake much commending their patience and noble spiritts, and applauding so good an accion, consulted with his captaines, and concluded to leave them a barke of seventy tonne, called the Frauncis, to serve them upon occasions, with two pinnaces, four small boats, and two experimented sea maisters, Abraham Kendall, and Griffeth Herne, to tarry with them with a supply of collivers,[1] hand-weapons, match, lead, tooles, apparell, and such like, with victualls for one hundred men for four monthes; all which, whilst they were in hand, in all hast to be prepared for them; and in two daies, almost dispatcht, the officers accepting of their charge, and the two maisters busy abourd the said appointed barke. The 13th of the said month of June, there arrose such an unwonted storme, and contynued four daies, that had like to have driven the whole fleet a shoare. The only shift was to weigh anchor and put to sea to save themselves; and [they being] in the same barke appointed to stay, [she] freeing herself, was carried with the violence of the storme so far in fower dayes, that at length she was forct to make for England, with others of the fleete.

Howbeit, Sir Frauncis Drake, riding yet out after the storme, examyning the losse, would have left them another goodly shipp, of the burden of one hundred-and-seventy tonne, called the barke Bonner, with maisters and guydes to tarry there; but yt being better considered, and the harbour so unfitt for a ship of that burthen to be winter roader in, and many other things considered, the determinacion of all was altered, and yt was conceaved more convenient to take in all the planters and come for England, which, unhappely, was accordingly performed, and soe, the 19th of June setting saile, the 27th of July they arrived in Portsmouth, Anno 1586.

[1] Doubtless a culverin; that word being derived from "coluber," a snake. The word "culiver" occurs not unfrequently in writing of this period.

CAPUT IV.

A new supply sent by Sir W. Raleigh unto his colonie unhappily brought away before by Sir Francis Drake.

YET, as the colony that whole yeare did their endeavour there, Sir W. Raleigh did as carefully intend the supplying of them here, preparinge a fleet of three shippes, well appointed, to accompany Sir Richard Greenvile with a bark of aviso,[1] freighted with all manner of things, in most plentifull manner, for the relief of the colony, and to give them intelligence of the generall's speedy hasteninge after him. The only fault and erroure was, that both his fleete and bark of aviso were not sett out till the spring was far spent, and yt was after Easter before this bark of aviso sett forth, whoe arrived at Hatarask, and not finding the colony (brought away as you have heard), returned with all the aforesaid provision into England againe.

Not fully forty or fifty dayes after the departure of this barke of aviso from Hatarask, Sir Richard Greenvile arrived with his three shippes, well appointed, and not finding the said barke nor any newes of the English colony (himself travelling up into divers places of the country), yet unwilling to losse the possession of the same, after good deliberacion, he left fifteen men in the islands of Roanoak, furnished plentifully with all manner of provision for two yeares, and departed agayne for England.

These checks found this pious busines even in her early daies and first begynning; howbeyt, yt did not yet make weary the forward mynd of Sir W. Raleigh to have this country by a full possession added unto our owne, who therefore prepared a fourth voyage and a new colony of one hundred and fifty howsholders, who, the 18th of May in the yeare following, 1587, weyed anchor from Plymouth, under the

A second colony, sent by Sir W. Raleigh, of 150 howseholders, anno 1587, under the commaund of John White.

[1] An advice-boat,—a small vessel employed to carry expresses or orders with all possible despatch.

charg of John White, whome he appointed governour, and
also appointed unto him twelve assistents, unto whome he
gave a charter, and incorporated them by the name of Governour and Assistents of the city Raleigh, in Virginia,—which
fleet, consisting of three sayle, the 22nd of July following,
arrived at Hatarask, where they came to an anchor. From
whence, the governour, accompanied with forty of his best
men, in a small pynnace, stood in for Roanoak, meaning to
take in the aforesaid fifteen men left there by Sir Richard
Greenvile the yeare before, and so to alter their seat unto
the Chesapeak Bay, according to directions from Sir W.
Raleigh; but the governour, being overruled by some of
the company, was diverted from that purpose, and in a manner constrained to seeke no further, but to sett downe in
that island againe, who accordingly brought all the planters
and provisions ashoare, where they beganne to fitt and ac-
commodate themselves. Nor could they heare of any of the
aforesaid fifteen, but found of the bones of one : and the people of Croatan gave our people to understand how they were
slayne, sett upon by thirty of the men of the Sequota, Aquas-
cogoc, and Dasamoquepeuk, conveying themselves upon a
tyme secretly behind the trees neere the howses, where our
men carelessly lived, and in the encounter, knockt out the
braynes of one with a woodden sword, and killed another with
an arrowe shot into the mouth of him, whilst the rest fled to
the water's side, where their boat laye, and all of them taking
the boat, rowed towards Hatarask, and re-landed on a little
island, on the right-hand of our entraunce into the harbour
of Hatarask, where they remayned a while, but afterward
departed, and could never after be heard of.

The governour, calling to councell his assistants, found that
the colony stood in want of many necessary things, both to
secure and settle them in their plantation, wherefore yt was
consulted upon, that some one should be forthwith dispatcht
into England, to ymportune the better supplie to be there

betymes the next yeare. And at length, by a generall consent, the governour himself was thought to be the fittest to undertake the busines, and therefore prepared the admirall and fly-boat to sett forward with all speed, the whilst he established some things amongst them; and having christened a grand-child of his owne, borne there (his daughter being married to one of the company), and calling yt Virginia,[1] he caused, likewise, Manteo, the savage, to be christened, by Sir W. Raleigh his appointment, and in reward of his faithfulnes, entitled him lord of Roanoak and of Dasamonquepeuk; after which, in August, he departed for England with the foresaid fly-boat and admirall, and about the beginning of November, the one landed at Hampton, the other at Portsmouth.

Uppon this arrivall he left not to sollicyte for a supplye; accordingly he sent betymes the next yeare, and as carefull was Sir W. Raleigh to provide him; howbeit, such were the occasions of the ymployment of our shippes in '88 and the yeare following, that yt was March 1590 before Captain White could be dispatcht for Virginia, who then, with three shippes, put to sea from Plymouth, and the 23rd of July had sight of the cape of Florida, and the broken islandes thereof, called the Martyrs, and the 15th of August came to an anchor at Hatarask, from whence he man'd two boats to row to Roanoak, shooting off twoo mynions and a falcon,[2] to give warning to the colony; but the billow was so rough, and the wynd rose so high at norwest, and the indiscreet steerage of the master's mate in a boat where a chief captaine was (Captaine Spicer), such a dangerous sea breaking on the quarter oversett yt, and the boat twice or thrice turned the keile upwardes, nor could the men save themselves in swymming in so great a sea, insomuch, that of eleven, seaven of the chiefest were drowned, Captaine Spicer himself and six more.

[1] The name of this first Anglo-American was Virginia Dare. She was born August 18th, 1587.   [2] Names of pieces of ordnance.

The which mischaunce did so much discomford the lazie and unfaithfull saylers, that they were all in an uproare and murmore not to go any further to seeke the planters; howbeit, Captaine White and Captaine Cooke compelled them, who, therefore, being nineteen persons in both boats, put off from Hatarask once more, and rowed to that parte of the island of Roanoak where the colony was left seated; but yt was so darke before they fell with the shoare, that they overshott the place a quarter of a mile, where yet espieing of a light towards the north end of the island, they made towards yt, and letting fall their grapnells neere the shoare, sounded with a trumpett a call, and afterwards many familyer English tunes and songs, and called out friendly to the shoareward, but all the while had no answere. At breake of day they landed, and went through the woodes to that part of the island directly over against Dasamanquepeuk, and from thence returned by the water-syde rownd about the northeren point of the island, untill they came to the place where the colony was left 1586. Some tracts of feeting they found, and upon a sandy banck, on a tree, curiously carved, these romaine letters, "CRO", which gave them hope they might be removed to Croatan, for their agreement was, indeed, to remove when Captaine White left them. Howbeit, Captaine White sought them no further, but missing them there, and his company havinge other practizes, and which those tymes afforded, they returned covetous of some good successe upon the Spanish fleete to returne that yeare from Mexico and the Indies,— neglecting thus these unfortunate and betrayed people, of whose end you shall yet hereafter read in due place in this decade.

CAPUT V.

The unfaithfulnes of such who were imployed miscarried the colony.

THUS Sir W. Raleigh, weried with so great an expence, and abused with the unfaithfulnes of the ymployed, after he had sent (as you maye see by these five severall tymes) collonies and supplies at his owne charges, and nowe at length both himself and his successors thus betrayed, he was even nowe content to submit the fortune of the poore men's lives, and lief of the holy accion ytself, into the favour and proteccion of the God of all mercy, whose will and pleasure he submitted unto to be fulfilled, as in all things ells, so in this one particuler.   By which meanes, for seventeen or eighteen yeares togeather, yt lay neglected, untill yt pleased God at length to move againe the heart of a great and right noble earle amongst us,

It is anew revived by the Rt. Hon. Henry Earle of Southampton.

"Candidus et talos a vertice pulcher ad imos,"

Henry Earle of Southampton, to take yt in consideration, and seriously advise how to recreat and dipp yt anew into spiritt and life; who therfore (yt being so the will of the Eternall Wisdome, and so let all Christian and charitable hearted believe in compassion to this people) begunn to make new enquiries and much scruteny after the country to examyne the former proceedings, togither with the lawfulnes and pious end thereof, and then, having well weighed the greatnes and goodnes of the cause, he lardgley contributed to the furnishing out of a shipp to be comaunded by Capt. Bartholomew Gosnoll and Capt. Bartholomew Gilbert, and accompanyed with divers other gentlemen, to discover convenyent place for a new colony to be sent thither, who accordingly, in March, anno 1602, from Falmouth in a bark of Dartmouth, called the Concord, sett forward, holding a course for the north parte of Virginia.   At which tyme, likewise, Sir W. Raleigh once more bought a bark, and hired all

Samuell Mace last dispatched into Virginia by Sir W. Raleigh.

X

the companye for wages by the month, ymploying therein, for
chief, Samuell Mace[1] (a sufficyent marriner, who had been
twice before at Virginia), to fynd out those people which
he had sent last thither (as before remembered) by Capt.
White, 1587; and who, if so be they could happely light
uppon them, were like enough to instruct us the more per-
fectly in the quality of the natives, and condicion of the
approved country, which barke departed from Waymouth
the said moneth of March, anno, likewise, 1602, to hold a
southwardly course for Virginia, and which accordingly fell
forty leagues to the so-westward of Hatarask, in 34 degrees,
or thereabouts, and having there spent a moneth trading
with the people for their owne, when they scoured along the
coast, and, according to their charge, should have sought the
people, both in the islands and upon the mayne, in divers
appointed places, they did yt not, pretending that the extreamity of weather and loss of some principall ground tack-
ling forced and feared them from searching the port at
Hatarask, the isle of Croatan, or any parte of the mayne of
Dasamonquepeuk, and therefore taking in some quantity of
saxafras, at that tyme of a good value, worth some three
shillings the lb., Chyna roots, benjamin, *cassia lignea*, and
the rynd of the tree which growes there, more strong then
any spice, the vertue whereof, at length, is nowe well knowne,
with divers other commodities, they returned, and brought
no comfort or new accesse of hope concerning the lives and
safety of the unfortunate English people, for which only they
were sett forth, and the charg of this imployment was undertaken.

[1] See Purchas, vol. iv. f⁰. 1653.

CAPUT VI.

The success of the good ship called the Concord, set forth by the Earle of Southampton, and commaunded by Capt. Bartholomew Gosnoll, for discovery, upon a right lyne, falling about Sachadehoc.

THE good ship the Concord, as you have heard, setting forth with this about the fourteenth of Maye followinge, making land in 43 degrees of the north latitude, had better successe; for the commaunders therein, intending faithfully the end of their goeing forth, discovered many goodly rivers, islands, and a pleasant contynent, and the Indians in the said height, in bark shallops, with maast and sayle, iron grapples, and kettles of copper, came boldly abourd them, apparelled with wastcoats and breeches, some of black serdge, some of blew cloth, made after the sea fashion, with hose and shooes on their feet: a people tall of stature, broad and grym visaged; their eye browes paynted white; and yt seemed by some wordes and signes which they made, that some barks, or of St. John de Luz,[1] had fished and traded in this place.

But the ship riding here in noe good harborow, and with all the weather doubted, the master stood off againe into the sea southwardly, and soone after found himself imbayed with a mighty headland, where, coming to an anchor within a league of the shoare, Capt. Gosnoll commaunded the shallop to be trymed out, and went ashore, where he perceaved this headland to be parcell of the mayne, and sondry islands lying almost round about yt; whereupon, thus satisfied, he repaired abourd againe, where, during the tyme of his absence, which was not above six howers, he found the ship so furnished with excellent cod fish, which they had hauled, that they were compelled to through nombers of them overbourd agayne: insomuch yt left this belief in them all,—

[1] So in MS. The port of St. Jean de Luz, in the Basses Pyrenees, became subsequently the seat of extensive commerce with the French possessions in North America.

that in this season, namely, April and Maye, there maye, upon this coast, in this height (as I said of about 43) be as good fishing, and in as great plenty, as in the Newfoundland; and they were the more probably confirmed herein by the skulls of mackarells, herrings, cod, and other fish, which they daily saw as they went and came from the shoare; the place, besides, where they tooke these codds being but in seven fathome water, and within lesse than a league of the shoare, where, in Newfoundland, they fish forty or fifty fathome water, and far off upon the banck.

This headland, therefore, they called Cape Cod, from whence they sayled round about the same almost all the points of the compasse, the shoare very bold; at length they came amongst many faier islands, three especyally, those which they had discerned upon the land, all lying within a league or two one of another, and not above six or seven leagues from the mayne; the one whereof Capt. Gosnoll called Marthaes Viniard, being stored with such an incredible nombre of vynes, as well in the woody parte of the island, where they runne upon every tree, as on the outward parts, that they could not goe for treading upon them; the second, full of deare, and fowle, and glistering minerall stones, he called by his owne name, Gosnoll's Island; the third, about some sixtene miles in compasse, conteyning many peeces and necks of land little differinge from severall islands, saving that certaine bancks of small breadth, like bridges, seemed to joyne them to this island, he called Elizabeth Island. Upon this island they did sow, for a tryall, in sondry places, wheate, barley, oats, and pease, which in fourteen dayes were sprounge up nyne inches and more. On the nor-west side of this island, neere to the sea-side, they found a standing lake[1] of fresh water, almost three English miles in compasse, in the midst whereof stood a little pretty plott or grove of wood,

[1] He would seem to refer to the lake, or rather lakes, near Middleborough, Plymouth county, Massachusetts.

an acre in quantity, or not much above ; the lake full of
tortoises, and exceedingly frequented with all sorts of fowle,
which bredd, some lowe on the bancks, and others on low
trees about the lake, in great aboundance, whose younge ones
theye tooke and eate at their pleasure; also therein they
found divers sorts of shelfish, as shallops, mushells, cockles,
lobsters, crabs, oysters, and wilks ; and the mayne against
yt had manye meadowes, large, and full of greene grasse,
even in the most wooddy places, the trees growing so distinct
and apart, one tree from another, as was passable for horse
or coach, with a broad harborow, or river's mouth, which
ran up into yt, most comodious, and promising a goodly seat.
The people theron (for they will appeare forty or fifty at a
tyme togither upon the water in severall canoas) would come
downe and trade for furs of beavers, luzernos, marternes,
otters, wild catt skyns, seale skyns, and other beast' skines
to ours unknowne, and which they would exchange for
knives, babies' beades, and such toyes. There were also
great store of copper about them, some very redd, and some
paller cullour. None of them but had chaines, earings, and
collers of this mettall, as also they had large drincking cupps
made like skulls, and other thine plates of copper, made much
like our boarspeare blades; and when our people were desirous to understand where they had such store of this mettell,
and made signes to them concerning the same, they tooke a
peece of copper in their hands, and made a hole with their
fingers in the grownd, and, withall, pointed to the higher
growndes.

Within the aforesaid grove, in the midst of the lake mentioned, Capt. Gosnoll did determyne, with eleven more besides himself, who promised to tarry with him, to sitt downe
and fortefye, purposing to send the pynnace home into England by Capt. Gilbert, for new and better preparations, to be
returned the next yeare againe ; and for the same purpose
he built a large howse, and covered yt with sedge, which

grew about the lake in great aboundance, in buylding whereof were three weekes and more spent.

But after the trading with the Indians, and the bark had taken in so many furrs, skyns, some saxafras, and other commodities, as were thought convenyent, most of those eleven, who before had given their   ¹ to stay with Capt. Gosnoll, having now possest themselves with a covetous conceipt of their unlookt for marchandize, that they would be very profitable to them at their returne home upon the sale thereof at the best hand, making nothing but present gayne the end and object of this good work, would not nowe, by any meanes, be treated with to tarry behind the shipp, casting many doubtes as how if the shipp should miscarry going home; or arriving, not to be supplied ; or supplied, miscarry in the returne, and suche like, Captaine Gosnoll was faine to yield to the presente necessity, and leaving this island with many sorrowful, loth to departe, about the mydst of June weyed, with faire wyndes, and the mydst of July arrived againe safe in Exmouth in five monthes, thus finishing this discovery, and returning with giving many comforts, and those right true ones, concerning the benefitt of a plantation in those parts.

CAPUT VII.

Capt. George Weymouth's voyage, upon a right lyne (not seeking the wynde in the accustomed height of the West Indies), and falling with Sachadehoc, and the discovery of that river.

Much was comended the diligence and relation of Capt. Gosnoll; howbeit this voyage alone could not satisfye his so intent a spiritt and ambition in so great and glorious an enterprise as his lordship, the foresaid Earle of Southampton, who laboured to have yt so beginne, as that it might be con-

---

¹ A similar gap in the original.

tynued with all due and prepared circumstances and saffety, and therefore would his lordship be concurrant the second tyme in a new survey and dispatch to be made thither with his brother in lawe, Tho. Arundell, Baron of Warder, who prepared a ship for Capt. Georg Weymouth, which set sayle from Ratcliff in March, anno 1605, and which, about the midst of Maye following, fell with the land, an island unto the mayne of the coast of America, in the height, as he found yt, of about 42, who from thence casting yt norward to 44,—what paines he tooke in discovering,—may witnes the many convenyent places upon the mayne, and isles, and rivers, togither with that little one of Pamaquid, and of his search sixty miles up the most excellent and beneficyall river of Sachadehoc, which he found capable of shippinge for trafique of the greatest burden, a benefitt, indeed, alwaies to be accompted the richest treasure to any land; for which we for our Severne and Thames, and Fraunce for Loire, Seine, and the river of Burdeux, and the Lowe Countries for their ynnumerable navigable rivers, receave our and their greatest wealth. Next he found the land faire, and the whole coast bold to fall with, and then, a safe harbour for shipps to ride in, which hath besides, without the river, in the channell and soundes about the island, adjoyning to the mouth thereof, so desired a road, as yt is capable of an infinite nomber of shippes. The river, likewise, ytself, as yt runneth upp into the mayne for very neere forty miles towards the high inland mountaines, he found to beare in breadth a myle, sometymes three quarters, and half a mile the narrowest; never under four or five fathom water hard by the shoare, and six, seven, eight, nine, and ten fathomes all along on both sides; every half mile very gallant coves, some almost able to conteyne one hundred sayle, where the grownde ys soft ouze, with a tuffe clay under, for anchor hold, and where shipps maye lye without eyther anchor or cable, only moared to the shoare with a hauser; and which floweth eighteen or twenty foot at

high water, with fit docks apperteyning to graine or carine
shippes of all burthens, secured from all windes, which is so
necessarye and incomparable a benefitt, that in few places in
England, or in any parts of Christendome, art, with great
charges, can make the like; besides, the bordering land most
commodious and fertill, trending all along on both sides in
an equall plaine, neither mountaynes nor rockye, but virged
with a greene border of grasse, sometymes three or four
acres, sometymes eight or ten togither, so making tender
unto the eye of the surveyor her fertility and pleasure, and
which would be much more if, by clensing away her wooddes,
shee were converted into goodly meadowe; and the wodd she
beareth is not shrubbish, fitt only for fuell, but goodly oake,
birch, tall firre and spruse, which in many places grow not
so thick together, but may, with small labour, be made feeding grownd, being plentifully stoared, like the outward islands, with fresh water springs, which streame downe in
many places. The woddes here are full of deare, hares, and
other beasts, and reasonably well inhabited by the natives,
of mild and good condicions; many provinces (as about us
within the Chesapeak Bay, and about Roanoack) governed
in chief by a principall commaunder or prince, whom they
call Bashaba, who hath under him divers petty kings, which
they call Sagamoes, the same which the Indians in our more
sowardly parts call weroances, all rich in divers kinds of
excellent furrs.

To take possession of this land and goodly river for his
Majestie, Captain Weymouth thought it fitt to make up to
the head of the river, which he did well sixty miles in his
barge; and as the streame trended westward into the mayne,
and at that height yt beganne to narrowe, so he there sett
upp a crosse with his Majestie's inscription thereon, observing all the waye, that in noe place, eyther about the islands,
or up in the mayne, or all alongst the river, there could be
discerned any one token or signe that ever any Christian

had been there before, of which, eyther by cutting wodd, digging for water, or setting up crosses (memorialls seldome omitted) by Christian travellers, they might have perceaved some testimony, or mention might have been left; and after this search, Capt. Weymouth being well satisfied, with instruction and knowledg, of soe commodious a seat, sett sayle for England, and the eighteenth of July following arrived before Dartmouth.

Upon his returne, his goodly report joyning with Capt. Gosnoll's, cawsed the busines with soe prosperous and faire starrs to be accompanied, as it not only encouraged the saide Earle (the foresaid Lord Arundell being by [t]his tyme chaunged in his intendments this waye, and engaged so far to the Archduke, before returne of this ship, that he no more thought upon the accion), but likewise called forth many firme and harty lovers, and some likewise long affected thereunto, who by comyng, therefore, humble peticioners to his Majestie for the advancemeat of the same (as for the only enterprize reserved unto his daies that was yet left unaccomplisht; whereas God might be aboundantly made knowen; His name enlarged and honoured; a notable nation made fortunate; and ourselves famous), yt well pleased his Majestie (whoe, in all his practizes and consultations, hath ever sought God more than himself, and the advauncement of His glory, professing deadly enmity—noe prince soe much—with ignoraunce and errour), adding to her Christian prænomen, Virginia, the surname of Britannia, to cause his letters to be made patents the tenth of Aprill, 1606, in the fourth yeare of his Majestie's raigne of England, and thirty-ninth of Scotland, for two colonyes; the one consisting of divers knights, gentlemen, marchants, and others of the citty of London, called the first colony;[1] and the other of sondry knights, gentlemen, and others of the citty of Bristoll, Exeter, and the

---

[1] Otherwise called the London Company.

towne of Plymouth, and other places, called the second colonye.[1]

This last, since yt had his end so untymely, by the death
of the upright and noble gentleman late Lord Chief Justice
of England, chief patron of the same, Sir John Popham,
knight ; and since the order and methode of a full history
doth clayme of me the remembrance of the most materiall
poincts at least, as well of this late northern colony as of
the first planted more to the south, I have not thought yt
amisse to epithomize a fewe things (and which have not yet
by any one bene published, or written of) of the same; by
which, likewise (as I maye the better descend into the oc-
curraunces of our owne), maie be the clierer confirmed the
story of all three—the one by the other—where the congruity
(meaninge the commodityes of the country, nature of the
soyle, and qualities of the people) betweene all three is so
full and answerable.

CAPUT VIII.

A colonie sent out to settle, within the river of Sachadehoc, by the
    Honourable Sir John Popham, Knight, Lord Chief Justice of Eng-
    land, under the government of Capt. Popham and Capt. Gilbert ; of
    the Spaniards surprising of a ship of Bristoll, sent for the use of the
    colonie.

AT what tyme the adventurers of the first colonye, anno 1606,
had prepared all things fitt, with a fleet of three saile, for
Capt. Christopher Newport to transport a colony of one
hundred, to begynne the plantation within the Chesapeak
Bay, the foresaid Sir John Popham likewise prepared a tall
ship well furnished, belonging to Bristoll and the river of
Severne, with many planters, which sett out from Plymouth
about Maye   ,[2] Haines maister, to settle a plantacion in

----

[1] Otherwise called the Plymouth Company.
[2] A similar gap in the original.

the river of Sachadehoc, which, making his course for the islands of Flores and Cornez,[1] one morning, about the islande of Gratiosa, the Spanish fleet comynge from Mexico, had sight of yt, gave yt chase, and soone tooke yt; and understanding by examinacion whither she was outward bound, and for what purpose, they tooke the captaine, whose name was Martyn Pryn, out of her, togither with the maister and most of the passengers, dispersing them into divers shipps of their owne, and soe held their course, carrying ours along with them for Spaine; howbeyt one of the fleete, wherein three or four of the English were togither, by the steerage of the English, who tooke their turnes at the helme, and not being observed, altered their course, or whither by contrary wynds compelled, true yt is upon observacion, the Spanish pilott not knowing where he was, unlooked for fell upon the coast of Fraunce, within the river of Burdeux, where they would have concealed the English, and stowed them therefore under hatches, had they not happely bene perceaved by some of the French, which came abourd and obteyned them of the Spaniard, and carried them ashore, at what tyme one of them, Daniell Tucker, gent., made complaint unto the officers of the place of this wronge offred unto them, and, in his Majestie's name, caused this shipp to be staied and arrested untill the court in Paris might determyn of the same; but the Spaniard had too golden an advocate, a West Indian purse comynge newly from thence, and therefore, after some litle attendaunce, easily freed himself from the incumbraunce and made for Spaine, with malice inough to entreat the other captived English, whome they had dispersed and made slaves in their gallions.

Howbeyt, the aforesaid late Lord Chief Justice would not, for all this hard hansell and Spanish mischief, give over his determinacion for planting of a colony within the aforesaid so goodly a country, upon the river of Sachadehoc; but

[1] *i.e.* Corvo.

against the next yeare prepared a greater number of planters, and better provisions, which in two shipps he sent thither; a fly boat, called the Gift of God, wherein a kinsman of his, George Popham, commaunded; and a good ship, called the Mary and John, of London, wherein Raleigh Gilbert commaunded; which, with one hundred and twenty persons for planters, brake ground from Plymouth in June, 1607, which the twenty-fifth fell with Gratiosa, and the twenty-eighth tooke in wood and water at Flores and Cornez, from whence they allways kept their course to the westward as much as wynd and weather would permitt; in which course to the west, and west nor-west, as the wynd would give leave, they ran twoo hundred leagues from Flores, and in the latitude of 42 degrees they found the compasse to be varied one whole pointe.

From whence they stood still to the westward untill the twenty-seventh of July, being then in the latitude of 43 and two thirds, where they threw out the dipsing lead, and had grownd, but twenty fathome and twenty-two fathome, upon a banck, and here they fisht some three howers, and tooke neere two hundred of cod, very great fish, and where they might have laden their ship in lyttle tyme.

From hence they stood in for the mayne, the wynd being at so-west, and as they ran in for the land, they alwaies sounded from this banck, and having run some twelve leagues from the banck nor-west, they sounded, and had sixty fathome ouze, ground black. The wynd now growing scant, they were constreyned to stand for the so-ward, and made south so-west way, and sounded againe the next daye, being the twenty-eighth of July, and had thirty fathome; small stones and white shells, fishing grownd.

29. They made a west waie untill noone, and then sounded; had one hundred and sixty fathome black ouze.

30. About   [1] of the clock in the morning, they had sight of the land, and yt bore of them nor-west. They

[1] A similar gap in the original.

sounded, being ten leagues from the shoar, and had one hundred fathomes black ouze. They made towards the shoare, but could not recover yt before the night tooke them; for which they were constrayned to beare of a litle from the land, and lye a hull all that night, where they found aboundance of fish very large and great, and the water deepe hard abourd the shoare, eighteen or twenty fathome.

31. Standing in for the shoare in the afternoone, they came to an anchor under an island, for all this coast is full of islands, but very sound and good for shipping to passe by them, and the water deepe hard abourd them; they had not bene at anchor two howers, when there came a Spanishe shallop to them from the shoare, in her eight salvadg men and a little salvadg boy, whoe at the first rowed about them and would not come abourd, notwithstanding they proffered them bread, knives, beades, and other small trifles; but having gazed awhile upon the ship they made shewe to departe; howbeyt when they were a little from them, they returned againe and boldly came up into the shipp, and three of them stayed all night abourd, the rest departed and went to the shoare, shewing by signes that they would returne the next daye.

The first of August, the same salvadges returned with three women with them in another biskey shallop, bringing with them many beaver skyns to exchaunge for knyves and beades; the saganio of that place they told them Messamot, seated upon a river not farr off, which they called Emanuell. The salvadges departing, they hoisted out theire bote; and the pilott, Captain R. Davies, with twelve others, rowed into the bay wherein their ship road, and landed on a galland island, where they found gooseberries, strawberries, raspices, hurts, and all the island full of huge high trees of divers sorts: after they had delighted themselves there a while, they returned abourd againe and observed the place to stand in 44 degrees one-third.[1]

August.

[1] The latitude here given would lead to the supposition that the island

2. About midnight, the moone shining bright and the wynd being fayre, at nor-east they departed from this place, setting their course so-west, for soe the coast lieth.

3. Early in the morning they were faire by the shoar, a league from yt, and saw many islands of great bignes and many great sownds going betwixt them, but made proofe of none of them, but found great stoare of fish all along the coast.

4. They were thwart of the cape or headland, which stands in 43 degrees,[2] the shipp being in 42 degrees 50 minutes; betwixt the place they were now at and the said cape or headland, yt is all full of islands and deepe sounds for any

referred to was Mount Desert Island, in Frenchman's Bay ; but nearly all other histories record Manhegin island as the point at which they first landed.

[2] In order to verify and define, in modern nomenclature, the description of the course held by the adventurers, as given in this and the following three pages, a very elaborate and beautiful manuscript map of this coast, in the British Museum, on a scale of two miles to an inch, has been consulted. The examination leads unequivocally to the inference, that the observation of the latitude, as here quoted, is incorrect by rather more than half a degree. The conclusion which, from a careful study of the map, the editor has adopted as most consistent with *all* the details here described, is, that the headland referred to is Cape Small Point, and that the three islands are Damiscove island, Wood island, and Outward Heron island, with the Pumpkin island ledges lying (as described) southward of the eastern-most of the three. The two latter of the three islands lie agreeably with the description, east and west of each other, but Damiscove island is to the *southward* of Wood island. If no allowance be made for this discrepancy, it appears impossible to find any other trio of islands so nearly approaching the description, either as to their bearing with reference to each other, and to the headland, or their distance respectively from Penobscot and the St. George's islands. The inference that the headland is Cape Small Point is based on the fact that no more southerly cape would offer a great number of islands between itself and the ship while lying southward of such cape ; and if we assume it to be more northerly, we wander still further from the latitude quoted by our author, and with still less correspondence with the description in other minor points ; this would be the case, for example, if we were to adopt the supposition, which the examination has sometimes suggested, that the Matinicus Islands and Moose Point were referred to.

shipping to goe in by them, and where is exceeding good
fishing for cod, great and small, bigger then what comes from
the banck of the Newfoundland. This cape is lowland, shewing white like sand, but yt is all whit rocks, and a strong
tyde goeth there. They ran within half a league of the cape,
and from thence the land fell awaye and falls in from this
headland, nor-west and by nore, and nor-west. They keept
their course from this headland and came to three islands,
where they found a ledge of rocks to the so-ward, which
made them hale off from them, and the wynd being at nor-
est, they passed them, keeping their coast still west and by
south, and west so-west, untill twelve of the clock at night,
and made from this headland, in all thirty leagues.

5. They made a west nor-west way, from four of the clock
in the morning untill three of the clock in the afternoone,
and made fifteen leagues, and then they saw the land againe;
for from the cape before named, they saw noe more land but
those three islands untill now, in which tyme they ran forty-
five leagues, and the land bore of them, when they saw yt
firste, nor-west and by north, and yt shewed yt self in this
forme.

Nine leagues or more from yt, there be three high mountaynes that lie in on the land, the land called Segohquet,
neere about the river of Penobscot.[1] They stood towards
this high land untill twelve of the clock noone the next daye,
and they found the ship to be by observation in 43.

---

[1] The mountains of Penobscot stand in three clumps, each of which
would probably have the appearance at a distance of a single mountain.

6. From twelve of the clock noon they kept their course due west and came neere unto the three islands, lying low and flatt by the water, shewing white to the water as if it were sand; but yt is white rock, making shew afarr off almost like Dover Cliffes. There lyeth so-west from the easter-most of the three islands a white rockye island, and those other three islands lye one of the other east and west; soe they stood their course west fast by them, and as they stood to the westward, the high land before spoken made shewe of this forme, bearing of them then nore-nor-west.

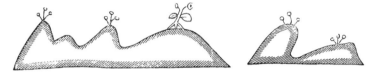

From hence they kept still their course west and by nore towards thrẹe other islands, which they saw lying from those islands eight leagues; and about ten of the clock at night, having sent in their boat before night to make yt, they bore in for one of them, the which they afterwards named St. George his Island; they sounded all along as they came in, and found very deepe water, hard about yt forty fathome. In the morning they were envyrouned every way with islands, they told upward of thirty islands from abourd their shipp, very good sayling out betweene them.

7. They weyed anchor, therby to ride in more saffety howsoever the wind should happen to blow; how be yt before they put from the island they found a crosse set up, one of the same which Captain George Weyman, in his discovery, for all after occasions, left upon this island. Having sayled to the westward, they brought the high land before spoken of to be north, and then it shewed thus,—

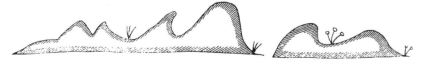

About midnight, Captain Gilbert caused his shipp's boat to be mannde with fourteen persons and the Indian Skidwares, (brought into England by Captain Wayman) and rowed to the westward from their shipp, to the river of Pamaquid, which they found to be four leagues distant from the shipp, where she road. The Indian brought them to the salvadges' houses, where they found a hundred men, women, and childrene; and theire chief commander, or sagamo, amongst them, named Nahanada, who had been brought likewise into England by Captain Wayman, and returned thither by Captain Hanam, setting forth for those parts and some part of Canada the year before ; at their first comyng the Indians betooke them to their armes, their bowes and arrowes ; but after Nahanada had talked with Skidwares and perceaved that they were English men, he caused them to lay aside their bowes and arrowes, and he himself came unto them and ymbraced them, and made them much welcome, and entertayned them with much chierfulnesss, and did they likewise him ; and after two howers thus enterchangeably spent, they returned abourd againe.

CAPUT IX.

Of some accidents happening in the firste setlement of this northerne colonie.

9. Sonday, the chief of both the shipps, with the greatest part of all the company, landed on the island where the crosse stood, the which they called St. George's Island, and heard a sermon delivered unto them by Mr. Seymour, his preacher, and soe returned abourd againe.

10. Captain Popham manned his shallop, and Captain Gilbert his ship boat, with fifty persons in both, and departed for the river of Pemaquid, carrieng with them Skidwares, and arrived in the mouthe of the river ; there came forth

z

Nahanada, with all his company of Indians with their bowes and arrowes in their handes.   They being before his dwelling-house, would not willingly have all our people come on shoare, using them in all kind sort after their manner; never-thelesse, after one hower, they all suddenly withdrew them-selves into the woodes, nor was Skidwares desirous to returne with them any more abourd.   Our people loth to proffer any vyolence unto him by drawing him by force, suffered him to stay behind, promising to returne to them the next day fol-lowing, but he did not.   After his departure they imbarked themselves, and rowed to the further side of the river and there remayned on the shoare for that night.

11. They returned to their shipps towards the evening, where they still road under St. George's Island.[1]

12. They weyed anchors and sett saile to goe for the river of Sachadehoc; they had little wynd and kept their course west.

13. They were south of the island of Sutquin,[2] a league from yt, and yt riseth in this form hereunder; but they did not take yt to be Sutquin.

Sutquin, being sowth of it.   The high mountains being north from you rise thus.

Soe the weather being very faire, they sought the islande further to the westward;[3] but at length fynding that they had overshott yt, they bore up helme, but were soon be-calmed; by which means they were constreyned to remayne at sea, when about midnight there arose a mighty storme upon them, which put them in great danger, by reason they were so neere the shoare and could not gett off, the wynd all

[1] Capt. John Smith makes them to fall in with Manhegin island on the eleventh of August.

[2] Seguin island.

[3] Damiscove island ?

the while at south, and yt blew very stiffe, soe as they were compelled to turne yt to and agayne, hard abourd the lee shoare, many rocks and islands under their lee hard by them; but, God be thancked, they escaped untill yt was daye, the storme still contynuyng untill noone the next daye.

14. Soe soone as the daye gave light, they perceaved that they were hard abourd the shore, in the bay that they were in the daie before, which made them look out for some place to thrust in the shipp to save their lives; for towing the long boat, yt laye suncke at the sterne two howers and more, yett would they not cutt her off, lyving in hope to save her; so bearing up helme, they stood in right with the shoare, when anon they perceaved two little islands, to which they made, and there they found (God be thancked) good anchoring, where they road untill the storme broak, which was the next daie after. Here they freed their boat, and had her ashore to repaire her, being much torne and spoiled. These islands are too leagues to the westward of Sachadehoc. Upon one of them they went on shoare, and found four salvadges and one woman. The islands all rockye and full of pine trees.

15. The storme ended, and the wynd came faire for them to goe for Sachadehoc, the river whether they were bound to and enjoyned to make their plantacion in; soe they weyed anchor and sett sayle, and came to the eastward and found the island of Sutquin, and anchored under yt, for the wynd was of the shoare, by which they could not gett into Sachadehoc; yet Capt. Popham, with the fly-boat, gott in.

16. In the morning, Capt. Popham sent his shallop to helpe in the Mary and John, which weyed anchor, and being calme, was soone towed in and anchored by the Guift's syde.[1]

17. Capt. Popham, in his pynnace, with thirty persons, and Capt. Gilbert in his long boat, with eighteen

[1] This ship, it will be remembered, was called the "Gift of God".

persons more, went early in the morning from their shipp
into the river Sachadehoc, to view the river, and to search
where they might find a fitt place for their plantation.   They
sayled up into the river neere forty leagues, and found yt to
be a very gallant river, very deepe, and seldome lesse water
then three fathome, when they found sest;[1] whereupon they
proceeded no farther, but in their returne homewards they
observed many goodly islands therein, and many braunches
of other small rivers falling into yt.

18. They all went ashore, and there made choise of a
place for their plantacion,[2] at the mouth or entry of the
ryver on the west side (for the river bendeth yt self towards
the nor-east, and by east), being almost an island, of a good
bignes, being in a province called by the Indians Sabino, so
called of a sagamo or chief commaunder under the graund
bassaba.   As they were ashoare, three canoas full of Indians
came to them, but would not come neere, but rowed away
up the river.

19. They all went ashoare where they had made choise
of their plantation and where they had a sermon delivered unto them by their preacher; and after the sermon,
the president's commission was read, with the lawes to be
observed and kept.   George Popham, gent., was nominated
president; Captain Raleigh Gilbert, James Davies, Richard
Seymer, preacher, Captain Richard Davies, Captain Harlow,
the same who brought away the salvadges at this tyme shewed

[1] Query, rest,—as in our old word "zest", an afternoon's nap ; as, "to
go to one's zest,"—from " siesta".—*Port.*

[2] Belknap, in his "American Biography," says that they landed on a
peninsula ; but in the collection of the Mass. Historical Society it is
called Parker's island, which, according to the MS. map already alluded
to, is formed by the waters of the Kennebeck on the west, Jeremysquam
bay on the east, the sea on the south, and a small strait dividing it from
Arrowsick island on the north.   It is called Parker's island because it
was purchased of the natives, in 1650, by one John Parker, who was the
first occupant after the year 1608, when this colony was broken up.

in London, from the river of Canada, were all sworne assistants; and soe they returned back againe.

20. All went to shoare again, and there began to entrench and make a fort, and to buyld a storehouse, soe
contynewing the 21st, 22nd, 23rd, 24th, 25th, 26th, 27th.

28. Whilst most of the hands laboured hard about the
fort and the carpenters about the buylding of a small pinnace,
the president overseeing and applying every one to his
worke, Captain Gilbert departed in the shallop upon a
discovery to the westward, and sayled all the daye by many
gallant islands. The wynd at night comyng contrary, they
came to anchor that night under a headland, by the Indians
called Semiamis;[1] the land exceeding good and fertile, as appeared by the trees growing thereon being goodly and great,
most oake and walnutt, with spatious passages betweene, and
noe rubbish under, and a place most fitt to fortifye on, being
by nature fortifyed on two sides with a spring of water
under yt.

29. They departed from this headland Semiamis, in the
heigh of 43½ degrees, and rowed along the shoar to the
westward, for that the wynd was against them, and which
blewe so hard that they reached no farther than an island
two leagues off, where, whilst they anchored, two canoas
passed by them but would not come neere them.

30. They returned homewards before the wynd, sayling
by many goodly and gallant islands; for betwixt the said
headland and Semiamis, and the river of Sachadehoc, is a
very great bay;[2] in the which there lyeth soe many islands
and so thicke and neere togither, that can hardly be discerned the nomber, yet may any shipp passe betwixt, the
greatest parte of them having seldome lesse water than eight
or ten fathome about them. These islands are all over-

[1] Cape Elizabeth.

[2] Casco Bay, which is said to contain as many islands as there are days
in the year.

growne with woods, as oak, walnutt, pine, spruse trees, hasell
nutts, sarsaparilla, and hurts in abundaunce, only they found
no saxafras at all in the country, and this night they arrived
at the fort againe.

September.   31. And 1st of September, 2nd, 3rd, and 4th, nothing was
done, but only for the furtheraunce and buyldinge of the fort
and storehouse to receave ashore their victualls.

5. About noone, there came into the entraunce of the
river of Sachadehoc and soe unto the fort, as our people were
at their worke, nine canoes with forty salvadges in them,
men, women, and children, and amongst them was Nahanada
and Skidwares. They came up into the fort, and the president gave them meat and drinck, and used them exceeding
kindly. Two or three howers they remayned there and then
they parted, Skidwares and an other salvadge staying still,
with whome at night Captain Gilbert, James Davies, and
Ellis Beast, went over to the farthest side of the river, whether all the rest had withdrawen themselves, and there remayned with them all the night; and early in the morninge,
the salvadges departed in their canoas for the river of Pamaquid, promising Captain Gilbert to accompany him in their
canoas to the river of Penobscott, where the bassaba dwells.

6. And 7th, the busines of the fort only attended.

8. Captain Gilbert, with twenty-two others, departed in
the shallop for the river of Penobscot, taking with him
divers sorts of marchandize to trade with the bassaba; but
by reason the wynd held easterly, being contrary, yt was
three daies before he gott into the river of Penobscot.

11. Early in the morning they came into the river of
Pamaquid, there to call Nahanada and Skidwares to goe
along with them; but, being arrived there, they found that
they were all gone from thence unto the river of Penobscot
before, wherefore, they sett sayle for that river; and all that
day, as likewise the 12th and 13th, they sayled and searched
to the eastward, yet by noe meanes could find the river, for

which they returned, their victuals spent, and the wynd large and good, and in too dayes arrived againe at the fort, having had a sight, the 15th in the morning, of a blasing starr in the nor-east of them.

The 16th, 17th, 18th, 19th, 20th, 21st, 22nd, all labored about the fort and buylding up of the storehouse.

CAPUT X.

The death of Capt. Popham ; Capt. Gilbert disposeth of himself for England when the companie woud then stay no longer, albeit Capt. Davies returned unto them with a great supply from England.

23. Captain Gilbert, accompanied with nineteen others, departed in his shallop, to goe for the head of the river of Sachadehoc. They sayled all this daye, and the 24th the like, untill six of the clock in the afternoone, when they landed on the river's side, where they found a champion land and very fertile, where they remayned all that night.

25. In the morning, they departed from thence and sayled up the river and came to a flatt low island where ys a great cataract or downfall of water, which runneth by both sides of this island very shold and swift.[1] In this island they found great store of grapes, both redd and white ; good hopps, as also chiballs and garlike ; they haled their boat with a strong rope through this downfall perforce, and went neere a league further up, and here they lay all night ; and in the first of the night there called certaine salvages on the further side of the river unto them in broken English ; they answeared them againe and parted long with them, when towards morning they departed.

[1] Query, Swan island, a few miles up the river ; the fall of water round which may be more properly called a downfall of water than a cataract. The first great fall of water from the mouth of the river is that at Waterville : but there is no island at that spot laid down in the best modern maps.

26. In the morning there came a canoa unto them, and in her a Sagamo and four salvages, some of those which spoke to them the night before. The Sagamo called his name Sebenoa, and told us how he was lord of the river Sachadedoc. They entertayned him friendly, and tooke him into their boat and presented him with some triffling things, which he accepted; howbeyt, he desired some one of our men to be put into his canoa as a pawne of his safety, whereupon Captain Gilbert sent in a man of his, when presently the canoa rowed away from them with all the speed they could make up the river. They followed with the shallop, having great care that the Sagamo should not leape overbourd. The canoa quickly rowed from them and landed, and the men made to their howses, being neere a league on the land from the river's side, and carried our man with them. The shallop making good waye, at length came to another downefall, which was so shallowe and soe swift, that by noe meanes they could passe any further, for which, Captain Gilbert, with nine others, landed and tooke their fare, the salvadge Sagamo, with them, and went in search after those other salvages, whose howses, the Sagamo told Captain Gilbert, were not farr off; and after a good tedious march, they came indeed at length unto those salvages' howses, wheere found neere fifty able men very strong and tall, such as their like before they had not seene; all newly painted and armed with their bowes and arrowes. Howbeyt, after that the Sagamo had talked with them, they delivered back again the man, and used all the rest very friendly, as did ours the like by them, who shewed them their comodities of beads, knives, and some copper, of which they seemed very fond; and by waye of trade, made shew that they would come downe to the boat and there bring such things as they had to exchange them for ours. Soe Captain Gilbert departed from them, and within half an howre after he had gotten to his boat, there came three canoas down unto them, and in

them some sixteen salvages, and brought with them some tobacco and certayne small skynes, which were of no value; which Captain Gilbert perceaving, and that they had nothing ells wherewith to trade, he caused all his men to come abourd, and as he would have putt from the shore; the salvadges perceiving so much, subtilely devised how they might put out the fier in the shallop, by which meanes they sawe they should be free from the danger of our men's pieces, and to performe the same, one of the salvadges came into the shallop and taking the fier brand which one of our company held in his hand thereby to light the matches, as if he would light a pipe of tobacco, as sone as he had gotten yt into his hand he presently threw it into the water and leapt out of the shallop. Captain Gilbert seeing that, suddenly commanded his men to betake them to their musketts and the targettiers too, from the head of the boat, and bad one of the men before, with his targett on his arme, to stepp on the shore for more fier; the salvages resisted him and would not suffer him to take any, and some others holding fast the boat roap that the shallop could not putt off. Captain Gilbert caused the musquettiers to present their peeces, the which, the salvages seeing, presently lett goe the boatroap and betooke them to their bowes and arrowes, and ran into the bushes, nocking their arrowes, but did not shoot, neither did ours at them. So the shallop departed from them to the further side of the river, where one of the canoas came unto them, and would have excused the fault of the others. Captain Gilbert made shew as if he were still friends, and entertayned them kindlye and soe left them, returning to the place where he had lodged the night before, and there came to an anchor for that night. The head of the river standeth in 45 degrees and odd mynutts. Upon the continent they found aboundance of spruse trees such as are able to maast the greatest ship his majestie hath, and many other trees, oke, walnutt, pineaple; fish, aboundance; great store of grapes, hopps, and chiballs, also they found certaine codds in which they supposed the cotton wooll to grow, and also upon the bancks many shells of pearle.

27. Here they sett up a crosse and then returned homeward, in the way seeking the by river of some note called Sasanoa. This daye and the next they sought yt, when the weather turned fowle and full of fog and raine, they made all hast to the fort before which, the 29th, they arrived.

30. and 1 and 2 of October, all busye about the fort.

3. There came a canoa unto some of the people of the fort as they were fishing on the sand, in which was Skidwares, who badd them tell their president that Nahanada, with the Bashabaes brother and others, were on the further side of the river, and the next daie would come and visitt him.

4. There came two canoas to the fort, in which were Nahanada and his wife, and Skidwares, and the Basshabaes brother, and one other called Amenquin, a Sagamo; all whome the president feasted and entertayned with all kindnes, both that day and the next, which being Sondaye, the president carried them with him to the place of publike prayers, which they were at both morning and evening, attending yt with great reverence and silence.

6. The salvadges departed all except Amenquin the Sagamo, who would needes staye amongst our people a longer tyme. Upon the departure of the others, the president gave unto every one of them copper beades, or knives, which contented them not a little, as also delivered a present unto the Basshabae's brother, and another for his wife, giving him to understand that he would come unto his court in the river of Penobscot, and see him very shortly, bringing many such like of his country commodityes with him.

You maie please to understand how, whilst this busines was thus followed here, soone after their first arrivall, that had dispatch't away Capt. Robert Davies, in the Mary and

John, to advertise of their safe arrival and forwardnes of their plantacion within this river of Sachadehoc, with letters to the Lord Chief Justice, ymportuninge a supply for the most necessary wants to the subsisting of a colony, to be sent unto them betymes the next yeare.

After Capt. Davies' departure they fully finished the fort, trencht and fortefied yt with twelve pieces of ordinaunce, and built fifty howses therein, besides a church and a storehowse; and the carpenters framed a pretty Pynnace of about some thirty tonne, which they called the Virginia; the chief ship wright being one Digby of London.

Many discoveries likewise had been made both to the mayne and unto the neighbour rivers, and the frontier nations fully discovered by the diligence of Capt. Gilbert, had not the wynter proved soe extreame unseasonable and frosty; for yt being in the yeare 1607, when the extraordinary frost was felt in most parts of Europe, yt was here likewise as vehement, by which noe boat could stir upon any busines. Howbeyt, as tyme and occasyon gave leave, there was nothing omitted which could add unto the benefitt or knowledg of the planters, for which when Capt. Davies arrived there in the yeare following (sett out from Topsam, the port towne of Exciter, with a shipp laden full of victualls, armes, instruments, and tooles, etc.), albeyt, he found Mr. George Popham, the president, and some other dead, yet he found all things in good forwardnes, and many kinds of furrs obteyned from the Indians by way of trade; good store of sarsaparilla gathered, and the new pynnace all finished. But by reason that Capt. Gilbert received letters that his brother was newly dead, and a faire portion of land fallen unto his share, which required his repaier home, and noe mynes discovered, nor hope thereof, being the mayne intended benefit expected to uphold the charge of this plantacion, and the feare that all other wynters would prove like the first, the company by no means would stay any longer in the country, especyally Capt.

Gilbert being to leave them, and Mr. Popham, as aforesaid, dead; wherefore they all ymbarqued in this new arrived shipp, and in the new pynnace, the Virginia, and sett saile for England. And this was the end of that northerne colony uppon the river Sachadehoc.

FINIS.

A DICTIONARIE

OF

THE INDIAN LANGUAGE.

A

DICTIONARIE

INDIAN LANGUAGE,

FOR THE BETTER ENABLING OF SUCH WHO SHALBE THITHER YMPLOYED.

A.

Ahone, *God*
Apome, *the thighe*
Apooke, *tobacco*
Apokan, *a tobacco pipe*
Ananson, *a matt*
Assentamens, *pears*
Anath, *farewell*
Assimnims, *walnutts*
Assimoest, *a fox*
Amahoth, *a targett*
Ampkone, *a frying pan*
Akontant, *a playster*
Ammomū, *to sowe*
Aayxkehake, *a spade*
Atapahañ, *a kixe*[1]
Asapan, *a hasty pudding*
Apquammon, *a show*
Amosens, *a daughter*
Aramiath south, } *I am sick*
Neire, }
Auppes, *a bow string*
Anaskomens, *acornes*
Asasqueth, *the clay they make pipes of*
Amonsoquath, *a beare*
Attomois, *a dog*
Arrokoth, *the skie*

Apones, *bread*
Arathkone, *a beast like a fox.*
Aposon, *a beast in bignes like a pig and in tast alike*
Aquintayne manggoy, *a great ship*
Aquintayne taux, *a little boate or canoa*
Assahampehooke, *a lobster*
Above, *oskeitch*
　　　, *vsquỹh*
　　　, *vspeuwh*
Abroad, *vscound*
Acorn, *anaskimmins*
Adder, *keihtascooc, sassacomu- wah*
Afternoone, *aunshecapa*
Ague, *chowhwasuw*
A king of the head, *nindgapamut- la mecreentecoh*
A king of the teeth, *vneghiawm- dupmeputs*
All, *cheisk*
An aule pin or needle, *pocohaac*
All is out, *tashoac, metatvwh neckatam*
Alive, *kekewh*
Angry, *pererrimuw*
Angle, *uamowk*

[1] So in original MS.

Apple, *maracah*
Apron or any kind of dressed leather, *mataheigh catommoik*
Arrow, *asqweowan*
Arme, *mese*
Armes, *meascoh*
Arse, *kensekit*
Ashes, *pungwe*
Aunts, *ariqwossac*
Awake, *aumaumer*
Aire, *rarascaū*

B.

Boketawh, *fier*
Bagwanchy basson, *a girdle*
Bmseran apook, *fill the pipe with tobacco*
A bag, *porasap vttamancoch*
To bark, *cuttoundg*
A barrell, *ohtamocan*
A batchellor, *matawiowijh*
A ball, *aitowh*
Bald, *paatchkiscaw*
A beare, *momonsacqweo*
A bell, *maucaqwins*
Beanes, *peccatoas*
A beard, *weihsatonowans*
A bed, *cawwaivwh, petaocawin*
To beat out with a cudgell, *auntemdun, nooueshetun*
To beat corne into meale, *vshvccohomen*
To beat any iron to an edge, *vtssetecuttawsew*
To bend, *accongaivwh*
Not to bend, *sansaqivawwh*
Before, *vtcharund*
Behind, *taangoqwaȳk*
Below, *nousomon*
Beneath, *vtshemaijn*
A beggar, *cuttassamais*
Better, *wingutscaho*
A bird, *tshehip, tshetcheindg*
A small bird or chicken, *cawahcheims*

A bird with carnation-coloured wings, *ahshowcutteis*
A bird like a lapwing, collour grey, which useth the water, *monahamshaw*
A bird called a Divedapper, *osasianticus*
The bill or beak, *mehkewh*
To bite, *amin, nussacun*
A bitch, *vsqwausum*
Black, *mahcatawaiuwh*
Blew, *osaih*
To blow any thing, *nepotatamen*
Blew beades, *vnetagwushomon*
Blew berries of the bignes of grapes, very pleasant, *accoondews*
Blunt, *wijhwaivwh*
To make any thing blunt, *neihpunsannvwh*
Block, *taccahooc*
Bluid, *nehpaangunnū*
A bow, *auhtab*
A bowstring, *aupeis*
A boat, *acomtan*
A bottle, *poheewh*
A bourd, *cutsotahwooc*
To boyle up, *potopotawh tawh*
A bone, *woskan*
A boy, *vscapess*
A box in which they play at a certain kynd of game, *assowpook*
The bob of the gynny wheat without corne, *okisher, okinsher*
Bread, *appoans*
Bread made of a woat called *taccaho appoans*
A braser, *qwunnumsc*
A bridge, *metucs*
To broyle or toast bread, *apetawh poan*
To breake with one's fingers any thing, *vdesinamun*
To break with stryking on any thing, *paskeaw, vdeistahamū*
To break all in pieces, *ketarowksunah*

To be broken or crackt, *perew*
Bright or plaine all over, *muscaussum*
To bring into the boat, *paaksetower*
To bring agayne, *patow*
Brasse, *osawas*
To bruise any thing small, *vnetawrnnū*
A brother, *nemat*
A brush, *vnepawahumā*
A bramble or brier, *cawmdguc*
A broome, *tshekehicawwuns*
A butterfly, *manaang-gwas*
To burne as if a shake light on any thing, *cutchow matowran*
A bunch of grapes, *metucsmarakimmins.*

C.

Camange, *a tobacco bag*
Chapant, *a shew*
Curcye neire, *I am a cold*
Commotins, *a turtle*
Cheawanta, *a robin read-breast*
Cursine, *sister*
Chippsin, *land or earth*
Chichiquāmins, *a kind of graine to eat*
Camatinge, *six in number*
Chakasowe, *a crack in any thing*
Cucheneppo, *a woman*
Crenepo, *a woman*
Cheskchamay, *all freinds*
Ceader, *maraak*
Calme, *cohqwaivwh*
To call one, *otassapnar*
A canoa or small boat, *aquointan*
A can or any such like thing to drinck in, *oktamocan*
A candle or gummy stick which will keepe light, *osanintak*
A cap or hat, *puttaiqwapisson*
To carry a thing up and downe, *nawwiowashim*
To carry a thing betweene twoo, *necussagwns*

To carry upon one's showlder, *ahcohkinnemun*
To catch in the mouth as dogs doe, *onascandamen, opassontamen*
A cat, or wild beast much bigger, and spotted black under the belly as a luzarne, *vtchoonggwai*
Caviare, or the roe of sturgeon, *woock*
To chaw, *tawhtagwountamen*
Cheyne, *rarenaw*
A chayne of copper with long lincks, *tapaantaminais*
Chesnutts, *opommins*
Cheese, or any curded matter made of milke, *ootun*
A chamber, *vtshecommuc*
A child, *nechaun*
A chest, *pacus*
A chicken, *cawahcheims*
To chop wood, *catchcahmun mushe*
A circle, *mussetaqwaioh*
A civet cat, *attowrin*
Clay. *pussagwuñ*
To clap one's hands, *passahicaan*
The claw of a crab, *ohtindge*
To clense a pipe, *jacuttehwoon*
To clense the grownd and make yt fitt for seed, *monascunnemū*
To climb a tree, *ahcoushe*
The clowds, *mammaum, arrahqwotuwh*
To take hold of any thing, *mammun*
Copper, *matassuñ*
A comb, *reihcoan*
Cold, *nonssamats*
A cord or small lyne, or a threed, *pemanataon*
A coat of plate, *aqwahussun*
A coat, jerkin, doublet, or ells what, *mantchoor*
To come (being spoken familiarly or hard by), *caumorowath, caumeir, caumear-ah*
To come (being spoken a far off to one), *pijah, pijarowah, pijarah*

To come in, *peintiker*

To come agayne, or we will come
againe, *oiacpijann, naantuc-ah,
pijautch*

To come quickly, *vskepijah, vske-
pewh*

To come up, *vtacqwowsun*

To come downe, *neighsawhor*

To coffe, *nussuccum*

The cock crowes, *moninaw, cutse-
cammo*

A covering or mantle made of
feathers, *cawassow*

A cockle, *osakescai*

To cover one, *ahgwur*

A cob-web, *muttassapec*

A cookold, *wmpenton*

A copper kettle, *aucutgaqwassan*

A crab, *tuttascuc*

A crane, *vssac*

A crack or crackt, *paskasew, ta-
tumsew*

A creeke, *meihsutterask*

A crowe, *ohawas*

Crooked, *ohorinne*

To cry, *neighseum*

To cut the haire of a man's head,
*moundg, nummundgū, cum-
mundgū*

To cut any thinge *vnekishemū*

Curled haire, *vtchepetaiuwh, awre-
whmerersk*

A woman's secrett, *mutusk, mocosijt*

D.

Dawbasonquire, *warme yourself*

A day, *cuttepacus, raieawk*

Darke, *pahcunnaioh*

I dare not, *necqurissaw, nequtahke*

A deare, *vttapaantam*

Dead, or to be dead, *tsepaih*

Deipe to the middle, *tsaqwomoi*

Deepe over the head, *nuttahcaam*

Deafe, *cuppotaw*

To devide a thing in half, *rickewh*

The devill, *riapoke*

A dish, *outacun*

To dive, *poohkewh*

To doe, *noungat*

A dog, *attemous*

Doe so, *vtsseneind*

To drincke to one, *vyaucopen*, or
kucopen

I would drinck, *vgaucopessum*

To dry by fier or otherwise, *tse-
tewh, gaukenates*

To be dry or thirsty, *paougwns-
senttawh*

To dresse or pitch a boat, *asca-
hamū*

A dram, *ahqwohhooc*

A duck, *piscoend*

Dust, *nepensun*

Durt, *keshackaivwh*

To dwell, *nahapuc*

A red dye, *pohcoons, mataqui-
wun*

E.

The eare of a man, *meihtawk*

The eares of a hare or any other
beast, *weihtaooes, mechijn*

To eate, *mecher*

I will eate, *nummechijn*

I'le eate by and by, *mechocusk*

Eate with me, *meihtussuc*

The earth, *aspamū, ottawm*

The east, *vtchepwoissuma*

An eagle, *opotenaiok*

An eare of wheat, *autowtaoh*

An eare of new wheat, *maucata-
watsomeon*

Ebbing water, *seiscatvwh*

An eele, *ascamauk*

An egg, *wouwh*

An elboe, *meisquan*

Elder, *nussaandg*

The elements, *poomp arrathqwa-
tuwh*

Enemy or naught, *macherew,
marapo*

Enough, *warnat, neimbat*

Entombing, *paiamasuw*

The eye, *muskiendguk*

The eyes, *muskiendues*

F.

Farewell, or the word at parting, *anah*

The face, *vscaentur*

The fall of the leaf or the autome, *punsaos*

To fall, *ammawskin, adamoin, adamosū*

To be like to fall, *cawesewh*

To fall downe from a tree, *raqwas-sewhmushe*

To let anything fall, *vtmoiahken*

The falls at the upper end of the king's river, *paqwachowng*

To be faint, *nettencrianges, num-mamuntam*

A father, *nows*

A faune, *nonattewh*

Fatt, *wiraohawh*

A fart, *poket*

A long feather, *meqwanoc*

Feathers, *ahpewk*

The feathers of an arrow, *assa-ovnsawh*

Feet of a hawk, *oremgeis*

Feet by a generall name, *messetts*

To feed with a spoon, *accopaata-mun*

To fetch some fier, *meshpataan bocotaoh*

Fish, *nammais*

A fishhooke, *auketuttawh*

The fore finger, *nummeisutteing-wah*

The long finger, *nuttawwuttemdg*

The ring finger, *nowqweitut*

The little finger, *nummeisutteidg*

Filther, *moieh, moiowat*

The fins of a fish, *wijhcats*

To fight at fisty cuffs, *nummecax-uttenax*

A fine or small thread, *vscook*

The flame, *catzahanzamusheis*

Flowing water, *tammuscamauwh*

The flower of the apple maraccih, *tsemahcaug*

To fly, *awassew, bauqweuwh*

A fly, *mowchesoh*

Flax, *tshehaoah*

A flea, *nuttaqwon*

To flea any thing, *poshenaan*

A flying squirrell, *aiossapanijk*

A fly, *mowcheson*

A fowle like a teale, with a sharp bill like a black bird, *ceumeats*

A waterfowle in bignes of a duck, finely coulored with a copit crowne, *meihteams*

A foole, *wintuc, wintuccum*

Froth, *peihtaoh*

Frost, *tacqwacat*

A freind, or the principall word of kindnes, *netab*

My foot is well, *wingan outssem-etsumneic*

The fur of the beast arrathcune, *wehsacanoc*

I am full, *negeisp*

To be full, *geispun*

Fier, *bocuttaw*

A cole of fier, *mahcatois*

A spark of fier, *accecow, pah-quarra*

To make a fier, *socaquincheni-mum, neusakaqwan*

The fier is out, *otawiaac bocataw*

G.

A garden, or plot of ground to sow corne, *oronocah*

A garter, *kispurracautapus*

A gate, *cuppenauk*

A garfish, *tatamaho*

Give yt me, or let me see yt, *tan-goa*

To give, *paatch-ah, pasemeh*

Give me some tobacco, *paseme vppooke*

Give me some water, *mammahe sucqwahum*

Give me some meat, *meishnah-mecher*

Give me some butter or fat to spread on my bread, *paatch nah rungan, vdamushcan*

Give this to the child, *meishmi-coan, chessoyowk*

Give yt him, *cummeish yoowah*

A girle, *vsqwaseins*

Girles, *vsqwasenis oc*

The gills of a sturgeon or any other fish, *woskeqwus*

Glew or gum that fasteneth on their arrow heads, *vppeinsaman*

A glove, *oteingas, oteincas*

Glorious, smooth, or beautiful, *mus-caivwh, wingaivwh*

A gnatt, *poenguwh*

Good, *wmgan*

It is good meat, *necoondamen*

To goe, *ireh, paspeen*

To goe abroad, *ireh vscoend*

To go along, *cawcawmear, asca-maner*

To go downe, *ireh cuppeintanaan*

To go in, *vscomtain*

To go softly, *vdasemeodaan*

To go home, *nummacha*

To go before, *nepopawinin*

To go after, *apahhammundg*

Now lett go togither, *caumenaan, cowichawwotun*

The shipps go home, *vppoushun, mushower*

Gone, *maentchatemayoac*

Not gon up, *kekenohaivwh, vspewh*

God, *rawottonemd*

A goose, *kahangoc*

A goosling, *marahungoc*

Good morrow, or the word of salu-tation, *kencuttemaum*

The grownd, *petawin*

To grow hie, *otsetuns, cutterewh*

The grissle of a sturgeon, *vsocan*

Grasse, *mehteqweins*

Grapes, *marrakimmins*

A grape's stone or the stone of any plum, *macauqs, caunomel*

A grashopper, *tatacaunshewah*

A grave, *ourcar*

A grownd nut, *ouhpunnawk*

A great deale, *moowchick*

A great way, *amaiuwh, netacoon*

Gymy wheat, *pohcuwtoah*

A gun or piece, *pacussac-an*

The gum that yssueth out of a certaine tree called the Vir-ginian maple, *pickewh*

The gutts of anything, *otakeishe-heis*

A gull, *coiahqwus*

A gust or horrocado, *tohtummo-cunnum*

H.

Hauquequins, *a little stone pot*

Hamkone, *a ladle*

Husque, *by and by, or quickly*

Hawtoppe, *a bow*

Husquequenatora, *now I under-stand you*

Huskpemmo, poketaws, *to sow wheat*

Howghweyh takon neire, *I am hungry*

Hawtorinkanaske, *a black fox skyn or an overgrowne sables*

A hare, *wijhcutteis*

The haire of the head, *merersc*

The haire of a deare, *vsheqwon-naih*

Hard by, *yowhse*

Hard, *esepannuwh*

A hand, *meihtinge*

To hang one, *wawapunnah*

A hatchet, *taccahacan, tamahaac*

An Indian hatchet, *cunsenagwus*

To have, *nohaivwh*

I have bene, *nearnowwan*

A hazell nut, *paaugahtamuns*

The head of a man, *mendabuccah*

The head of an arrow that is rownd, *assamuwh*

The head of an arrow, *raputtak*

The head ake, *kawmdvppaan*

Heaven, *mounshaqwatuwh*

To heare, *nowwuntamen*

Not to heare, *mata-nowwontamen*

He, *yoowah*

Hemp, *weihkippeis*

Hell, *popogwussur*

He hath not or none, *tahmocassewh*

The height of any thing at a good growth, *mangeker*

Of a little height, *tangasuw*

Hearing, *aumpsuwk*

To hide or cover from the rayne, *cushe*

A hill or small mount, *romuttun*

A hill or mountaine, *pomotawh*

Hidden under a cloud, or overcast, *reihcahahcoik*

A howse, *yohacan*

A great howse, *machacammac*

A husband, *wiowah*

A hole, *woor*

To make a hole, *mbococotamen*

A great hole, *maangairagwatowh*

The hornes of a deare, *wawirak*

Hold yt aside, *hatacqwoear*

Hot weather, *vneshawocanassup*

How many, *keis*

Hungry, *noiatewk, vnapootain*

The husk of their wheat, *pocututauha*

A hurt or cut, *wapewh*

To hurt, or a thing hurts me, *ahkij, vwwaap*

It hurts my leg, or my legs ake, *vnegapamutta mennetatakij*

It hurts me not, or yt is whole or well, *mamoindgakij, potterakai*

I.

Ire assuminge, *go and run quickly*

Ioughqueme wath, *let us go or come awaie*

Iakesan apooke, *light tobacco*

I myself, *near*

I or yea, *nim*

The jaggs of the salvadges habit, *rassawans*

Ice, *oreih*

An island, *memnunnahqus*

The itch, *vnechikutchikussa*

Certayne phrases put under

this letter, because they begin with I.

I am lither or lazier, *mushawuacat*

I am your friend, or at your comaund, *netab, netapewh*

I care not for it, *nummaskatamen*

I will not give it, *malacommeir*

I must keepe yt, or I love yt, *nuwamatamen*

I thanck you, *kenah*

I have none, *mahmaindg-nohaivwh*

I will go home, *nummacha*

I must put tobacco in yt, *vpococaheih*

It stincketh, *ahtur*

I cannot tell, *caivwh*

I have noe tobacco, *matavppoannonuwh*

I will not, *matush*

I have no shooes, *matamawcasunneh*

I have no hose, *matacawqweowanneth*

I understand you not, *matagvenatoroth*

I love you, *nouwmais*

You love, *commomais*

I give yt you gratis, *thaigwenvmmeraan*

I have bene asleepe, *mummascushenepo*

K.

Kenah, *I thanck you*

Kayquiose, *a boat*

Kuttchawe, *I burne*

Kameyhan, *rayne*

Kowse, *father*

Kicke, *mother*

Kemotte, *brother*

Kouppathe, *yea truly*

Kenorockonoren quire, *come look at my head*

Kanyough, *I know not*

Kawwin, *sleepe*

Kawkopen quier, *I drinck to you*

Kicketen quier, *speak, or tell me*

Kikithamots, *the wynd*

Kykeytawe, *nine in number*

Koske, *ten in number*

Kantokan, *to daunce*

Kantikantie, *sing and daunce*

Kequasson, *a pot to drinck in*

Kahunge, *a goose*

A king or great lord, *wiroance*

The king's name of Roanoak, *Nanamachauwh*

To kick or spurn, *keiskecamon*

A kixe, *natapahan*

To kisse, *tsepaantamen*

A kettle, *aucogwins*

A knife, *damisac*

To knot up haire tye upon their heads, *vdansqwapissun*

L.

Land, *cheipsin*

A ladle, *tshepoijn*

Lame, *nepawironowh*

A lampray, *rahtaws*

To laugh, *kesshekissun*

To lay downe a thing, *nawhpomind*

Leather that covereth their hips and secretts, *paqwantawun*

Leather, *uttocais*

Leather stripes or stringes, *rahsawans*

Leaves, *maangwipacus*

Dead leaves, *moincaminge*

To leap as men leap in dauncing, or otherwise, *netuspus*

To leap, *huspissaan*

To leane against a thing, *atcheisqwansun*

The leane of any flesh, *oiawh, wiaaws*

Lead, *windscup*

To light any thing, *iahcasomaw*

It is not lighted, *matackesa*

Light, *keshawtewh*

A lyon, *vttacawai*

To lift up any thing, *vdespunnemun*

Lightning, *kecuttannowas*

A little peece, *paangun*

Give me a little piece, *kapessemapaangun*

A little, *taux*

A lizard or elfe, *vtacaskis*

You have no lice, *matavtapawpeak*

The lippes, *nusshaih*

To looke ones head, *cuttahcum meis*

Lost, *nowwanus*

A lobster, *ahshaham*

Long, *cunnaivwh*

Low, *machess*

A lowse, *metacum*

Alone, *apopaqwatecus*

To lye downe to sleepe, *machenecawwun*

To lye with a woman, *saccusac*

To tell a lye, *vtchepitchewain*

To lye togither, *cowijhpaantamū*

M.

Metmge, *a hand*

Miske, *heare*

Mintabukhan, *the head*

Muskan, *the forehead*

Muskins, *the eyes*

Meskew, *the nose*

Mettone, *the mouth*

Mepit, *the teeth*

Maxatsno, *the tongue*

Muckatahone, *the arme*

Meskott, *the leg*

Messeate, *the foot*

Mekouse, *the nayles of the fingers and toes*

Metawke, *the eares*

Mowhkohan, *a fish hooke*

Maskowhinge, *a parrot*

Monowhauk, *a sword*

Maquiquins, *small bells*

Makateweygh, *pearle*

Mattanahayyough, *I have yt not*

Machequeo, *a show*

Mangoite, *great*

Muskefkimmins, *strawberries*

Matchkore, *a stag's skyn*

Minchin quire, minchin, *eat you*

Mattaquenatorath, *I understand you not*

Matassumitohook, *a small bird of divers cullors*

Mahawke, *a gourd*

Meroathachessum, *a young boy*

Mayanse, *I have yt not*

Momuscken, *a mole in the ground*

Monynawgh, *a turkey*

Moroke, *ceader*

Makique, *snot*

Musken, *to run*

Mayis, *going in a path*

Matakuske, *the leafe of a prickle peare*

Mattath, *noe*

Manote, *a basket*

Moussomko, *a squirrel*

Mussane, *a beast so called*

Messetonaance, *a beard*

A man, *nimatewh*

A mat made of reeds, *anansecoon*

A martern, *mouhwacus*

A married man, *nowiowijh wiowah*

Maneaters, *mussaangegwah*

The marrow of a bone, *weimb*

A marryner or seaman, *cheiksew*

A match, *nmtawooc*

To make bread, *apoanocanosutch*

To make a spoone, *ampconomindg*

To make a dish, *ackohican*

To make a frame or boate, *cowcacunnemuñ, ahtowvun*

To make a grave, *cuttahamunourcar*

To make a mat, *chessunnaansun*

To make a basket, *mannottaihcaun*

Meale and flower, *rouhcat, rowksewh*

Meale made of gynny wheat called *vsketehamū*

To melt, *pussepuffactawas*

To be melancholy or sad, *maskihaan*

Milke made of walnutts, *pocohiquara*

Milke, *mutsun*

To misse the hole, *nembobatsoho*

A morter, *taccahooc, rttawh.*

The morning or sun rise, *papasowh*

The morning is faire, *paspasaat, vscantewh*

A moath, *mohwhaiok*

To morrow, *raiab, vimawh*

A mother, *nek*

A mouse, *apegwus*

A mulbery, *muskmuims*

A mushell shell, *tshecomah*

A muskcat, *osasquus*

N.

Numerothequier, *your companion*

Neir, *myself*

Nissakan, *a reed*

Nisake, *a cane*

Nepausche, *the sun*

Nepunche neir, *I am dead*

Nehapper, *sit downe*

Nuppawē, *sleepe*

Nechañ, *a child*

Netap, *my deare friend*

Noewanathsoun, *I have forgotten*

Nekut, 1 *in nomber*

Ninge, 2 *in nomber*

Nousough, 3 *in nomber*

Nuscawes, 8 *in nomber*

Ningepoke, 20 *in nomber*

Nocmchamino boketaw, *mend up the fier*

Nehapper kupper, *sit further*

Namaske, nameche, *fish of any kind*

Nethkeon, *the nose*

Neputte, *the teeth*

Noraughtoan, *put on your hat*

Nahayhough, *I have yt*

Naked, *nepowwer*

A napkin or any lynnen, *matassaih*

The neck of any thing, *nusqwoik*

A nett, *aussab, nacowns*

Next, *vtakijk*

A nettle, *mauhsaan*

The nest of a bird, *wahchesao*

Neere by or next hand, *patewh*

New moone, *suckimma*

Night, *tapacoh, reihcawh*
No or nay, *matah, tah*
None, *rawwaiend*
The noise of a peece, or fall of a tree, *penim*
No more, *tawhs*
I will drink no more, *nutsseqwa-cup*
The north, *vtcheiks*
A nut like a small acron, good meat, *chechmqwanims*

O.

Oyykerough, *a bren, a fowle like a goose*
Oteyquenimin, *to teare or rent any thing*
Ockquetath, *a tausell of a gos-hauke*
Oughtamangoyth, *a tobacco bag*
Owanough, *who hath this*
Onxe, *a fox*
Ockquins, *a watchet coulored bird*
Opomens, *chesnutts*
Ough, *yt is well*
Oughrath, *far off*
Owaugh, *an egge*
An oare, *tshemacans*
An oake tree, *poawamindg*
Oysters, *cauwaih*
An old man, *rawerunnuwh*
An old woman, *vtumpseis*
To open the dore, *tenuecatower, rassicokear*
To open ones eyes, *vdapungwaren*
An otter, or rather a bever, *poh-kevwh*
An otter, *cuttack*
Only one, *naantucah-necut*
Out, or yt is pluckt out, *aumpos-saish*
Out, away, or get you gone, *keij*
To overset, or a boat to turne keele up, *cotappesseaw*
An owle, *qwangatarask*

P.

Poketawes, *wheat*

Peketawes, *beanes*
Peache, *fetch or bring*
Penninaugh, *a rope*
Peymmatā, *threed*
Pasquehamon, *to eate*
Powtowhone boketan, *blow the fier with your mouth*
Punguy, *ashes*
Pettackqueth, *thunder*
Pokoranse, *a minerall stone*
Pokin, pokeyough, *to dive under water*
Pamyauk, *a goard*
Pokosack, *a gun*
Pichamnis, *an excellent plom*
Paskamath, *mulberries*
Poughkone, *the red paint or dye*
Peyeugh, *returning*
Pickutts, *the gum we hold balsome*
Potawaugh, *a porpus*
Porance, 5 *in nomber*
Paspene, *to walke about*
Pisquaon, *a duck*
Paskorath, *the gold sparkes in the sand*
Penonge, *jeron stone*
Pocohack, *a bodkin or ale*
Pattihquapisson, *a hat*
Pokontats, *a girdle*
A parret, *massacamwmdg*
Perle, *matacawiak*
Perle mushell shells, *vsasqwork*
Peaze, *ossantamens, otassanta-mens*
A peece of a pot or a pot sheard, *rummasvwendg*
A peece of bread, *rowcar appons*
A pestle, *pocohaac*
The pipe is stopt, *opoteyough*
A pin, *pocohaac*
To pinch, *nepkehanaan*
A pidgion, *towacqwoins*
A wood pidgeon, *qwanonats*
To pisse, *shekijn*
A pike, *wijhtoram*
Porredg or broth, *noumpqwaam*
A post, *meihtoram*
Porredg or broth, *noumpqwaam*

A polecat, *cuttenamvwhwa*
A pot, *ancagwins*
To powre out water, *qwatshacum-hcaan*
To powre in water, *vsowcunnemū*
The poxe, *nummagwais*
To pluck up, *nummonnemenndus*
A playster, *nuttacoondah*
A plomb stone, *maquascawnomell*
A plomb very delitious when yt is ripe, *pushenims*
A playse, *weiskis*
To play at any game, *mamantū terracan*
The privities or secret of a man, *pocohaac*
Prayer, *maunomommaon*
To come to praier, *pijahtamaon*
A pumpeon, *mahcawq*
A purse, *vttamainquoih*
To pull, *nummavmon*
To pull yt out, *necantowh*
To put yt in, *peinder*
To put on anything, *puttohiqwosur*
To put off any thing, *pussaqwun-nenidg*
Purple, *ourcrewh*
To put out a candle, *vtahtahamū*
To pull one downe, *cuttaqwocum*

Q.

Que quoy, *what is this*
Que quoy ternis quire, *what is your name*

R.

Rapantā, *venison*
Rungâ, *all kind of suet*
Rocoyhook, *an otter*
Rickahone, *a comb*
Rokohamin, *parched corne grownd small*
Reconack, *a tobacco bag*
Rassoum, *the wynd*
Riapoke, *to morrow*
Riokosick, *the devill*
Rekasque, *a knife*
Raw, *ascunnewh*

Rayne, *camzowan*
A raynbow, *qwannacut*
A rattle, such as they use in their ceremonies, made of a goard, *chmgawwonawk*
A ratt, *aotawk*
A reed, *nehsaakah*
Rent or torn, *tuttascwh*
A river, *yocaanta*
Ripe, *wingatewh*
Not ripe, *vscannewh*
To rise up, *passagwear*
The rynd of a tree like hemp, *chesawk*
A ring, *nekereinskeps*
A rose, *pussaqwembun*
To rowle or tose, as a ship, *vtuco-tucosa*
To row, *tchijmaoc*
To rost, *apowssaw*
The root of tobacco, *vppoo-chappoc*
A root, *vtchappoc*
A rope or cord, *pemuntnaw*
To run, *rasannear*
Rushes, *cakekesqus*
To cut rushes, *maniasc cake*
To rub a thing, *vsseqwahamun*

S.

Suckquohana, *water*
Sawwone, *salt*
Sakahooke, *the cleere stones we gather*
Sakahocan, *to write*
Secon, *to spitt*
Sekehekonaugh, *to write*
Sand, *racawh*
To sacrifice, *vtakaer*
To say or be said, *kekuttun*
A saile, *tsemaosoy*
To see, *vunamun*
Let me see it, *numpenamun*
A seat in a boat or a bench, *tussan*
Seedes, *amenacacac*
Sea weeds, *ascaxasqwus*
Sedge, *eskowwascus*
The sea, *yapam*
Scum, *peihtaoh*

c c

The scales of a fish, *wohaikank*
To scratch ones head, *vyvnnecus-sopisson*
To scratch, *vnecussopisson*
A skabb, *vmeqwussum*
Sharp, *keneiwuh*
Sheares, *mundgtacan*
Shells, *ohshaangumiemuns*
A ship, *mussowuxuc*
Yt shyneth, *assentewcaiah*
Shoos, *mawhcasuns*
To shoot, *nepomotamen*
Short, *tackqwaisuw*
Shut the dore, *kessohikear*
To skrub ones head, *necutchuc-skuw*
To sing or dance, *cante-cante*
To sit downe, *nawpin*
To sit nearer, *otassotagwopur*
To be sick, *aroummossouth*
The single of a deare, *wushaqwun*
A sister, *nuckaandgum*
The skyn or fur of a hare, *weisa-cannac*
A sheldrake, *rowhqwawh*
To sleepe, *nepaun*
A sloworme, *apouscase*
Smoake, *kekepengwah*
To smell, *nummeramin*
To snort, *neqwaxulloundwun*
To suit ones nose, *vtanneqwun*
Snow, *coan*
Yt snoweth, *rookewh coan*
A snake, vide adder
A snaile, *pomahaum*
To sow or sett wheat, *nuttaspin*
To sow with a needle, *husquamun*
A sore, *meihkeih*
To soake bread, *nepokeunnamū*
The soule or vitall breath of man, *netshetsunh*
A sparrowhawke, *fatacaumexan*
To speake softly, *kemaantuñ*
A squirrell, *missanek*
To looke asquint, *perrmgqwak*
A sturgeon, *cuppatoan*
A string, vide leather
A stone, *shacahocan*

A little stone, *mananst*
To steale, *commotoouh*
A stake, *weputtahoc*
A stalke, *mehtacooc*
To strike, *nepassingwahoon*
To strike with a sword, *vepaca-man*
Stockings, *cawqweawans*
A starre, *attaanqwassuwk*
A straunger, *vttassantassowaih*
To stand, *vannatassun*
Streight, *majawh*
To stirr ones self, *vummewsun*
To stop or put in a stopple, *mut-taqwohoons*
Strong, *towawh*
To step or go up, *accowson*
The stinging of a snake, *vtag-woong*
To strike fier, *bocata oc kok*
To stinck, *auutus*
The sun, *keshowse*
Sun rise, vide morning
Sun sett, *qwunsewh*
To sup, or to have bene at supper, *meatsun*
Summer, *cowwotaioh*
To suck, *anowwoninr*
A sword, *monohacan*
To sweat, *vebowchass*
To swym, *tooskean*
To swell, *cunnaqueis*
A swan, *wopussouc*
To swallow, *quantamun*
To sweepe, *tsekehica*
To swym as a peece of wood or feather on the water, *puppo-qwahauns*

T.

Tanggo, *let me see yt*
Towaughe, *a crome*
Tanx, *small or little*
Tamokin, *to swimme*
Tauosin, *a stoole*
Tangeqwath, *a furre like a sable's*
Tamohake, *a hatchett*
Take yt, *vntowh*

To take up with a spoone, *auut-sahamun*

To take off, *rassunnemum*

To take one prisoner, *necakes-suttun*

To take tobacco, *vespessemaanpooc*

To take heed, *amuwoir*

A targett, *amunwhokk*

The taile of any thing, *wushaqwun*

To tell one any thing, *cutterah*

To throw a thing away, *apacet*

Thunder, *vmdgtuppauk*

A thigh, *wnijqwans*

These, *yowhs*

This, *yowkk*

Thread, *penimathatoan*

The thumb, *vketeqwaivtteindg*

The throat, *vegwantaak*

Three, *nus*

Tobacco, *vhpooc*

A tobacco pipe, *vhpoocan*

A tobacco bag, *vttamancoih*

The tobacco is good, *wingutsee upooc*

The tobacco is naught, *keshemaik pooc*

A towne, *mussaran*

The trayne of a bird, *ottanueis*

A tree, *meihtucs*

A greene tree, *aqwataneik*

A walnut tree, *assunnoineindge*

An oake tree, *poawnncindg*

A turtle, *accomodemsk*

A sea turtle, *tuwcuppewk*

A turd, *moich*

A turkey, *monanaw*

A turkey cock, *ospanno*

To turne or take up the coales, *cuskessamun*

Twyned threed, *pemucqweraneind*

To tye or make fast any thing, *cuspurn*

V.

Veroanee, *a king or a great man*

Vndoth, *take yt*

Vsquion, *an arrow*

Vmpsemen apook, *drinck, tobacco*

Vmpsquoth, *the moone*

Vaugh, *a word of wonder*

A vaine, *abescur*

A village, *kaasun*

Virginia, *Tsenahcommacah*

Vnderneath, *vtshemandgij*

To unclose hands, *penumun*

I understand well, *kennehautows*

I understand not, *matakennown-torawh*

A vine, *wapapammdge*

W.

Weyans, *the leane of any thing*

Wekowehees, *a hare*

Wapin, *a stab*

Wysotonoans, *a beard*

Winpe, *marrow*

Woussicket, *a running brooke*

Woughtathe, *to swym*

Wecacke, *the yard of a racone*

Wousckan, *a bone*

Winggapo, *my beloved friend*

Wingan, *good*

Winganouse, *very good*

A waare to take fish, *neihsacan*

A walnut, *ahsmenuns, paukauns*

To wash the face, *keseiqwaan*

To wash the hand, *keseiceindcher*

To wash any thing, *ketssetawun*

Water, *secqwahan*

A wart, *meihkeis*

To warme one, *bahtanomun*

Yt is warme or hot weather, *chingissum*

To waken, *vnamun*

The waves of the sea, *aqwaskaw-wans*

To walke, *pawpawmear*

Weake, *kesshemauc*

Weary, *cuttoxeen*

Attasqwus, *weedes*

To weepe, *nummawh*

Yt is well or ynough, *wamattuwh*

Welcome, or the word of greeting, *wingapo, chamah, netab*

A well, *ohcawooc*

The west, *attagwassanna*

Wett, *neppe*
What is your name? *cacuttere-windg kear?*
What is his name? *cacutterewindg yowk?*
What is my name? *cacuttewindg near?*
When, *tanoo chinck*
Where have you been, *tanaowaam*
To whet, *nusseseqwus*
Whelpes, *apowhoh-homins*
Wheat, *pocuttawes*
A wheat plomb, *asseseim*
Wheat parcht in the fier, *aparou-menans*
White, *opaivwh*
To whistle, *qweisqwesun*
A whiting, *vtteitsouk*
The small wynd, *rowhsunnvwh*
A great wynd, *mahqwaih*
A wife, *noungasse*
A wing, *vttocannuc*
A widgeon, *ponomawus*
Will you goe home, *numma*
Winter, *puppaannoh*
To wind about, *pasqwuxxaws*
A woman, *cutssenepo*

A woman's breast, *otaus*
A woman with child, *pomevwh*
A woman queene, *wironausqua*
An old woman, *tumpseis*
A little worme or magot, *mowsah*
Wood, *muskeis*
A wound, *nepocuttokeau*
The world, *pamahsaivwh*
A woolf, *naantam*
To wrastle, *mamarenaretun*
To wrap or wind up any thing, *nuwweisqwaput*

Y.

Yeahaukan, *a howse*
Yeokanta, *a river*
Yeough, 4 *in nomber*
To yawne or gape, *tawatuttener*
Yellow, *oussawack*
Yesterday, *osaioh*
Yea or yes, *cuppeh*
Yonder or far off, *yoaxvwh*
Yonger, *wesaws*
You, *kear*

Z.

Zanckone, *to sneese*

FINIS.

INDEX.

Henlopen, Cape, formerly named Cape Lawar by Capt. Argoll, 43
Henry VII accepts the offer of Columbus, 4 ; gives letters patent to John Cabot, 6
Henry, Cape, 28 ; its bearings, necessity of fortifying, 44
Henry, Fort, built on Southampton river, 61
Houses of the Indians, 70
Howard river, or Susquehannah, 39
Hudson, his supposed discovery of the north-west passage, 23
Hunting excursions of the Indians, 75

I.

Images in the treasure house of Powhatan, 54
Immortality of the soul, Indian belief respecting, 96
Ingram, Capt., his expedition in search of the north-west passage with Capts. Button and Nelson, 23
Isenacommacah, Indian name of Virginia, 47

J.

James the First grants letters patent to the London and Plymouth companies, 161
Jopassus, Indian king, his conversation with Capt. Argoll concerning his religion, 98

K.

Kecoughtan, harbour at, 36
Kecoughtans, people living upon the King's river, 35 ; their conquest by Powhatan, and transportation to Payankatank, 36, 61
Kemps, an Indian, who gave information respecting Powhatan, 53
Kequotaugh, brother of Powhatan, 62
King's river, or Powhatan, description of, 33
Kiskiak, on the south side of the river Pamuncke, 36
Kuscarawoak, river of, 41

L.

Lane, Ralfe, made governor of the colony at Roanoak, 8, 145
Lawarr, Cape, so named by Capt. Argoll, 43
Lead, mine of, found by Capt. Argoll, 39

M.

Mace, Samuel, sent by Sir Walter Raleigh to Virginia, 153
Machumps, an Indian who gave information respecting Powhatan, 54 ; his sister one of Powhatan's wives, 54 ; repeats the Indian grace at Sir Thomas Dale's table, 94
Macock gourds, a fruit cultivated by the Indians, 72-119
Madoc's supposed voyage to the West Indies, 5
Maize cultivated by the Indians, 116
Mamanatowick, a title of Powhatan, 48
Mangoangs, people living near Powhatan, 41
Mannacans, people living near Powhatan, 41
Mannahocks, people living near Powhatan, 41
Mannahoacks, people upon the Toppahanock, or Queen's river, 37
Manteo, an Indian brought to England by Capts. Amadas and Barlow, 144 ; christened at Roanoak, and entitled lord of Roanoak and Dasamonquepeuk, 151
Mantles of feathers worn by the women, 65
Maratock, river of, now called Roanoke, 146
Maricock Apple, passion flower, bears fruit in Virginia, 60 ; cultivated by the Indian, 72 ; description of, 119
Marriages of the Indians, 109
Martha's Vineyard, discovered by Capt. Gosnold, 156
Massawomecks, enemies of the Sasquesahanougs, 40 ; enemies of Powhatan, 104
Mattapament, people upon the River Pawtuxunt or Duke's river, 36-39
Medicine of the Indians, 108
Melendes, Pedro, his cruelty to the French colony in Nova Francia, 9
Meta Incognita, 6
Mines of alum and copper, report of the Indians concerning, 33
Mine of antimony found by Capt. Argoll, 39
Mine of lead found by Capt. Argoll, 39
Minerals of Virginia, 131
Monuments of the Indian kings, 89
Monacans, people living near Powhatan's territories, 41
Moraughtacunds, people upon the Toppahanock or Queen's river, 37
Mountains of Virginia, 25
Mountgomery river, or Payankatank, 36

Moyoones, on the Patawomeck or Elizabeth river, 38
Music of the Indians, 79

N.

Nacothtank, on the Patawomeck or Elizabeth river, 38
Nahanada, chief of the Indians on the river Pamaquid, visited by Capt. Gilbert's company, 169 ; receives Capt. Popham and Capt. Gilbert, 170 ; with other Indians visits the fort, 178
Names, custom among the Indians of giving a variety, 111
Nandsamund, river of, 35
Nandsamunds, people living upon the King's river, 35
Nandfaughtacund, upon the Rappahanock or Queen's river, 37
Nelson, Capt., his expedition in search of the North-west passage, with Capts. Button and Ingram, 23
Nets for fishing made by the Indians, 75
Newfoundland, discovered by John Cabot, 6
Newport, Capt., takes Tackonekintaco and his son prisoners, 58
Nomopana, river falling into the river Occam, 143
North-west passage, supposed discovery, 23
Nuskarawaoks, people living near Powhatan's territories, 41

O.

Oaths used by the Indians, 113
Occam, river before Roanoak, 143
Oholasc, queen of Coiacohamanke, which Capt. Smith calls Quiyoughcohanock, 56
Onawmanient, on the Patawomeck or Elizabeth river, 38
Opechanckeno, brother of Powhatan, 62
Opusoquionusque, a weroancqua or queen of a village of Appamatuck, 56
Orapaks, the place where Powhatan removed after he left Werowocomoco, 49
Ottamack, a title of Powhatan, 48
Ozinies, people upon the Tockwogh or Sydney river, 41

P.

Pamacocack, on the Patawomeck or Elizabeth river, 38
Pameik, town on the river Occam, 143

Pamunck river, or Prince's river, 35
Paquippe, a lake discovered during the expedition under Sir R. Grenville, 145
Parahunt, one of Powhatan's sons, 56
Paspaheghes, people living upon the King's river, 35
Patawomeck, or Elizabeth river, 38 ; Indians, their religion, 98
Pawtuxunt, people upon the river Pawtuxunt, 39
Payankatank or Mountgomery river, the people surprised by Powhatan, 36
Pearls supposed to be found in the Lake of Virginia, 132
Pemaquid, river of, discovered by Capt. Weymouth, 159 ; visited by Capt. Popham and Capt. Gilbert, 169
Penobscot, mountains near the river of, 167
Percy, Capt. George, temporary president of the colony, 41 and 59
Pipisco, formerly weroance of Coiacohawauke, but deposed by Powhatan, 57 ; his chief wife, the state in which she lives, 57 ; hope of his conversion to Christianity, 97
Pochins, one of Powhatan's sons at Kecoughtan, weroance at the time Sir Thomas Gates took it, 60
Pochone root, used by the Indians to paint themselves, 64
Pochahuntas, daughter of Powhatan, 54 and 65
Pomeioke, a town discovered during the expedition under Sir R. Grenville, 146
Pope's, the, donation of America to Spain, 13
Popham, Sir John, sends out a colony to Saghadehoc, 162 ; sends another under Capt. Popham and Capt. Gilbert, 164
Popham, Capt., sent out with the colony to Saghadehoc, with Capt. Gilbert, by Sir John Popham, 164 ; goes with Capt. Gilbert to the river Pemaquid, 169 ; they seek a fit place for their settlement on the river Saghadehoc, 172 ; commence a settlement, 173 ; his death, 179
Potapoco, on the Patawomeck or Elizabeth river, 38
Powell, Ensign, with Ensign Walker, sent by Capt. George Percy to surprise and kill Wowinchopunck, 59
Powhatan or King's river, description of, 33
Powhatans, a people of Virginia, 27
Powhatan, his conquest of the people of Payankatank, 36 ; his conduct to

INSTRUCTIONS TO BINDER.

RICHARDS, 100, ST. MARTIN'S LANE

For EU product safety concerns, contact us at Calle de José Abascal, 56–1°,
28003 Madrid, Spain or eugpsr@cambridge.org.

www.ingramcontent.com/pod-product-compliance
Ingram Content Group UK Ltd.
Pitfield, Milton Keynes, MK11 3LW, UK
UKHW010343140625
459647UK00010B/794